SIERRA LEONE: INSIDE THE WAR
History and Narratives

*To the people of Sierra Leone,
in the spirit of understanding and reconciliation*

SIERRA LEONE: INSIDE THE WAR
History and Narratives

James Higbie and Bernard S. Moigula

Orchid Press

James Higbie and Bernard S. Moigula
SIERRA LEONE: INSIDE THE WAR
History and Narratives

First published 2017

Published by
ORCHID PRESS
P.O. Box 19,
Yuttitham Post Office,
Bangkok 10907, Thailand

www.orchidbooks.com

© Copyright 2017 by James Higbie and Bernard S. Moigula

Protected by copyright under the terms of the International Copyright Union: all rights reserved. No part of this publication may be reproduced in any form or by any means, electronic or mechanical, including photocopying, recording, or by any information storage or retrieval system without prior permission in writing from the copyright holder.

ISBN 978-974-524-198-5

TABLE OF CONTENTS

Preface vii

PART 1: HISTORY
Country and People 1
Before the War 17
The Rebel War: 1991-2002 31
After the War 91

PART 2: NARRATIVES
THE EAST: REBEL TERRITORY
Introduction 99
1. Sheku (Civilian) *They Called Themselves Freedom Fighters* 100
2. Lucia (Civilian) *It Was Rogues and Crooks* 102
3. Jusu (RUF Child Soldier) *Rebel Child* 104
4. Jeneba (Nurse with the RUF) *Saving the Lives of Others* 114
5. Michael (Civilian) *Things Became Difficult* 119
6. Jasper (RUF) *Voluntarily Recruited* 125
7. Fatmata (RUF) *I Became Involved* 132
8. Bolo (SLA–AFRC) *Why Am I Fighting?* 135

KONO DISTRICT: DIAMONDS AND BLOOD
Introduction 145
1. Allan (Civilian) *Everyone Wanted Diamonds* 146
2. Jammie (Civilian) *I'm Going To Die* 151
3. Kumba (Civilian) *A Command To Cut Off Our Hands* 154
4. Momodu (Kamajor) *The Kamajors were Fighting for Peace* 156
5. Massah (Civilian) *Remembering The War* 159
6. Finda (Civilian) *Massacre in Tombodu* 160
7. Tamba (RUF Child Soldier) *Helping The Men* 164

Designations for fighting factions
RUF—Revolutionary United Front rebel
SLA—Sierra Leone Army
AFRC—Army junta formed after 1997 coup
Kamajor—The main Civil Defense Force

THE SOUTH: SELF-DEFENSE
Introduction 173
1. Bobby (RUF–SLA–Kamajor) *Liberian Connection* 174
2. Ansumana (Civilian) *Southern Villager* 179
3. Foday (Kamajor) *Protecting the Village* 183
4. Baby Seiya (Civilian) *He Proposed Love* 185
5. Borbor (Kamajor) *Initiation* 186
6. Makambo (SLA–AFRC) *Soldier of This Country* 190
7. Bernard Sifoi (Civilian) *Bo School* 194
8. Mr Tucker (Civilian) *Around as a Young Man* 199
9. Margaret (Civilian) *It Pays to be Kind* 210

FREETOWN AND THE NORTH: CONFRONTATIONS
Introduction 217
1. Gibrilla (Civilian) *Trouble in Aberdeen* 218
2. Heavy D (RUF) *He was a Good Leader* 226
3. Samuel (AFRC Child Soldier) *Freetown Invasion* 236
4. Alfred (Civilian) *Brima Lane* 242
5. Isata (Civilian) *Victim* 244
6. Mahmood (Civilian) *A Devil Incarnate* 245
7. Kaiku (AFRC Child Soldier) *They Were Against Us* 251
8. Edward (Civilian) *Trying to Seize Power* 256

THE END OF THE WAR
Introduction 261
1. Mohamed (Civilian) *These Were the Thugs I Saw* 261
2. Fallah (RUF Child Soldier) *I Never Want to See Such Things Again* ... 265
Allan *Epilogue: Counseling and Reconciliation* 278

Appendix 1: Groups and Organizations Involved in the War 283
Appendix 2: Leaders and Commanders 285
Glossary 289
Footnotes 295
Sources 299
Index 302
About the Authors 311

PREFACE

In 1991 a brutal civil war broke out in Sierra Leone, a small, former British colony on the west coast of Africa. Known locally as the Rebel War, it was a shockingly violent conflict in a country that had been peaceful and friendly, though divided by political and tribal rivalries.

Many people outside Africa first learned about the war in 1999 when the Revolutionary United Front rebels and their army allies attacked Freetown, the country's capital, and killed or mutilated thousands of people. Reports of the attack were followed by news of child soldiers, amputations, and the "blood diamonds" that were mined by the rebels and exchanged for arms.

The war had actually begun eight years earlier when former Sierra Leone Army corporal Foday Sankoh and his RUF rebels invaded Sierra Leone with the support of Muammar Qaddafi, president of Libya, and Charles Taylor, a Liberian who was, at the same time, waging a war to take over his own country which is Sierra Leone's neighbor to the southeast. The conflict became more complex in 1997 when the army staged a coup d'état and asked the rebels to join them. This resulted in heavy fighting as pro-government forces fought the rebels and the army junta to control the country.

Western countries weren't willing to become involved in the fighting and supported stopgap peace agreements that were ignored by the adversaries. For most of the war West African troops were the only forces that kept the rebels from taking power, and many Nigerians and other West Africans died in the fighting. It wasn't until 2000-2001 when Britain sent troops, the United Nations imposed sanctions on Charles Taylor, and Guinean, Liberian, and Sierra Leonean fighters overpowered the rebels that the war finally ended.

The Rebel War was particularly violent because the RUF tried to take power through terror, believing the government would yield to the sheer brutality of their actions. A list of atrocities compiled after the war by the Sierra Leone Truth and Reconciliation Commission includes killing, rape, amputations, abduction and arbitrary detention, sexual slavery, drugging, forced labor, torture, looting, destruction of property, and cannibalism.[1] All the factions, which included the rebels, the army junta, and the Civil Defense Forces, committed atrocities during the war, and some of the torture and killing was done by children under the age of fifteen.

When the war was over many civilians and ex-fighters required counseling, and an extensive reconciliation process was implemented so that ex-fighters and civilians could accept the tragedies that had taken place and live together peacefully. A UN-sponsored Special Court tried the leaders of the three factions, a process that ended in 2012 with the conviction of Charles Taylor for war crimes.

After the war there was a great deal of discussion on human rights, child rights, gender issues, transparency, and fair elections, and Sierra Leoneans became more vocal on these issues and hopeful that their leaders would be honest and conscientious, and follow international conventions. However, political and tribal rivalries remain along with endemic corruption and mismanagement, and there is still the chance that the country could experience political violence, and that poverty, poor education and health services, and low life expectancy will persist.

History and Narratives: This book is divided into two parts. The first part includes an explanation of Sierra Leone's culture and historical background followed by a detailed history of the civil war. Sources for the history include the Sierra Leone Truth and Reconciliation Commission Report, testimony and judgments from the Special Court trials, and news articles, books, and academic papers written about the war. In addition, the Special Court Judgment (verdict) of Charles Taylor from 2012 presented significant information on Taylor's involvement in planning and supporting the war.

In the second part of the book the story of the civil war is retold by Sierra Leoneans who lived through it. As most of the reporting on the war was Freetown-based, we, as co-authors, aimed to explain how the war progressed through the country, starting with the first attacks in the east and south, through the guerrilla takeover of almost the entire country, to the climactic incidents in Freetown, the north, and along the Guinean border. We also wanted readers to understand how the war was experienced and perceived by both civilians and combatants. Therefore, we interviewed people from all parts of the country and fighters from all three factions, and presented our results in the form of narratives that follow the war from beginning to end.

Narrators who were civilians during the war were willing to tell their stories and were glad that others would hear what they had experienced. However, it sometimes took time to gain the trust of the former fighters who thought we might be exposing them to prosecution, while some ex-fighters refused to talk to us.

As in all wars men did most of the fighting, but the factions in the Sierra Leone war also had child soldiers and, except for the Civil Defense Forces, female soldiers. Our biggest challenge was finding female fighters who would tell their stories, as women and girls who fought in the war can be ostracized if people know about their past. In the end, we were able to interview a cross section of ex-combatants and gain significant information on details of the war and the attitudes and motives of the fighters.

Preface

The narratives provide not only details and experiences, but insight into the social, cultural, and economic aspects of the fighting. By combining the discourse of the narrators, the cultural background, and the history of Sierra Leone and the war, we hope that readers can gain an understanding of the causes of the war, the reasons for the sometimes confusing progression of events, and of the motivations, reactions, and feelings of individuals caught up in the fighting. We hope that this will, in turn, lead to an appreciation of the reconciliation process that has allowed Sierra Leoneans to live together in relative peace, though in truth, many people who experienced the war haven't reconciled with the violent and inhumane events that followed the invasion of the country by the Revolutionary United Front.

James Higbie and Bernard S. Moigula

* * * * *

Notes:
Narratives: Interviews took place from 2010 to 2013. Narratives were recorded in English, Krio, and Mende, and transcripts were edited for clarity and length. Some of the narratives contain first-hand descriptions of brutalities, and a few include descriptions of extreme violence, especially those of Finda, Tamba, Ansumana, and Fallah. All narrators gave permission to use their stories and photos. Names were changed and photographs omitted or obscured at the request of some narrators.

Distances: Sierra Leone uses miles to measure distance, and distances are expressed in miles without conversion to kilometers.

Town/town: "Town" is capitalized if it is part of the proper name of a town, as in Kossoh Town or Calaba Town. It is not capitalized if it is added informally or to distinguish a district headquarter town from a district of the same name, as in Kailahun town (the district headquarters of Kailahun District).

Acknowledgments:
Peter C. Andersen, former Chief of Outreach and Public Affairs for the Special Court of Sierra Leone, founded the Sierra Leone Web, a website that includes news archives of day-by-day events in Sierra Leone from 1994 to 2003 which

were used extensively in the account of the war, and Peter himself provided many details and photographs that were included.

We would like to give special thanks to all the people who told us their stories of the war. We would also like to thank Peter Andersen, Gary Schultz, and Fred Ligon for checking and commenting on the manuscript, and Nelson Nyandemoh, Alpha Sesay, Aiah Marrah, Issa Jawara, Bashir Bah, Mr. Bernard Matthew Moigula of Mano-Dasse, Bernard's sisters Edith, Abie, and Nyanda, his children Margaret and Jimmima, and his university comrades Maxwell T. Dakowa and Alie Tarawally. Also Robert McLaughlin, Jordene Hale, Dunrie Greiling, David Higbie, Janet Higbie, Kristian Lund Jespersen, Joseph Bullie, Tom Riddle, and other friends and family who gave us their support.

PART 1: HISTORY

COUNTRY AND PEOPLE

The State House in the early 1970s

Sierra Leone is a small country located on the West African coast between the Republics of Guinea and Liberia. About one-sixth the size of California, its land area is only 27,599 square miles, a tiny part of Africa's total land area of 11.72 million square miles. The country is roughly circular in shape and approximately 200 miles across. The population is estimated at seven million people.

Freetown, the capital, is a city that preserves much of its historic character though it is overburdened by a population that doubled during the civil war. The city is located on a peninsula with the harbor, the broad estuary of the Sierra Leone River, on its east and the Atlantic Ocean on the north and west. The backdrop of the city is a range of low mountains.

The country is tropical and green with vegetation similar to the Caribbean or Hawaii. Lumley Beach, on Freetown's Atlantic coast, is lined with hotels and restaurants and is the first of a string of beaches along the peninsula that support a small tourist industry.

History

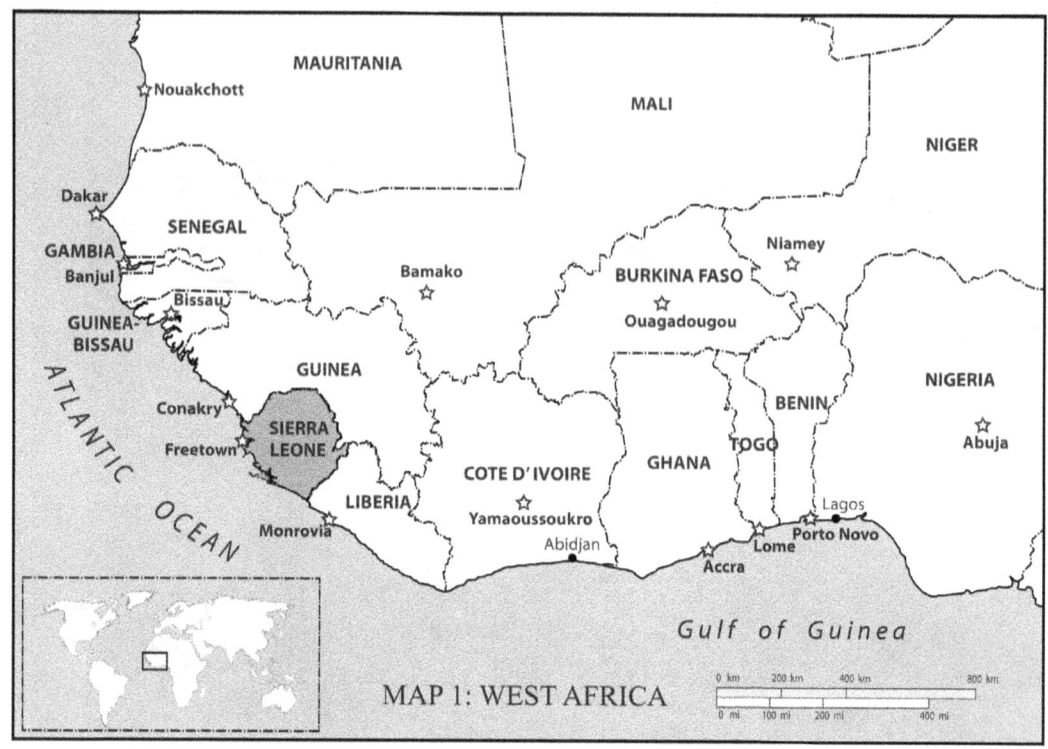

Map 1: West Africa, countries and capitals

Sierra Leone has two main seasons—the rainy season from May to October and the dry season from November to April. The south and east of the country receive heavy rainfall during the rainy season and are covered with forests and cultivated land. The north is drier with sparser vegetation, and the whole country becomes dry and dusty during the dry season. The main export crops are coffee and cocoa which are grown in the south and east. Mining is the main industry and there are iron ore, bauxite, rutile (titanium dioxide), gold, and diamond mines owned and operated by foreign companies. The country has few factories.

Administratively Sierra Leone is divided into three provinces—Northern, Eastern, and Southern—which are further divided into twelve districts, with Freetown and the Western Area administrated separately. The war began in the Eastern and Southern Provinces which border on Liberia where the rebel army was first formed and trained. The Eastern Province was especially hard-hit and suffered heavy damage, as most of the country's diamonds are found in the two eastern districts of Kono and Kenema.

Country and People

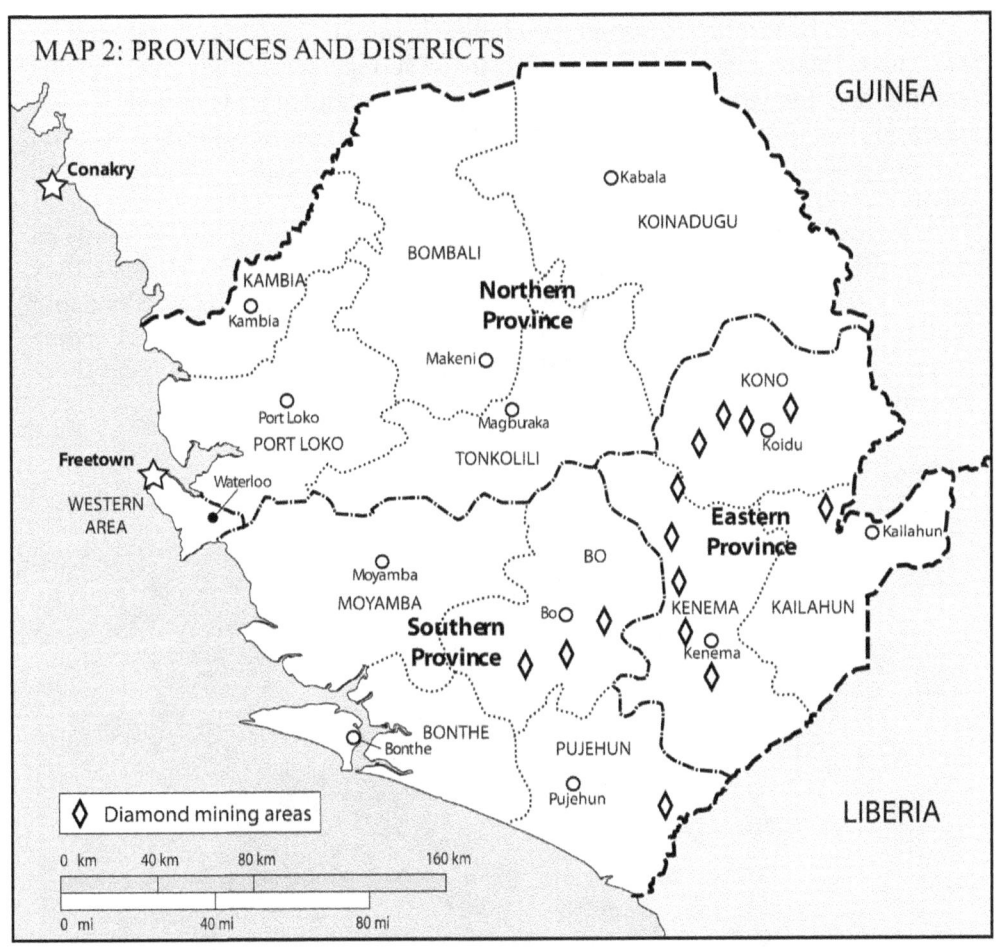

Map 2: Provinces and districts of Sierra Leone, with diamond mining areas

Sierra Leone was colonized by Britain and became independent in 1961. The national language is English though more people speak Krio, an English-based creole language that developed during the colonial period.

There are seventeen ethnic groups, or tribes, each with its own language. ("Tribe" is a word commonly used in Africa to denote ethnic groups.) The largest are the Temne in the north and the Mende in the south and east, each with around 30% of the population. Other groups are the Limba, Kono, Koranko, Mandingo, Loko, Susu, Fullah, Yalunka, Bullom, Sherbro, Vai, Gola, Krim, and Kissi. The Krio are a separate ethnic group who are the descendents of repatriated Africans and captives liberated from slave ships in the 19th century.

History

The Lebanese are another prominent group. They began arriving in the early 1900s and are the country's main shopkeepers. They are also the middlemen for exported produce such as coffee and cocoa, and they own diamond-buying offices in the diamond districts. The Lebanese in general are not well integrated into Sierra Leonean society though some marry local people.

Sierra Leoneans are friendly, outgoing, and very social, always ready to enjoy the company of friends and family. Living in a tropical climate, they spend most of their time outdoors working, chatting with friends, and listening to the radio, or walking around town greeting people and talking. Local people enjoy discussing and debating politics and local events, and it seems that there are always rumors in the air.

Lightfoot-Boston Street, downtown Freetown

Sierra Leoneans love music and dancing. All-night dances are held in cities and towns, and there is constant upbeat music from radios and loudspeakers. Types of music that are popular include afro-beat, soukous, hip-hop, reggae, and calypso (through the country's connection with the Caribbean). Gospel music is sung in all styles and there is even Muslim gospel music. Traditional musical styles are still common and include drumming and call-and-response singing.

Sierra Leoneans are very religious. The population is around 60 percent Muslim and 40 percent Christian, and there are elements of traditional beliefs in both religions. Muslims predominate in the north though people from both religions are integrated throughout the country. There is a high degree of tolerance and respect for both Christianity and Islam. People believe that the two religions share the same God. Meetings begin with both Muslim and Christian prayers, and when you meet someone they will usually ask what your religion is, expecting to hear either "Muslim" or "Christian".

Rice and Palm Oil
Rice is the staple food of the country. Sierra Leoneans eat rice every day with a spicy sauce called "plasas" made of oil, meat or fish, onions, peppers, and greens or peanut paste. In rural areas people eat what they grow, and in towns there are crowded markets selling rice, fruit, vegetables, meat, and spices. Cattle are raised in the drier areas of the north or in Guinea. There are chickens and goats from villages and fresh and dried fish from the coast, but the country also imports large quantities of chicken, fish, and eggs. In some towns bakers from Guinea make French-style baguettes and people occasionally eat cassava, yams, and fufu (starch paste) but rice is by far the preferred food. The specialty food of the Krios is fufu made of fermented cassava that is traditionally cooked on Saturdays.

Women going to market, Tonkolili District

History

Sierra Leonean farmers raise both dry upland rice and swamp rice. The farming cycle is the basis of rural life. During the dry season the forest and bushy areas become dry and are cleared (or "brushed") and burned, the work usually done by men. Planting takes place when the rainy season starts in May and June. Women plant and take care of the crop and children use slings to scare away birds. The rice is harvested from October to January. In villages there may be a "hungry season" when rice from the previous season runs out and people rely on cassava and other starches. The country used to be self-sufficient in rice but is now dependent on imports.

Palm oil is another important food. Palm oil is produced from palm nuts harvested from the wild oil palm trees that grow throughout the country. Palm nuts are harvested in the dry season and the outer, fleshy layer is processed into bright orange oil that is the basis for plasas. The inner seed or kernel, called "banga", can be eaten or is processed to produce clear oil. Palm wine, or "poyo", is a favorite alcoholic beverage that is tapped and drunk fresh from the same tree. Sierra Leoneans eat few sweets and processed foods.

Rice farm and oil palms, Kailahun District

Lebanese-owned produce buying shop (cocoa beans spread to dry)

Poverty—Corruption
If the following description sounds harsh and disheartening it should be remembered that the events that took place and the current conditions in Sierra Leone are a result of the country's history and of the age-old customs and beliefs that have existed for centuries.

Only a few generations ago, before it was taken over by Europeans, West Africa was divided into tribal areas under the leadership of chiefs or kings who generally held autocratic power for life, their terms ending only if they died or were deposed. These chiefs and kings also had control over the land and other resources of the tribal territory, with the right to grant temporary use of land and other resources to families and individuals. Land was not bought and sold.

The population consisted mainly of farmers and traders living in villages connected by footpaths, and there was constant communication and movement among villages and tribes. Some tribes were larger and more dominant than others and rulers might form alliances and wage war for territory, and also for captives who could be bartered or used as domestic slaves. When Europeans began trading in West Africa in the 1500s and 1600s they exploited this by buying captives to be shipped to the Americas as slaves, and a new era of intensive slave raiding began.

History

Britain demarcated the borders of Sierra Leone in the 1890s, establishing the borders without regard to tribal territories. Some of the tribes within the new country of Sierra Leone (or the "protectorate") were already rivals, and when Sierra Leone became independent in 1961, less than seven decades after it was first formed, expectations were that it would function as a democracy with an effective civil service and loyal citizenry, when in reality the country had no experience in democratic governance or locally-led administration.

The results of this experiment in nation-forming were disastrous. The first generation of elected leaders in Sierra Leone, and in many other African countries, became corrupt autocrats who continued the old traditions of holding power for life and keeping personal control of the country's treasury and other resources. Economies collapsed, and politics became violent as rival tribes fought for control of central governments. In Sierra Leone, the battle for power resulted in an eleven-year war that left the country in a worse state than at any time in its short history.

Sierra Leone is currently one of the poorest countries in the world. During the civil war it ranked at the bottom of the UN Human Development Index and in 2015, thirteen years after the end of the war, it still ranked 181 out of 188 countries.[1] 57% of the population lives below the poverty line of $1.25 per day and 44% are in extreme poverty.[2] Most families live without electricity and running water. Markets are full of cheap used clothing from Western countries, and very few people own vehicles.

The majority of Sierra Leoneans are subsistence farmers with little cash income to pay for medical needs and schooling. Paid employment is limited mainly to government, NGOs, and the mining sector. Many people work as petty traders, drivers and mechanics, carpenters, construction workers, and tailors. Wages are very low, usually under $100 per month. In most villages the only paid workers are the local primary school teachers.

In the past, unemployed men traveled to the country's diamond districts and mined the alluvial, or surface, diamonds found in deposits of sand, gravel, or clay in river and stream beds. During the war most of these areas were mined out and artisanal mining (as it is called) is no longer a viable occupation, though it continues in some remote areas. Most diamond mining is now done underground with heavy equipment.

Many of Sierra Leone's problems can be linked to the high incidence of corruption. Transparency International ranked Sierra Leone 119 out of 167 countries on its 2015 Corruption Perception Index.[3] Sierra Leoneans pay bribes during most interactions with the government such as when they report crimes to the police, receive injections at a government hospital, or apply for a

Mined-out diamond pits at Namadu Bridge, Kono District

driver's license. The people demanding the bribes say their low salaries require them to make extra money.

Higher-level corruption is also common. In such a poor economy politics is seen as a way to become wealthy and, as in many African countries, leaders skim off government money so they can live in a Western style with electricity and vehicles and send their children to study in foreign countries. People in power often have a high sense of privilege and exploit others for their own gain. They steal money meant for communities, schools, and hospitals without regard for development, quality of life, or even human life. Managers demand free labor from subordinates and male teachers may ask for sex from girl students in exchange for good grades.

People in power can also be lax in their duties. Government workers sometimes sit and chat all day or they may not show up for work at all. Many are political employees with little knowledge or interest in their fields. The government moves slowly and without any sense of commitment or accountability. Everyone complains about the government, songs are written about it, but most people feel they are powerless to do anything.

History

Low Life Expectancy

Because of the extreme poverty and poor quality of health care, the life expectancy (at birth) of Sierra Leoneans is very low, estimated by the United Nations Development Program to be only 50.9 years.[4] People can die at any age. Children, teenagers, and young adults can meet sudden death, usually from preventable or treatable illnesses. The most common fatal diseases are malaria and typhoid fever, and there are occasional outbreaks of cholera. Intestinal worms and shistosomiasis are common parasites. Lassa fever and Ebola are viral hemorrhagic fevers affecting local people and HIV/AIDS is also present, though not at high levels.

In 2013 the country had the worst under-five mortality rate in the world at 161 per 1000 births, compared with only three for Norway and seven for the United States.[5] Babies and young children die mainly from diarrhea, respiratory infections, malaria, and malnutrition. Sierra Leone also has the world's highest maternal mortality rate. In 2013 the UNDP estimated that women giving birth died at the rate of 1,100 per 100,000 live births, compared with four for Norway and twenty-eight for the United States.[6] Many women die because they give birth at home and are unable to find help if there are complications. (The statistics for Sierra Leone are approximations and could be worse, because there is little accurate data collection and record keeping in the country.)

There is a severe lack of public health education. Most Sierra Leoneans are unable to recognize symptoms of common diseases and don't take measures to prevent them, and the population in general has little knowledge of science and modern medicine. Most people believe that illness is caused by witchcraft and go to traditional healers when someone becomes ill. The high cost of medicine and the poor treatment patients receive in government hospitals are other reasons why people avoid Western medicine.

There is also a religious factor in the high mortality rate. Sierra Leoneans believe that God decides when you will die and that nothing can change God's decision. Many people show resilience to the death of children, family members, and friends, something that happens often in their lives.

Witchcraft

The belief that humans can attain supernatural powers is almost universal in Sierra Leone, and magical happenings are a topic of everyday conversation. People use magic for two purposes: to harm others and to bring benefits to themselves.

The most-rumored method of harming others is through the use of a "witch gun". A person who wants to harm someone can hire a witch doctor (or "ju-ju man") who performs a magical ceremony in which the victim is "shot" with

Connaught Hospital, the country's main government hospital in Freetown, built in colonial times

a witch gun, resulting in illness, a violent headache or other symptoms, and possibly death. Actually seeing a real witch gun or finding a witch doctor who will perform the ceremony is difficult, but almost everyone believes they exist.

A common reason given for witch gun shootings is hatred or jealousy. For example, if a child dies the parents may think that a neighbor was jealous and had the child killed with a witch gun. People are also shot in struggles for positions or from simple "wickedness". The use of witch guns is illegal in the country and allegations of witch gun shootings are taken seriously and sometimes go to court. (Most lawmakers and judges believe in witch guns.)

Witchcraft is used in beneficial ways to cure disease and for protection. People who are ill can go to traditional healers and receive magical treatments combined with herbal medicines. People who have been shot by witch guns can have the witch bullets removed from their bodies by magic.

Many Sierra Leoneans fear they have enemies who want to harm them and carry magical objects on their bodies or clothes or have their bodies "washed" with herbal solutions for protection. This type of magic was used extensively in the war, and some of the narrators in this book describe having their bodies washed so they couldn't be killed by bullets. Sierra Leoneans also use religion for protection, calling on God, Jesus, or Allah to protect them from enemies or to have their enemies destroyed. Pentecostal Christian churches are popular and preach the protective power of Christianity.

Another common belief is "African airplane" where witches (both male and female) magically travel around the world at night and visit various locales. People can also change into animals, and powerful magicians stage magic shows in town centers where they pierce themselves with knives and disappear.

A small number of people may try to gain benefits for themselves through human sacrifice, believing that ceremonies involving human body parts can give them power and wealth and protect them from evil forces. There have been historical incidents of human sacrifice/cannibalism in the country, for example, there is a report available online on the trials of "Human Leopards" by the colonial government, written in 1915.[7] Before the war there was the "Lodge" in Freetown and other major towns. This was an organization of leaders and those who wanted to become leaders, and it was rumored that Lodge members practiced human sacrifice in their chapter houses to give themselves formidable powers. When Charles Taylor came to power in Liberia it was widely rumored that he practiced it.

There are still occasional reports or rumors of bodies found with missing parts that people assume were used in rituals. However, with the general modernization of the country the practice has probably lessened, though there is little valid documentation of incidents.

The Sierra Leone Truth and Reconciliation Commission Report states that all the fighting factions in the war practiced cannibalism, both as a scare tactic and from the old belief that the body parts will give power and strength to the person eating them.[8] Some fighters ate human hearts, livers, and muscle tissue either raw or cooked. This type of cannibalism emerged as part of the extreme violence of the war.

Education

The country's modern education system was set up by Britain and was geared toward academic studies to enter university with few vocational or technical courses. Today, classes still focus on rote learning and there is little emphasis on usable skills or creative thinking.

Freetown had the first university in West Africa—Fourah Bay College in Freetown, founded in 1827. In the 19th century the city was known as the "Athens of West Africa" and people from English-speaking West African countries traveled to Freetown to study for degrees. However, following independence and especially after the war, corruption, poor administration, and emigration of educated people to other countries led to the deterioration of education at Fourah Bay and other institutions.

Families are required to pay fees for their children's education and many students quit after the 6th grade because of poverty. In 2013 the World Bank estimated that only 46% of the population over fifteen was literate.⁹ Many schools were destroyed in the war and textbooks and other teaching materials are scarce. Rural schools may be poorly organized with low attendance of both teachers and students, and parents have little control over what goes on in schools and classrooms.

Secondary schools are especially corrupt. Teachers charge students for lessons and high grades while principals steal school funds for their own use. Since the end of the war, the West African secondary school examination for English-speaking countries has been taken by thousands of Sierra Leonean students, but only a few pass it each year.

Primary School children in Kono District

It is common for both parents and teachers to employ corporal punishment, using cut sticks or "canes" to "beat" or "flog" children. Co-author Bernard Moigula describes it as follows:

Physical violence is not a new problem in Sierra Leone. It is a habit for the majority of Sierra Leoneans to beat their children, even for educated people. Many Sierra Leonean homes have canes for beating the children and they are used often. My father was not an exception. As a child I got used to beatings and came to accept it, then do what I wanted.

Most teachers believe in being tough. For example, teachers play a game called "Hot Mental" where students are required to recall random multiplications in seconds, and if they make a mistake they are given a beating. A punishment for coming to school late is to kneel under the sun, and a group of teachers makes a circle around the student and take turns flogging him or her.

In colleges and universities it's more mental violence. For example, during my first semester in one of the Sierra Leone universities lecturers hid reading materials from students so we would be embarrassed in the exams.

In Sierra Leone when someone is caught stealing, the whole area will fall on him or her with heavy kicking and beatings using anything they can find—sticks, iron rods, and stones. I once saw a pickpocketer caught in Freetown near the Eastern Police Station. A crowd of people beat him until he was unconscious. This is practiced country-wide.

Girls and Boys, Women and Men

Education is valued, but after leaving school most young people remain unemployed because of the poor economy. Many of them don't want to live a life of poverty as village farmers so they stay in towns and try to exist on petty trading or other low-paid work. Sierra Leone suffers from ongoing marginalization and disaffection of youth. Young people must defer to elders who are given a high level of respect, and older people may discriminate against and exploit them. During the war feelings of powerlessness, bitterness from poverty, and the political, social, and physical violence around them led some young people to become brutal fighters.

Young people gain their traditional education through secret society training which includes a period of instruction followed by an initiation ritual. The country's tribes have separate secret societies for women and men with different names by ethnic group—the most common are the Sande or Bundu for women and the Poro for men. Secret society training takes place in rural areas in "society bush" located near villages with separate areas for men and women. In the past, society training could last for one or more years, but currently it is shortened and sometimes takes place during school holidays. Men's societies are very secretive and asking questions about their activities isn't allowed.

The women's society traditionally prepared girls for marriage by training them in domestic skills. The men's society trained boys in farming, hunting, marriage responsibilities, and warfare. Initiation ceremonies include ritual scarring for boys and female genital cutting (FGC, also called FGM—Female

*Mende women's society Sowei and attendants.
The masked Sowei makes appearances during society activities.*

Genital Mutilation) for girls which in Sierra Leone involves excision of the clitoris. There is currently some resistance to initiation among young men and women who prefer to live a modern life. There is also a movement to prohibit female genital cutting until a girl is eighteen years old and able to make her own decision. UNICEF estimates that 88% of Sierra Leonean women have undergone FGC.[10]

Women and girls suffered tremendously during the war from rape and other physical violence and the country is still male-dominated, though there are many strong and vocal women who take positions of leadership nationally and in towns and villages. Traditionally women had a low status in the family with no influence in decision making, and they received no property if their husband died. In the more Muslim north girls may be forced into marriage and fewer of them are sent to school. Since the war laws have been passed that give women more rights including the right to inherit their husband's property, and there are laws that require all parents to send their children to school.

In the past, sex was never discussed, but public education on AIDS, FGC, and women's issues have made it a more common topic, especially among young people. Birth control isn't commonly available and is rarely used. Girls may become pregnant in their mid-teens, and both women and men often have children by more than one partner. In addition, polygamy is practiced by Muslims, so many people have half sisters and brothers. This doesn't mean that Sierra Leoneans aren't monogamous: there are many types of family structures with extended families of grandparents, aunts, uncles and cousins forming close bonds. It's customary for couples to wait to get married until they are older—men often waiting until they are around thirty years old and financially stable—and when a couple does get married, there is a grand wedding celebration.

Radio discussion on gender issues

BEFORE THE WAR

Arial view of central Freetown (photo by Peter Andersen)

Prior to contact with Europeans, the area that is now Sierra Leone lay on the southern periphery of the great West African empires: the Ghana Empire of the 10th century, the Mali Empire of the 13th to 17th centuries, and the Songhay Empire of the 15th and 16th centuries. These empires controlled the trans-Saharan trade routes to North Africa, sending gold, ivory, kola nuts, and slaves north in exchange for metal, cloth, and manufactured goods. The coastal forest regions to the south where Sierra Leone is located weren't directly ruled by these empires, but were connected to the trade routes as sources of goods, and possibly slaves, that were transported across the Sahara.

In Europe it was known that West Africa was an important source of gold but the Sahara Desert was too dangerous for Europeans to cross, and in the 15th century Portuguese ships began exploring the West African coast. By the mid-15th century the Portuguese had given the name "Serra Lyoa", meaning "Lion Range" or "Lion Mountains", to the mountainous peninsula where Freetown is now located. Various reasons are given for the name: the shape of the mountains, the roaring of thunder, or the sound of surf on the shore.

The harbor that is the estuary of the Sierra Leone River is the largest and best protected on the West African coast and it became a provisioning spot for European ships. Portuguese traders settled there and at other river estuaries and were joined by British, French, Dutch, and Danish traders who set up "factories" at points along the coast from present-day Senegal to Angola. They engaged in trade with local rulers and middlemen, exchanging commercial goods, rum, and firearms for gold, ivory, and agricultural produce. There was also trade in humans. People kidnapped or taken captive in wars and raids, along with debtors and criminals, were shipped to the new world to live and work as slaves.

The slave trade grew in the 16th and 17th centuries and by the 18th century the British were the dominant slave traders in the region and the United States, Brazil, and Sweden had joined the other nations in the trade. Millions of Africans were transported to the Caribbean, South America, and North America. People from what was called the Grain Coast or Rice Coast, which included present-day Guinea, Sierra Leone, and Liberia, were valued for their rice-growing skills and many were sent to rice plantations in the southeastern United States. Presently their descendents include the Gullah people of the Sea Islands off the coast of South Carolina and Georgia who still have traces of Sierra Leonean language and traditions in their local culture.

The indigenous people of Sierra Leone also had their own form of slavery, buying and selling captives and debtors to use for domestic and farm work. Indigenous slavery was abolished by the colonial government in 1928.

Freetown is Settled
In 1787 a British charity brought a group of 400 "black poor" to settle on the Sierra Leone peninsula. The group included former slaves, indentured servants, and sailors who had been living on the streets of London, and also some white women and men. They settled by the harbor near the site of present-day Cline Town and named their settlement Granville Town after the abolitionist Granville Sharp. Most of these settlers died from disease and warfare with the local Temnes.

In 1792 the settlement was re-established by a group of 1,000 "black loyalists"—African-Americans who had fought for Britain in the American Revolutionary War and who were resettled in Nova Scotia after Britain lost the war. Unable to tolerate the weather, poor farmland, and racism they encountered in Nova Scotia, they moved to Sierra Leone and built a new town they called Freetown on the same site, to the east of the enormous cotton tree that still dominates the center of the capital.

In 1800 a group of Jamaican Maroons arrived. "Maroon" was a term used in the Caribbean and Americas for runaway slaves who lived in independent settlements. In Jamaica, Maroons had established villages in remote mountain areas and fought two wars with the British. When they lost the second war a group was expelled to Nova Scotia then transferred to Freetown. Their descendents still live in Sierra Leone and St. John's Maroon Church on Siaka Stevens Street in Freetown is a local historic site.

Britain outlawed the Atlantic slave trade in 1807 and Sierra Leone, consisting of Freetown, the peninsula, and adjacent coastal areas, became a British crown colony in 1808. The British navy used Freetown as a base for an anti-slavery squadron that intercepted slave ships and seized captives who were released in the colony. Some of them returned to their homelands but others stayed in Freetown or lived in new villages on the peninsula such as Regent, Goderich, and York. British missionaries established churches and schools and many African residents of the colony became Christians, though there were also Muslims among the colony's residents. (Islam had come to West Africa from North Africa, and the area around present-day Guinea and the Sahel was already Islamized at the time.)

Africans from many ethnic groups lived in Freetown and at first they settled by tribe, but by the second and third generations they developed into a distinct ethnic group called "Krio". This term is the phonetic spelling of "creole", a word from Portuguese and Spanish that was used during the colonization of Africa and the Americas to refer to locally-born descendents of foreigners, at first for white descendents but later for descendents of any non-native person.

The language of the Krios is also called "Krio". It is a mixture of English, African, and Portuguese words and is similar to the English creole languages spoken in former British colonies in West Africa and the Caribbean such as Nigeria and Jamaica. Krio is now the lingua franca of Sierra Leone. Its use expanded during the civil war as people moved around the country and to refugee camps in neighboring countries, and currently almost everyone in the country speaks it.

After Fourah Bay College was established Krios became the main businessmen, traders, pastors, professionals, and civil servants of the colony. They assimilated aspects of British culture including Victorian clothing and manners and built wooden houses in the style of the colonies they came from. Many of these charming, old-fashioned houses still exist in Freetown and surrounding areas.

Krio and European traders moved into the interior regions followed in the mid-1800s by British officials who made treaties with local rulers, by force if necessary, to counter France as it expanded its influence to the north and east of the colony in the area of present-day Guinea. In the 1880s European powers made claims to territory throughout Africa in what is known as the "Scramble for Africa" and in 1895 an agreement was signed in Paris between France and Britain that fixed a border between Guinea and Sierra Leone. The interior became a British protectorate in 1896.

Britain required the colony to finance itself and efforts were made to increase the export of agricultural products such as palm nuts, coffee, cocoa, and ginger. A narrow-gauge railway for freight and passengers was constructed beginning in 1896 and the Freetown-Pendembu line was completed in 1907 followed by a branch to Makeni in 1914. During this period Freetown was known locally as "Salone" while the interior regions were "upcountry" or "upline" ("up the railway line"). Later the entire country was called "Salone".

To assure their authority the British weakened the power of local kings and chiefs and gave them the new title of "Paramount Chief". The British also imposed protectorate-wide laws including a tax on dwellings. This "Hut Tax" resulted in a rebellion in 1898 known as the Hut Tax War in which both major tribes—the Temnes in the north and the Mendes in the south—battled the British and their African colonial troops. In the north the Temne chief Bai Bureh fought an organized campaign, but he was captured and deported. In the south Mende fighters seized and killed Europeans and Krios, but colonial troops captured and executed many of their fighters and leaders and the Hut Tax War ended.

However, threats of local rebellions and skirmishes continued, and in response the colonial government demarcated revised areas of control for Paramount Chiefs known as "chiefdoms" and assigned the right of chieftaincy to only a few families in each chiefdom. The British paid stipends to Paramount Chiefs to ensure their loyalty and replaced those they considered troublemakers. The Paramount Chiefs continued to hold strict autocratic power over their people which allowed Britain to control the population indirectly through them. Some judicial powers were transferred from chiefs to District Commissioners and a force of Frontier Police was established to keep order. After these changes Britain had firm control of the protectorate.

The colony's economy changed in 1930 when diamonds were discovered in Kono District. A monopoly concession was given to De Beers, the world's largest diamond-mining company, but illegal mining couldn't be stopped and in 1956 a licensing system for the mining of alluvial diamonds was established that gave the power to grant licenses to Paramount Chiefs. There was a rush of thousands of miners to the diamond mining areas with enormous financial rewards for diamond buyers, government officials, and the Paramount Chiefs who controlled the diamond areas. With enormous riches for those in power, diamonds became a major corrupting force in the country.

Independence and the One-Party State
Following the independence of India in 1947 there was a move to grant independence to other British colonies, and in 1951 Britain created a

constitution and a framework for the independence of Sierra Leone. In 1953 Milton Margai, a Mende and the leader of the Sierra Leone People's Party, or SLPP, was elected Chief Minister. In the late 1950s an opposition party, the All People's Congress, or APC, was formed by Siaka Stevens, an ethnic Limba and trade union leader with his power base in the north and Western Area.

These two parties, the SLPP and APC, became the dominant political parties and split the country in half politically along ethnic and regional lines: the SLPP of the Mendes and their allies in the south and east, and the APC of the Temnes, Limbas, Krios and other tribes in the north and Western Area. This ethnic and regional divide became, and remains, the defining characteristic of politics in the country.

Milton Margai

The two parties clashed in the lead-up to independence. Ten days before the handover Chief Minister Milton Margai declared a state of emergency and had APC leaders arrested for threatening a strike and an alleged plot to blow up a bridge. Sierra Leone became independent on April 27, 1961 with the SLPP in power and APC leaders under detention.

In 1962 Milton Margai was elected the country's first Prime Minister, but he died after two years in office and was replaced by his brother, Albert Margai. To keep the SLPP and the Mendes in power Albert Margai tried to impose a one-party state, but he was forced to back down after strong opposition from Krios and northerners.

An election in 1967 was hotly contested between Albert Margai of the SLPP and Siaka Stevens of the APC. Siaka Stevens won the vote but at his swearing-in ceremony a group of soldiers announced a coup d'état. Brigadier Andrew Juxon-Smith declared himself Head of State and ruled the country for nearly a year when he was overthrown by Brigadier John Bangura, and Siaka Stevens was finally instated as Prime Minister.

Siaka Stevens

History

From the beginning Siaka Stevens was a suspicious and heavy-handed leader. In 1971 he accused Brigadier John Bangura of planning a coup and had him arrested and executed. This was the first officially sanctioned killing by the government and the first execution of a suspected coup plotter. Others in the plot were arrested and imprisoned including a corporal named Foday Sankoh, the man who would lead the attack on the country twenty years later as leader of the RUF rebels.

The APC controlled parliament and in 1972 Siaka Stevens made Sierra Leone a republic with himself as President. To gain total control he centralized the government, ending district-level elections and closing district offices. This resulted in the deterioration of education, health, and other services and gave Stevens and his loyalists more opportunities to steal government funds for themselves and their families.

Elections in 1973 and 1977 were rigged and violent. Groups of APC youth and Steven's personal police force, the Special Security Division, intimidated opponents, attacked polling stations, and arrested SLPP candidates. In 1975 Stevens had six political enemies executed for an alleged coup plot, and in 1978 he declared a one-party state. Stevens became an absolute dictator with control of both parliament and the courts. No open debate was allowed and newspapers and broadcasting were tightly controlled.

Fearful of coups, Stevens surrounded himself with Guineans who served as his personal bodyguards. He reduced the size of the army and filled its ranks with northerners and others loyal to him. The army received little training or equipment, and at the beginning of the war had only 4,000 troops led by poorly trained and corrupt officers. The fact that the army was dominated by northerners also caused tremendous problems during the war.

The Sierra Leone economy was dependent on exports of bauxite, diamonds, and agricultural produce, and because of mismanagement and fluctuations in export prices the economy stagnated through the 1970s. The railway was discontinued, a victim of poor management and the increased use of roads. The economy finally broke down completely, many Sierra Leoneans believe, in 1980 when Stevens decided to host the Organization of African Unity conference in Freetown and built lavish facilities at the cost of $200 million which bankrupted the country.

Stevens and his loyalists also had control of the diamond trade. They smuggled gems out of the country for their own profit, and after DeBeers pulled out of its contract in 1984 most of the country's diamonds were traded illegally with no tax revenues for the country.

In agriculture, the government set up marketing boards that required farmers to hand over their produce for government purchase, but corrupt officials paid farmers less than market price and stole the remaining funds. Education came to a standstill as unpaid teachers refused to teach. Even the power system in the capital ceased to function and Freetown became possibly the only capital city in the world without electricity.

In 1985 Siaka Stevens was 80 years old. He retired from office and handed over power to Major General Joseph Momoh, the highest ranking officer in the army. Momoh wasn't a tyrant like Stevens but he was weak and ineffectual, and criticized for his frequent drinking parties.

The economy continued to decline and President Momoh turned to the IMF and the World Bank for help. They demanded an end to subsidies for fuel and food and the Leone, the country's monetary unit, was floated which resulted in rapid inflation. Sierra Leoneans were powerless and destitute. As the report of the post-war Sierra Leone Truth and Reconciliation Commission states:

> *It was years of bad governance, endemic corruption and the denial of basic human rights that created the deplorable conditions that made conflict inevitable. Successive regimes became increasingly impervious to the wishes and needs of the majority....Institutional collapse reduced the vast majority of people into a state of deprivation. Government accountability was non-existent. Political expression and dissent had been crushed. Democracy and the rule of law were dead.[1]*

Conditions were bad and the country may have been ready for war, but the conflict that eventually took place wasn't initiated to improve the lives of the people. It was instigated by two power-hungry men—Foday Sankoh and Charles Taylor—with support from Muammar Qaddafi, the president of Libya, who was attempting to expand his influence in West Africa.

Student Activists and Qaddafi

In 1977, in response to the deteriorating political and economic situation, Fourah Bay College students held demonstrations that were put down violently by Siaka Steven's security forces and gangs of APC youth. A group of student activists at Fourah Bay founded an organization they called the Pan African Union, or PANAFU, to agitate for social justice and the restoration of democracy. The name of the organization linked it with pan-Africanism, a movement that promoted African and black solidarity and self sufficiency. In their search for political ideology the PANAFU students studied The Green Book, a revolutionary tract created by Muammar Qaddafi.

Muammar Qaddafi had taken control of Libya in a coup in 1969 and instituted a nationalistic and anti-Western agenda. He allied himself with the

Soviet Union and promoted himself as a pan-Arab and pan-African leader dedicated to ending Western influence in the region. Qaddafi was strongly pro-Palestinian in an era when the Palestinian cause was becoming radical and violent, and he supported acts of terrorism including the killing of Israeli athletes at the 1972 Munich Olympics by the Black September group. He sent his armed forces into conflicts in Uganda where he supported Idi Amin against a rebel invasion, and to Chad where he aided rebels fighting the French-supported government. In 1982 Qaddafi's plans to hold the OAU conference in Tripoli were cancelled when the conference was boycotted by pro-Western African nations, including Sierra Leone and Liberia.

Muammar Qaddafi as Pan-Africanist

Qaddafi's Green Book, which the Sierra Leonean students were studying, sets forth his "Third Universal Theory" of direct governance by the people rather than by a party, class, or ethnic group. This was a theory designed to appeal to activists from countries with oppressive regimes—regimes that were often supported by Western countries—and Qaddafi's plan was to attract militants to his World Revolutionary Headquarters near Benghazi and train them in revolutionary theory and guerrilla warfare, then support insurgencies against Western-supported governments.

In Sierra Leone, the PANAFU students set up Green Book study groups around the country including one in Bo, the country's second largest city. One person who became involved with the study group in Bo was the former corporal Foday Sankoh, who had left prison in 1978 and become a commercial photographer in Bo, then later in the town of Segbwema in far-eastern Kailahun District, deeper into strongly anti-government Mende territory.

Charles Taylor, Foday Sankoh, and Blaise Campoaré
At the same time, events were taking place next door in Liberia that would set the stage for wars in both countries. Liberia, a heavily forested country with sixteen indigenous ethnic groups, had an early history similar to Sierra Leone's. Beginning in the 1820s a group in the United States called the American Colonization Society bought land along the coast for the resettlement of free African-Americans. The settlement grew and expanded into the interior and in 1847 the Republic of Liberia was established with Monrovia, named after U.S. President James Monroe, as its capital.

The settlers were known as Americo-Liberians. They dominated politics and became the elite of the country, keeping power out of the hands of the local tribes and leaving the interior of the country undeveloped. In 1980 the last Americo-Liberian president, William Tolbert, was overthrown by Master Sergeant Samuel Doe in a coup that included the murder of the president and the public execution of the cabinet on a beach in the capital.

Doe allowed indigenous people into government and was popular at first, but he began to favor his own tribe, the Krahn, and his popularity with other ethnic groups declined. Doe's regime was supported by the United States, which was using Liberia as its main Cold War ally in West Africa with a communications center and broadcast facilities for the Voice of America.

Charles Taylor in his fighting days

In 1980 a young and ambitious Liberian named Charles Taylor returned to Monrovia from university studies at Bentley College in Massachusetts and joined Doe's administration as head of purchasing. In 1983 he was accused of embezzlement, and he fled to the United States where he was arrested on an extradition warrant. Taylor was put in prison but he escaped in 1985 and traveled to Mexico.

The same year an insurgent group called the National Patriotic Front of Liberia attacked Liberia from the Ivory Coast (or Côte d'Ivoire) in an attempt to overthrow President Doe, but they were fought back and defeated by the Liberian army. The NPFL was predominantly from the Gio and Mano tribes, and in revenge Doe had the two tribes singled out for killings by the Liberian army.

From Mexico Charles Taylor returned to Africa and traveled to Ghana where he met with remnants of the NPFL taking refuge there. Together they moved to Burkina Faso, a former French colony located to the north of Ghana, where Taylor became leader of the group. He also became friendly with Blaise Campaoré, second in command of Burkina Faso.

Muammar Qaddafi had been involved in Burkina Faso since 1983 when he supported a coup that brought Thomas Sankara, a charismatic pan-Africanist, to power, and Sankara had named his friend Blaise Campaoré second in command. In 1987 Qaddafi supported a second coup in which Blaise Campaoré replaced Thomas Sankara, with Sankara killed during the takeover.

Charles Taylor and the NPFL were in Burkina Faso at the time of the coup but it's not known if they were involved in bringing Blaise Campaoré to power. Nor is it known how they met Muammar Qaddafi, though at some point Taylor and his group became friendly with Qaddafi and he agreed to support them in an overthrow of the Liberian government, and they began military training and lessons in political theory at the World Revolutionary Headquarters.

In 1987 a group of Sierra Leonean PANAFU students went to Libya for a training course, but when they returned to Sierra Leone they split over strategy. A majority of the PANAFU members opposed a violent overthrow, preferring a revolution through education. A smaller group wanted to stage an armed insurgency, and in April 1988 they returned to Libya. This group of militants included two committed student activists named Abu Kanu and Rashid Mansaray. Foday Sankoh was also with them, having become more involved with anti-government factions in eastern Sierra Leone. Sankoh, who was the oldest, and who had military experience in the Sierra Leone Army, became the group's leader.

Foday Sankoh, leader of the RUF rebels

In Libya Foday Sankoh met Charles Taylor and the two men agreed to help each other with their insurgencies. Blaise Campaoré agreed to transship arms through Burkina Faso and supply Burkinabé troops for the invasion forces. Muammar Qaddafi provided funds and links to arms dealers and mercenaries. The group was now formed that would instigate long wars in Sierra Leone and Liberia.

Taylor and the NPFL Invade Liberia

In 1989 Charles Taylor began his moves to take over Liberia. He traveled to Sierra Leone and asked President Momoh for permission to use the country as a base to attack Liberia. Momoh refused and had him arrested. Taylor was quickly released and he traveled to the Ivory Coast where he assembled a group of NPFL fighters. On December 24, 1989 Taylor and his troops invaded Nimba County in Liberia from the Ivory Coast. A contingent of Sierra Leonean fighters led by Foday Sankoh joined them in the invasion.

On entering Nimba County the NPFL recruited large numbers of Gio and Mano fighters who were embittered by President Doe's revenge killings. They quickly defeated Doe's Liberian Army forces in Nimba Country and moved toward Monrovia. The tribal antagonisms provoked by Doe and Taylor turned the Liberian war into an ethnic conflict with the Gio and Mano fighting the Krahn (Doe's tribe) and Mandingos which resulted in many civilians deaths as the opposing tribes attacked and killed each other.

In May 1990 Charles Taylor and the NPFL established their headquarters at the town of Gbarnga on the main highway to Monrovia. At this point the NPFL split into two factions, one headed by Taylor and the other by a rival named Prince Johnson. ("Prince" is a name, not a title.) Prince Johnson's forces arrived in Monrovia first and took control of parts of the city.

In response the Economic Community of West African States (ECOWAS) sent a force to stabilize the country, using Lungi Airport in Sierra Leone as a backup base. The force was named ECOMOG, an acronym for Economic Community of West African States Monitoring Group. The majority of the ECOMOG troops were Nigerian with smaller contingents from Sierra Leone, Guinea, Gambia, and Ghana. The U.S. didn't intervene to help Samuel Doe.

On September 9, 1990 Samuel Doe visited the ECOMOG headquarters near Monrovia and was captured by Prince Johnson's troops who tortured and killed him, and Prince Johnson took over Monrovia. Fighting between Taylor, Prince Johnson, and Doe's supporters continued and thousands of refugees fled to Guinea and Sierra Leone. Guinean President Lansana Conté responded by sending Guinean army troops to the Liberian border and to strategic towns and bases in Sierra Leone.

The RUF Prepares to Attack
After helping Charles Taylor invade Liberia, Foday Sankoh turned his attention to attacking his own country. The invasion force he formed was named the Revolutionary United Front, or RUF. Sankoh's troops included volunteers from Sierra Leone and others who were abducted and forced to join. To find fighters Sankoh and his commanders also visited Sierra Leoneans in detention in Liberian prisons and convinced them to join, or forced them under threat of death.

Military training for the RUF began in October 1990 at Camp Naama, a base located around 20 miles from Taylor's headquarters at Gbarnga. Charles Taylor and Blaise Campaoré provided trainers, arms, and additional troops, mainly Liberian NPFL fighters with women and boys among them. The Truth and Reconciliation Commission Report puts the number of Sierra Leoneans trained at 400 and the initial invasion force at 2,000.[2]

In addition to military training, the group received lessons in the rudimentary ideology that Foday Sankoh developed for the RUF—demands for local representation in government, an end to corruption, and the equitable use of natural resources—and when the fighting started Sankoh used his skills as a speaker to repeat these points over and over to keep up the morale of his troops and to convince civilians of the righteousness of his invasion. It seems that Sankoh believed the mostly Mende, anti-government civilians living in the eastern and southern districts would support him and that he could move on Freetown for a quick takeover, and he told his initial group of fighters that the war would be over in three months.

In the overall plan Taylor would take control of Liberia and Sankoh would take over Sierra Leone, and the two men would become rulers of their respective countries. The diamonds in Sierra Leone were also a target as both a source of funds for the fighting and a means for Taylor and Sankoh to enrich themselves. Charles Taylor advised and supported Foday Sankoh and the RUF throughout the war, though Taylor's prosecutors in his Special Court trial weren't able to prove that Sankoh and the RUF were actually under his command.[3]

What were the motives of Foday Sankoh and Charles Taylor? Charles Taylor seems easy to interpret as a power-hungry megalomaniac willing to say or do anything to take power. Foday Sankoh, on the other hand, sometimes seemed confused, as if he believed his own revolutionary rhetoric and actually cared about the people of Sierra Leone while at the same time ordering civilians to be amputated and murdered.

Taylor appears more articulate than Sankoh. When people made accusations against him he used his sharp focus to deny what they said or to turn the argument back on the accusers. Sankoh more often spoke with vague promises, lame excuses, and the continual recitation of his revolutionary goals. As the war progressed the statements and arguments the two men made were often preposterous, but enough people believed them, had vested interests in their campaigns, were afraid of them, or had reasons not to get involved to keep them fighting for many years.

Where did the brutal tactics used in these wars originate? All the factions in both Sierra Leone and Liberia employed violence as a tactic that included rape, looting, abduction, use of underage fighters, and killing of civilians and prisoners, so the fighters may have been using tactics they already knew about or had experienced, possibly the traditional tactics used in past wars in the region. Sankoh, Taylor, and other high-level commanders surely understood modern warfare conventions while their fighters possibly didn't, so it can be argued that these commanders exploited their fighters' ignorance, having them commit international-level war crimes for their own aims, and when the war was over some of them were rightly convicted and imprisoned.

Were Foday Sankoh and Charles Taylor psychopaths? Monsters like other mass murderers? The two men certainly had no empathy for the thousands of people who were killed and mutilated in the wars they initiated, including many of the fighters they conscripted or abducted. They were single-minded in their individual drives for power and there is no evidence that they were politically motivated, that their coming to power would yield anything but dictatorial, exploitative regimes. However this classifies the two men psychologically, they were egocentric murderers who took advantage of their people and culture for their own ends.

But this is getting ahead of the story. It's up to the reader to comprehend the motives of these leaders and their fighters from what follows in the history of the war and the narratives.

* * * * *

So, in March 1991, as Charles Taylor and the NPFL were still fighting to take over Liberia, Foday Sankoh's troops moved from Camp Naama to the Sierra Leone border. They traveled in two groups, one to the border of Kailahun District in the Eastern Province and the other to the border of Pujehun District in the Southern Province. The Sierra Leone-Liberian border was lightly defended and the fighters mingled with the civilians, refugees, and soldiers at the border and prepared to attack.

History

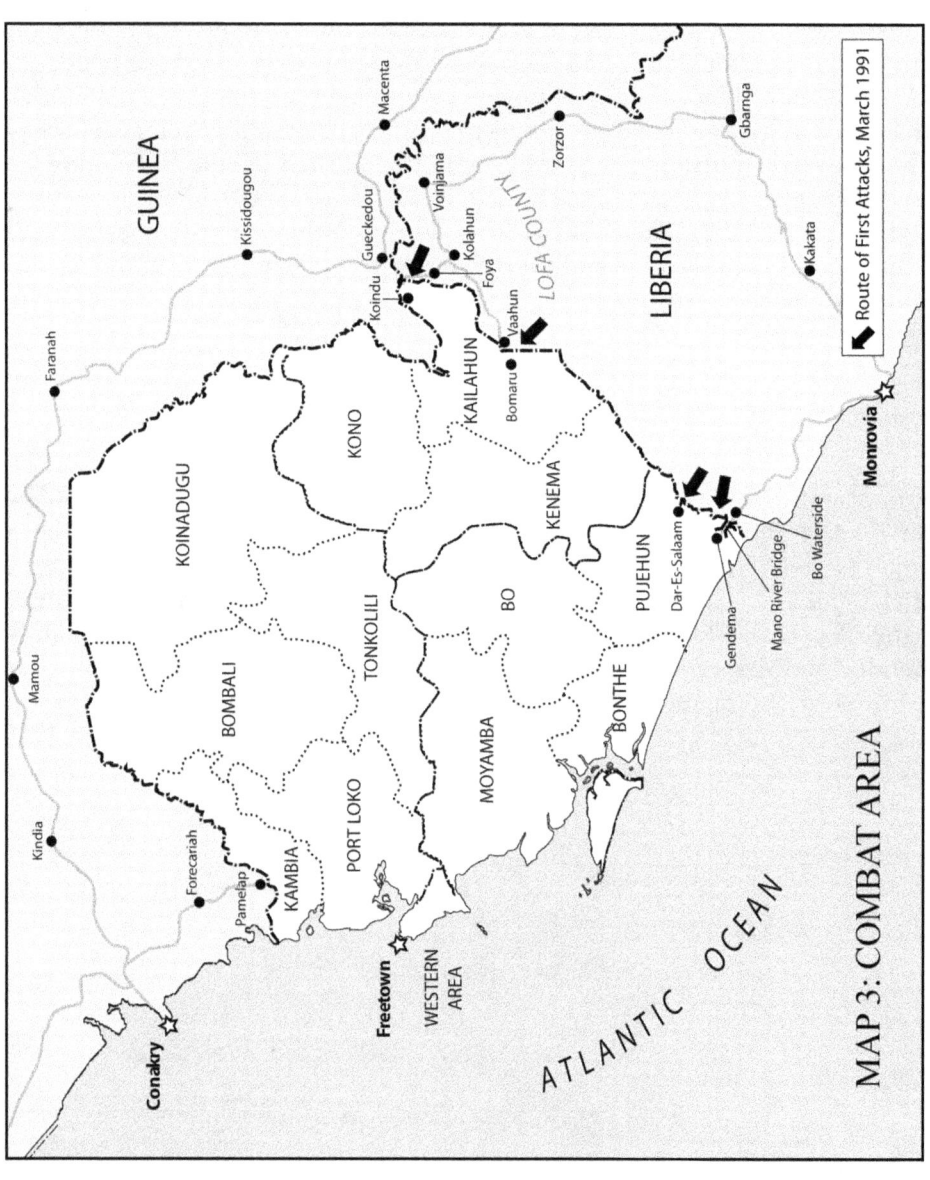

Map 3: Combat areas in Sierra Leone, Liberia, and Guinea including the route of initial attacks from Liberia into Kailahun and Pujehun Districts

THE REBEL WAR: 1991-2002

1991: First attacks in the east, First attacks in the south, Tactics, Poor response from Freetown

First Attacks in the East
Fighting began in March 1991 with attacks by Foday Sankoh's combined RUF/NPFL forces on Kailahun District in the east and Pujehun District in the south. In the east the first attack was at Bomaru, a village on the border that is the crossing point to the town of Vaahun in Liberia. Sierra Leone Army troops were stationed at the crossing, and before the attack were doing business with Charles Taylor's NPFL troops across the border, buying items the NPFL looted in Liberia and selling them to Sierra Leoneans.

On March 23, 1991 the rebel forces attacked and captured Bomaru in the early morning hours, killing fourteen people. In response a contingent of Sierra Leone Army troops traveled to Bomaru from Moa Barracks, a nearby army base, and forced the rebels out. The army then reacted brutally against the villagers, beating and torturing those they thought were in collusion with the rebels. They also looted items the rebels left behind, and this started rumors that the soldiers conspired in the attack so they could loot. A few weeks later the rebels attacked Bomaru again and retook the village from the army.

Where the war began: the checkpoint at Bomaru and road to Liberia, Kailahun District

Four days later, the RUF made another attack further north in Kailahun District on the town of Koindu, located at the far end of the "parrot's beak" where Sierra Leone, Guinea, and Liberia meet. Koindu was a commercial town where a weekly market was held for traders from all three countries, and it was also a trading point for goods looted by the NPFL. The rebels captured and looted Koindu, then moved on and took over the town of Kailahun, the district headquarters of Kailahun District.

The rebels quickly captured other towns and villages and opened training camps, and within a month had upper Kailahun District under their control. The area was well situated for the rebels. It was at the point in the country farthest from Freetown, and was adjacent to Charles Taylor's territory in Lofa County in Liberia. The RUF used it as their headquarters for the entire war.

In June the rebels moved to attack Moa Barracks, located 34 miles southwest of Kailahun town, probably planning to push into Kenema District, link up with the contingent attacking the south, and move on to Freetown. Moa Barracks was built during the colonial period where a bridge crosses the Moa River, with the town of Daru on the opposite bank. At the barracks Sierra Leone Army troops were reinforced by soldiers of the Guinean army and volunteer fighters.

Moa Barracks, Kailahun District (on the Moa River)

The rebels attacked from the Daru side of the river and engaged the army at the bridge. After a fierce battle the army defeated the rebels, and a famous NPFL commander called Rambo was killed in the fighting. (He was the first of several Rambos in the war.) With this defeat the rebels' plan for a quick takeover failed and the demoralized fighters returned to Kailahun town, committing serious atrocities against civilians as they retreated. The atrocities were blamed on the Liberians, angry that their compatriots were being killed in a foreign country.

Foday Sankoh was in Kailahun District directing the fighting, and after the defeat at Moa Barracks (and defeats in the south) he changed his strategy and decided to move north to attack Kono District, the main diamond mining area of the country. Capturing Kono would give the RUF access to the diamonds and also to an alternate route to Freetown along the main highway through the north.

The rebels crossed the Moa River at the Manowa Ferry and, after losing a battle at Segbwema, fought their way up the road that leads to the town of Koidu, the district headquarters of Kono District (not to be confused with Koindu in Kailahun District). In October they captured the town of Gandorhun part way up the road but were stopped by army troops and volunteers who battled them back to Kailahun District.

First Attacks in the South

The initial attacks in the south were coordinated with those in the east. In the south, the border with Liberia is formed by the Mano River, and on March 28th the RUF/NPFL forces attacked at two places—the river-crossing point of Dar Es Salaam and the Mano River Bridge. They moved inland and quickly took control of Zimmi, Potoru, and Pujehun, three towns in Pujehun District, and also captured the local diamond mines.

A contingent of southern rebels then moved northeast to attack the major town of Kenema, probably planning to link up with the eastern contingent, but after many battles around Joru they were turned back by the army and troops from ULIMO (United Liberation Movement of Liberia), a faction of Liberians hostile to Charles Taylor who the Sierra Leone Army had organized and trained in camps for Liberian refugees.

At the same time other groups of rebels moved through the south into Bo and Bonthe Districts, two large southern districts, but they were also fought back by the army and ULIMO. The main towns were retaken and this left the southern rebels confined to the rural areas of Pujehun and Bonthe Districts. Unable to make headway they looted villages and terrorized civilians while mining diamonds in the areas they controlled. Southern RUF commanders Rashid Mansaray and Mike Lamin tried to maintain order by executing rebel fighters who committed crimes, but most crimes weren't reported and there were many abuses against civilians.

History

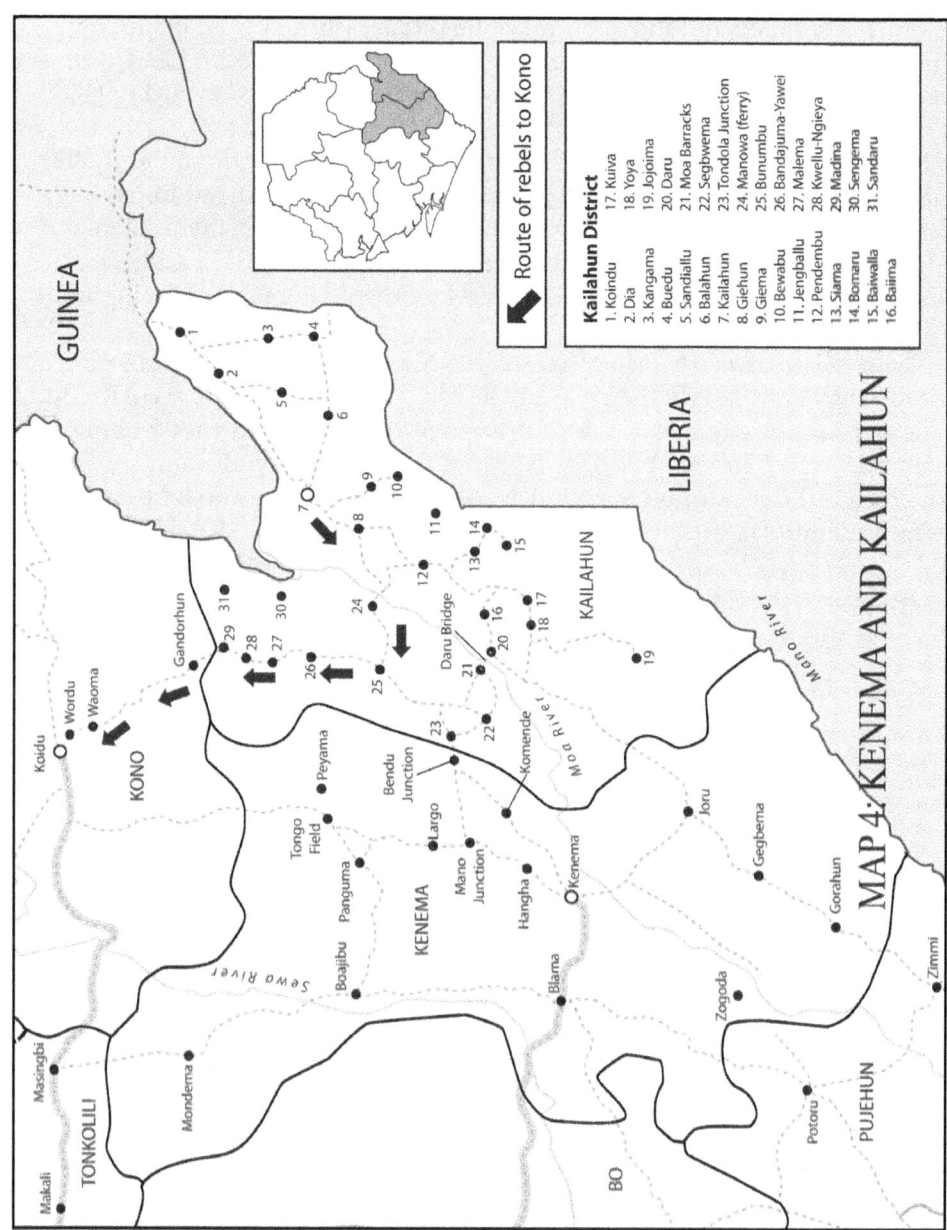

Map 4: Kenema and Kailahun Districts, with route the rebels used to attack Kono District

The Rebel War: 1991-2002

Potoru after the war

Foday Sankoh visited the south during the fighting, but after the failures of the southern contingent he returned to Kailahun and concentrated on taking over Kono District. The rebels weren't able to move past the border districts in their first year of fighting, and Sankoh's plan for a quick takeover failed.

Tactics
Both the rebels and the Sierra Leone Army fought a low-tech war. The rebels had only hand-held weapons including AK-47s, Berettas, and rocket-propelled grenades. They traveled on foot along bush paths or in stolen trucks, vans, and SUVs on the unpaved upcountry roads. The army had no surveillance aircraft, rudimentary communications equipment, and only a small number of armored vehicles. Telephones didn't exist outside the district headquarter towns and there were no local radio stations, so the rebels could attack towns and villages without warning and with little response from the army.

Foday Sankoh visited towns and villages in areas the rebels controlled and gave speeches to win over the local people. He criticized the one-party state and promised that his revolution would bring democracy, prosperity, and an end to corruption. The RUF also wore the symbols of the outlawed SLPP party—palm fronds and the color green—in their first attacks, trying to win over civilians through politics.

Sankoh was a persuasive speaker and some people joined the RUF willingly. However, many RUF commanders and troops used violence more than persuasion to scare the population into submission. To make themselves "fearful" rebel fighters wore combinations of uniforms and civilian clothing, painted their faces, and wore wigs. When they took over towns and villages they replaced local chiefs and other authority figures with their own fighters and supporters, sometimes torturing and killing APC chiefs. Civilians might also be killed including those who wouldn't submit to rebel demands, who tried to escape, or who wouldn't give up produce and livestock.

The rebels abducted young men (and some women) to become fighters. They forced civilians to carry looted goods and sacks of confiscated coffee and cocoa to Liberia where they were exchanged for weapons, ammunition, and market goods. Doctors and nurses were also conscripted, and people with skills such as drivers.

It's not known if the initial violence was part of Sankoh's strategy. The rebels also had poor communications and bands of rebel fighters could operate on their own. Some commanders and fighters were more interested in looting and violence than in winning over the population, and Sankoh couldn't control the actions of all of his troops. In addition, the majority of the rebel fighters were Liberian NPFL who had used violence against civilians as a tactic in their own country and for whom looting was a normal part of war.

Sankoh himself committed crimes. The Truth and Reconciliation Commission Report describes the case of a professor and his wife from Bunumbu College, a small college in Kailahun District, who were abducted during a rebel attack. The professor's wife was the sister of a high-level army officer and Sankoh repeatedly raped her in the presence of her husband.[1]

A 1992 Amnesty International report criticized both the rebels and the army for human rights abuses during the first year of the war:

> *Pushing back an invasion force which entered the country in March 1991, [the government forces] have reportedly executed suspected rebels and collaborators after perfunctory investigation and without any legal sanction. Suspects are alleged to have been tortured or ill treated....all were denied the chance to defend themselves in a court of law....The rebel forces have also been responsible for major human rights abuses, including both deliberate and arbitrary killings and torture. The invasion forces and the rebels they recruited have tortured and slaughtered hundreds of civilians.*[2]

Poor Response from Freetown
In Freetown neither President Joseph Momoh nor army headquarters put much effort into fighting the rebels. They failed to supply soldiers with sufficient arms and medical supplies and, following normal practice, officers stole salaries and rice meant for the soldiers. (SLA troops received a 50-kilogram bag of rice per month as part of their pay.) The army held a recruitment drive to increase the size of the army but failed to train and equip the new recruits adequately.

President Momoh was an incompetent administrator, but he understood that the country needed to return to multi-party democracy. He had the constitution revised and it was voted into law in a referendum in May 1991, though the country would have to wait five more years for multi-party elections.

1992: NPRC coup, RUF expels Liberians and attacks Kono, NPRC executes coup plotters

NPRC Coup

Sierra Leone Army troops had fought the rebels successfully but they weren't satisfied with the poor support from Freetown, and a group of junior officers decided to take action. They traveled from their upcountry barracks to the capital and staged a coup d'état on April 28, 1992. President Momoh fled to Guinea.

Valentine Strasser

The new military government called itself the National Provisional Ruling Council, or NPRC. The group named Captain Valentine E. M. Strasser head of government, giving him the position because of his popularity and speaking skills though he had just turned twenty-five. Besides Strasser, three men involved in the coup became major players as the war progressed: Brigadier Julius Maada Bio, Major Johnny Paul Koroma, and Lieutenant Solomon A. J. Musa, known as SAJ Musa (who was named NPRC Deputy Chairman).

The public was enthusiastic about the new government. The NPRC instituted popular campaigns including the mobilization of youth and the monthly cleaning of towns by the public. They reorganized the war effort and large numbers of young men were conscripted. The army also incorporated local volunteers or "vigilantes" into their ranks as official soldiers.

RUF Expels Liberians and Attacks Kono

Back in Kailahun District Foday Sankoh was having problems controlling the Liberian NPFL fighters who were committing serious atrocities against civilians including killings, torture, rape, and cannibalism. A series of violent campaigns called the TOP ("stop") campaigns took place in late 1991 and 1992 that included the killing of civilians and fighting between factions as

History

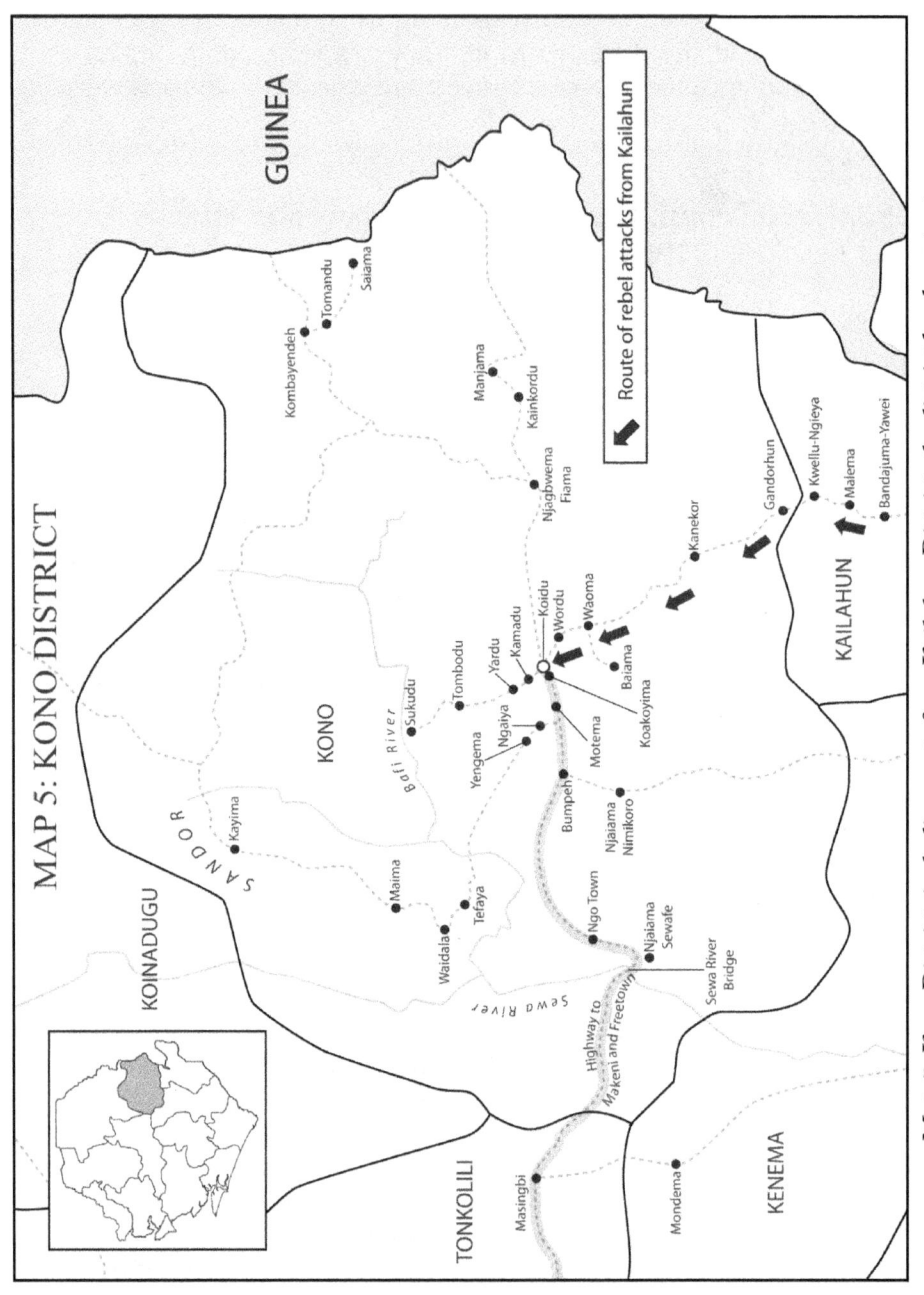

Map 5: Kono District, including route from Kailahun District, the district headquarter town of Koidu, and the main highway to Freetown through the north

commanders tried to control as many fighters and as much territory as they could. Sankoh took charge and in a final campaign ("TOP final") he ordered his Sierra Leonean RUF fighters to kill or expel the Liberians and other foreign troops from the country.

Around the middle of the year the RUF made another attempt to capture Kono District, reinforced with weapons supplied by Charles Taylor.[3] RUF troops again moved up the road linking Kailahun and Kono Districts and captured Gandorhun, the town where they had been turned back the previous year. In October they attacked Koidu and occupied the town for a week before the army forced them out. The rebels didn't leave the district but moved into rural areas where they mined diamonds or seized them from civilian miners and diamond dealers. This resulted in the first significant supply of conflict diamonds that the rebels sent to Charles Taylor to exchange for arms and ammunition.

Army troops weren't able to clear the rebels out of the villages and forests of Kono District on their own, and to assist them the first civil militias, or Civil Defense Forces (CDFs), joined the fighting. Two Civil Defense Forces took part in the fighting in Kono: the Donso force from the Kono ethnic group, and the Tamaboro force who were ethnic Korankos from Koinadugu District in the north.

The Donsos were a men's hunting society who fought with cutlasses and single-shot hunting rifles, while the Tamaboros were sorcerers, both male and female, who fought using the individual magical powers each possessed. Skills the Tamaboros had, or claimed to have, included changing into birds to reconnoiter enemy positions, changing into leopards or producing bees from their noses to attack enemies, and using medicines and incantations to become immune to bullets, immobilize enemies, shoot straight, see in the dark, and disappear.[4] The fighting in Kono District continued into 1993.

SAJ Musa

NPRC Executes Coup Plotters

The year ended with a crisis for the NPRC government in Freetown. On December 29th twenty-six soldiers suspected of plotting a coup were arrested in the capital. They were executed the following day without trial and it was reported that SAJ Musa, the Deputy Chairman of the NPRC, had personally tortured some of the suspects at his home the night before they were executed. The torture and summary executions were condemned both locally and internationally and to quiet the criticism the NPRC sent SAJ Musa to the U.K. with a scholarship to study at a university, though he returned in 1997 and took a major role in the war after the second coup.

1993: Army pushes RUF to the border, Ceasefire, Sankoh consolidates power

Army Pushes RUF to the Border, Ceasefire

At the beginning of 1993 the army and Civil Defense Forces were still fighting the RUF in Kono District with additional support from Nigerian ECOMOG troops. The combined forces were successful, and in February they expelled the rebels from the district. The troops then pushed the rebels through Kailahun District and up to the Liberian border, and by November 1993 had the main towns of Kailahun District under their control. The fighting caused the first major refugee crisis of the war as civilians fled to camps set up for internally displaced persons (IDPs) in the towns of Masingbi, Magburaka, and Makeni located to the west of Kono District on the main highway to Freetown.

In the south, the army and ULIMO also forced the rebels into Liberia. Fighting stopped along the border, and at this point NPRC leader Valentine Strasser made a serious error. Thinking the war was over he declared a ceasefire without disarming the RUF or capturing Foday Sankoh, and this gave the RUF a chance to regroup.

Sam Bockarie (a.k.a. Mosquito)

Sankoh Consolidates Power

Kailahun District is dense with low mountains and forest. The RUF had been pushed out of the towns but they still had camps in the forest along the Liberian border. After the ceasefire Foday Sankoh made a move to consolidate power, probably because of dissension over his failure to win the war. He had forty of his own commanders killed including the original revolutionaries Abu Kanu and Rashid Mansaray. Aiding Sankoh in the killings was Sam Bockarie (known as "Mosquito") who Sankoh appointed second-in-command. Mosquito became notorious in the war as a commander of extreme cruelty, known for summarily killing both fighters and civilians, including children.

In the south, RUF commander Gibril Massaquoi executed an additional twenty-five commanders. Foday Sankoh was now firmly in command with his RUF troops either loyal to him or frightened into submission, and in late 1993 he initiated a new campaign of guerrilla warfare to take over the country.

1994: Guerrilla warfare, RUF spreads through the country, Problems with the army, Rise of the Kamajors

Guerrilla Warfare, RUF Spreads through the Country
The rebels began by strengthening their forces. They attacked military garrisons and convoys for weapons, communications equipment, and army uniforms, and abducted civilians and government soldiers for guerrilla training. They quickly retook upper Kailahun District and re-established it as their home base with operations centers at Buedu, Giema, and Kailahun town.

Moving on bush paths along the border, the Kailahun rebels re-established communications with the southern flank. They built a large operations base called Zogoda Camp in Koya Chiefdom in the far south of Kenema District near the Moa River, away from roads and difficult to reach. Zogoda Camp was positioned for attacks on the Kenema-Bo Highway and gave the RUF access to the south, east, and north. Additional bases were established to stage attacks and train new fighters while Foday Sankoh moved between the bases to coordinate military actions. The Truth and Reconciliation Commission Report explains Sankoh's new strategy:

> *The movement set out to infiltrate deep into Government-held territory... territorial control was secondary to nationwide coverage, however thinly spread. The aim was not occupation but penetration; the objective was not to take control, but to carry out raids, ambushes, and arbitrary violations and abuses to such a disturbing extent that nobody would be genuinely in control... in pursuit of the belief that if it made the life of the people in the Provinces unbearable, it would render the Government devoid of alternatives but to engage in negotiations.*[5]

In a typical operation the RUF would encircle a village in the early dawn and fire their weapons, causing the villagers to panic and run into the bush. They captured those who couldn't escape, then entered the village and took food, livestock, and personal items. The captured civilians would be forced to carry the looted items back to RUF camps while others were taken to be fighters and "bush wife" sex slaves. They kept some of the villages as bases and

History

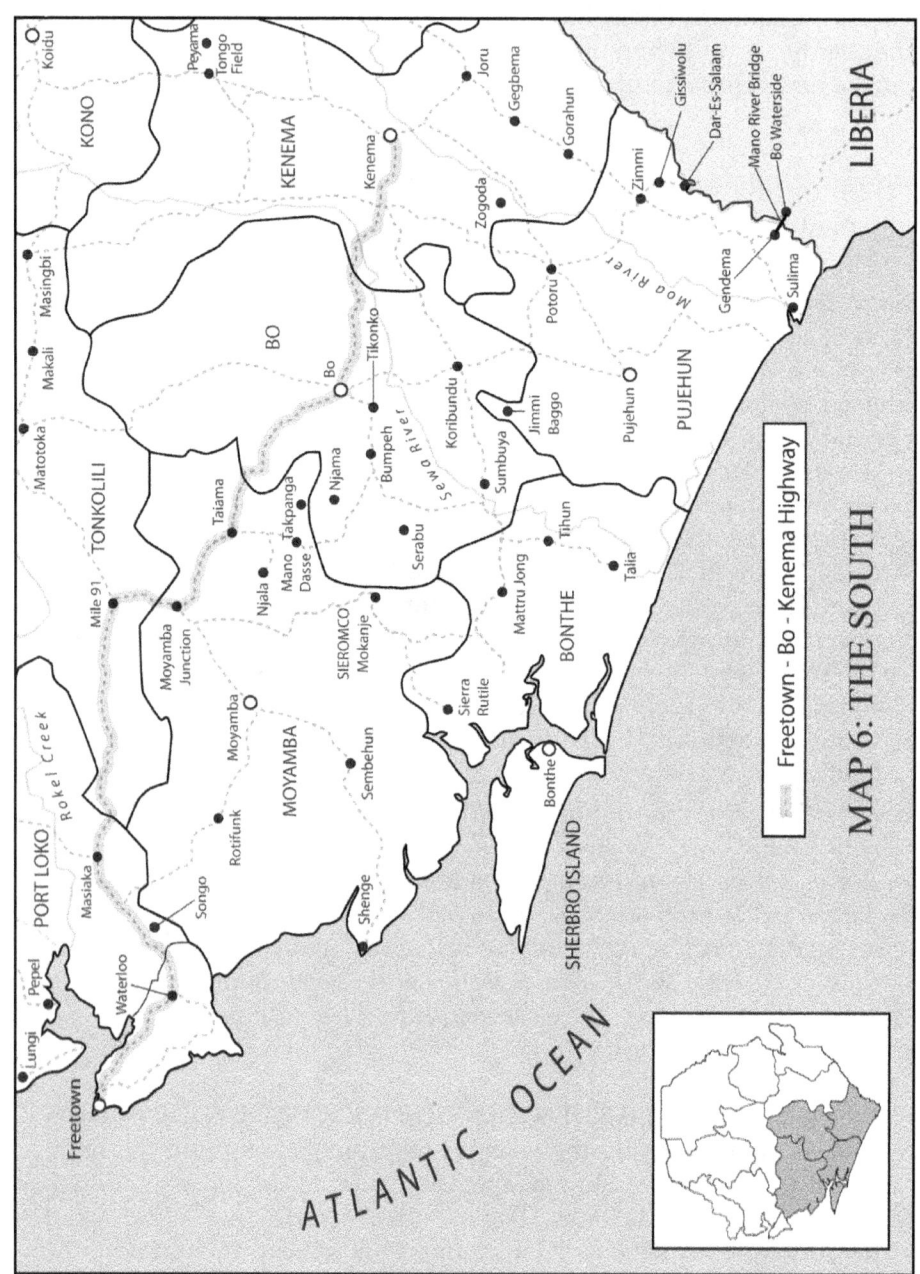

Map 6: *The South—Moyamba, Bo, Pujehun, and Bonthe Districts with the main town of Bo, the Freetown-Bo-Kenema highway, Mile 91, and mining companies*

moved on to others. The rebels also attacked and looted vehicles on roads and highways, and travel became dangerous for civilians.

The RUF committed brutal atrocities during these attacks including torture, murder, mutilation, and rape. They destroyed houses, schools, and clinics and locked people in houses and burned them alive. Abducted civilians became unwilling fighters, afraid to escape because they would be killed by either the rebels or the army if they were caught.

Abducted girls and women were repeatedly raped, and some of them were forced to take up arms and fight alongside the men, though some also did it willingly or for self-protection as female fighters had a higher status and could avoid being raped. The rebels called the youngest boys "Small Boys Unit". Boys as young as seven or eight years old were trained, given weapons, and sent on food-finding missions. Some RUF bases also had Small Girls Units for girls who were too young to be bush wives.

The rebels used drugs to enhance their confidence and endurance. Drugs included marijuana, rough heroin called "brown-brown", refined white heroin, amphetamines, and cocaine, and the drugs were sometimes mixed with gunpowder or put in cuts in the skin. Drugs were also given to children, and it was common knowledge that armed child fighters under the influence of drugs were dangerous and unpredictable.

In the Eastern Province the RUF fought intensively with attacks on Daru, Segbwema, Kenema, and villages in rural areas. The diamond-mining town of Tongo Field in northern Kenema District was an important target and the RUF established a base called Peyama Camp seven miles from the town. There were rebels and army troops around Tongo Field, and both groups engaged in diamond mining when they weren't fighting each other. In Kono District the rebels attacked and occupied Koidu town for a month before the army and allied fighters drove them out, though they stayed in rural areas and continued to mine.

The rebels were also successful in the north, a new area for them. They established a base in the Malal Hills in Tonkolili District to the east of Lunsar which gave them access to the north, Moyamba District, and the Western Area. They attacked vehicles on the Makeni-Koidu highway, and in July they fought for control of three major towns along the highway—Matotoka, Makali, and Masingbi. In August they attacked a large convoy on the Freetown-Bo highway, looting relief supplies and killing drivers and passengers. In November they moved into Koinadugu District and attacked the town of Kabala, and in December they attacked Mile 91, a major junction on the Freetown-Bo highway.

History

In the south the rebels moved into Bo and Bonthe Districts. In June they attacked Telu Bongor in Bo District, the home of Regent Chief Samuel Hinga Norman, a leader of the local civil militias, and killed over one hundred people. In November they attacked an IDP camp at Gondama near Bo and killed hundreds of people.

Becoming bolder, the rebels attacked the major towns of Kenema and Bo in late December. In Kenema the army fought off the attackers, while in Bo the army and a large group of civilians chased them out of town, killing those they caught. A humanitarian worker described the fighting in the south during this period:

Since the end of 1993, we have seen a significant increase in the level of fighting, and we now have the whole south and southeast of the country up in flames. The fighting is very violent, and is characterized by extreme ferocity. These are not minor incidents of small-time rebels or isolated elements simply looting: it is far more serious than that. These are organized forces, who have decided to go on the offensive to overthrow the Freetown government. [6]

Problems with the Army, Rise of the Kamajors

The Sierra Leone Army had expanded its forces and was receiving increased support from abroad including financial aid from Britain. Additional ECOMOG troops assisted the army in fighting the rebels and a mutual defense pact was signed with Nigeria in September.

However, the NPRC government was having serious problems managing the war. There was inadequate planning, and army staff in Freetown had little control over the haphazard military actions taking place upcountry. The army couldn't stage successful attacks on rebel bases and it was impossible to patrol the roadless forest and farmland that covers most of the country.

In addition, the behavior of some army troops and officers led to a decline in the army's reputation. Groups of Sierra Leone Army soldiers were committing crimes against the general population including looting and murder, and many civilians believed that government soldiers were colluding with the rebels to loot and sell stolen goods. Soldiers were accused of running away from RUF attacks and ignoring intelligence of coming attacks. Officers were accused of failing to follow up on civilian complaints of abuses, and there were rumors that the NPRC government was deliberately mismanaging the war to prolong it so they could stay in power and become wealthy.

People began calling the government soldiers "sobels"—soldier-rebels—or soldiers by day and rebels by night. The RUF exploited this by dressing in army uniforms and attacking villages in "false flag" operations so that civilians would think the army was attacking them, causing confidence in the army to decline further.

Mistrust of the army led to an increase in Civil Defense Forces to protect villages and stop rebel infiltration. The largest CDF to emerge was the Kamajor force (pronounced KAH-mah-joh) in the south and east whose members were ethnic Mendes. Other groups, smaller than the Kamajors and from other tribes, were the Kapra fighters who were ethnic Temnes, the Gbinti fighters from the Temne, Limba, and Loko tribes, and the Donsos from Kono who had fought the RUF in Kono District in 1992-1993. (The Tamaboros had disbanded after the fighting in Kono.)

The Kamajors used supernatural powers to fight, and they institutionalized an initiation ceremony that gave their fighters magical powers including the ability to withstand bullets. Kamajors also wore a special shirt (a *ronko*) and cap covered with protective amulets. It was believed that if a Kamajor followed the strict rules of the society he couldn't be killed (and by circular logic, if a Kamajor was killed in battle people believed that he had broken the rules). The initiation ceremony included eating human flesh which was thought to be a powerful type of magic.[7]

The Chief Initiator and High Priest of the Kamajors was Allieu Kondowai, (spelled Kondewa by the Special Court) a herbalist from Bonthe District. Local chiefs from the south and east sent men to Allieu Kondowai to be initiated, and a Kamajor training base called Base Zero was established at Tihun in Bonthe District. The Kamajors started taking a major role in the war, protecting the south and east from RUF attacks and abuses by government troops while working with the army to track RUF rebels in the bush.

A Kamajor in his war ronko
(Photo by Joseph Bullie)

Allieu Kondowai,
Chief Initiator of the
Kamajors
(Special Court photo)

History

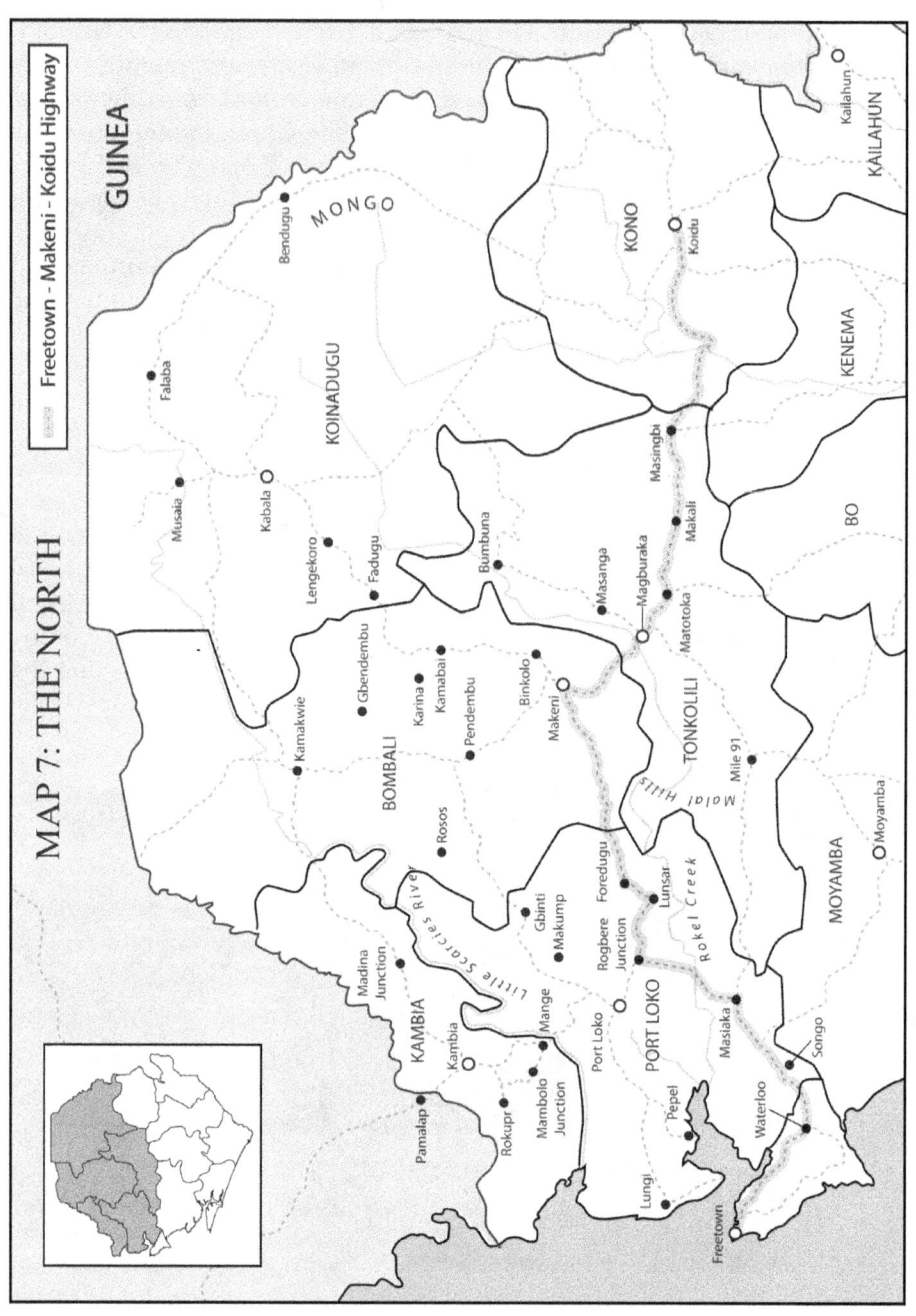

Map 7: *The North—Kambia, Bombali, Koinadugu, Tonkolili, and Port Loko Districts, with Freetown and the Western Area, the Malal Hills and the Freetown-Makeni-Koidu highway.*

By the end of 1994 the situation in Sierra Leone was critical. The RUF had returned from near defeat and infiltrated almost the entire country. The army was weak from mismanagement and lawlessness, and except for the ECOWAS countries of Nigeria, Guinea, and Ghana, no foreign country would intervene to bring an end to the war.

1995: Rebels spread further, Attacks on mining companies, NPRC hires mercenaries, Lead-up to elections

Rebels Spread Further, Attacks on Mining Companies

1995 was another year of intense fighting. In January the RUF moved into Kambia District in the far north, then attacked the towns of Foredugu and Lunsar in Port Loko District, advancing closer to the Western Area and Freetown. They attacked Njala University in Moyamba District where they killed staff, burned buildings, and abducted students and staff to become fighters.

After attacking Njala, and acting on advice from Charles Taylor,[8] the rebels attacked two large mining companies in the south: Sierra Rutile in Bonthe District and SIEROMCO (Sierra Leone Ore and Metal Company), a bauxite mine at Mokanji in Moyamba District. The attacks caused both companies to close which affected the country's finances, as the mines were Sierra Leone's largest employers. After these attacks the rebels continued moving through the south and captured Mattru Jong in Moyamba District where they established a training base. The army and its allies fought back throughout the country but weren't able to stop the rebels.

The RUF began taking hostages in late 1994 in an attempt to gain concessions from the government. They abducted two VSO volunteers during the attack on Kabala in November 1994, and in early 1995 they abducted seven foreign nuns in Kambia and a number of foreign and Sierra Leonean workers from the mining companies. Foday Sankoh demanded the removal of ECOMOG and Guinean troops from the country, but the government wouldn't agree and the hostages were released in March and April.

In the east, there were continued attacks and fighting for control of diamond mines. As villages were burned and civilians abducted and murdered rural areas became depopulated. People fled to major towns, IDP camps, and refugee camps in Guinea and Liberia. The comeback of the RUF was a shock to the public and the reputation of the NPRC government and the army deteriorated further, made worse by the stylish civilian clothes the NPRC leaders wore and the flashy cars they drove around Freetown.

The poor performance of the army and the growth of the Kamajors resulted in hostility between the two groups, and they began to attack each other. The antagonism followed the historic political divide between regions and tribes. The Kamajors, Mendes from the south and east, considered the army not only criminal but an institution controlled by the Temnes and Limbas of the north, who were their political rivals. Hostilities between the two groups were simmering at this point, but events two years later would turn them into full-fledged enemies.

NPRC Hires Mercenaries
In February 1995 the NPRC government turned to private security companies (or mercenaries) to stop the RUF onslaught. They hired Gurkha Security Group, a British company, to protect the Western Area and train the army but the company left after only a month when their commander was killed in an ambush.

In March the government contracted Executive Outcomes, a South African "private military company" that had successfully fought the UNITA rebels in Angola. The government couldn't afford Executive Outcome's fee so Branch Energy, a related company, was given a valuable mining concession in a diamond field near Koidu in Kono District. Branch Energy began intensive mining operations in Kono using a deep pit process, extracting and crushing kimberlite ore to recover diamonds.

In April the RUF attacked Newton, only 35 miles from Freetown. The following month two rebel commanders, C.O. Mohamed and Dennis Mingo (known as "Superman"), established a base near Fogbo and attacked Waterloo, a junction town just 18 miles from the capital. The first Executive Outcomes mercenaries arrived in May and immediately trained a task force that drove the rebels out of the Freetown area.

Executive Outcomes then trained a larger group of soldiers and Kamajors to expel the RUF from strategic upcountry locations. Their goals were to take back the SIEROMCO and Sierra Rutile mines, secure the diamond town of Koidu (where Branch Energy was mining), and destroy RUF bases in the south and east. Executive Outcomes and their troops fought the RUF using tactics described in an article from the website "Soldiers-of-Misfortune":

> *In guerrilla warfare in the African bush, where there is a lack of solid front lines, reconnaissance, concentration of firepower, speed and ambushes all play crucial roles. As former members of South African elite units during the war in Angola, most of the mercenaries had plenty of experience with these tactics. Reconnaissance was mainly carried out by the Kamajors and a special*

airplane, ambushes were avoided by transporting troops with helicopters, and firepower was provided by the dreaded Mi-24 gunships, along with two Alpha Jets dispatched by the Nigerian Air Force for support.

First, the enemy positions were precisely reconnoitred, followed by intense bombardment by the Nigerian Alpha Jets. The already demoralised enemy was then attacked by small mobile combat groups supported by mortar fire, armoured vehicles, land rovers with heavy machine guns and the helicopter gunships. Driven from their positions, the rebels usually fled directly into ambushes of Kamajor groups previously flown in by helicopters.[9]

Executive Outcomes was successful fighting the RUF in the target areas but they couldn't cover the entire country, and the rebels continued to terrorize rural towns and villages. In August the New York Times reported that hundreds of people in the south were starving to death as thousands of civilians fled rebel attacks.[10]

Lead-up to Elections
By the end of 1995 the NPRC government had been in power for nearly three years and the public was pressing for elections. The NPRC arranged for two consultative conferences to be held to discuss and debate a return to democracy. The conferences were held at the Bintumani Hotel in Aberdeen, a town on Cape Sierra Leone near Lumley Beach where major tourist hotels are located. The RUF was invited but didn't attend.

An important issue debated at the conferences was whether to have "elections before peace" or "peace before elections". The first option, elections before peace, meant that a new government would be elected that would then negotiate with the RUF to end the war. The second option, peace before elections, meant that the current government and the RUF would agree on a peace settlement before the elections were held.

The second option was Foday Sankoh's preference as it would give him control over when the elections would take place, and it would also allow him to run as a candidate for president. However, most of the representatives of the political and civil society groups attending the conference didn't trust Sankoh, and they voted overwhelmingly to hold the elections prior to a settlement with the RUF. A date was set for the elections early the next year. The new government would be organized under the constitution promulgated by President Momoh in 1991.

History

1996: NPRC palace coup, Operation Stop the Election, SLPP wins the election, Build-up of Kamajors, Abidjan Peace Accord, Anger in the army

NPRC Palace Coup, Operation Stop the Election, SLPP Wins the Election
The decision to hold elections resulted in a crisis in the NPRC leadership. Chairman of the NPRC Valentine Strasser decided to run for president though he was under the minimum age of forty required by the constitution. Strasser wanted to change the constitution, and this led Julius Maada Bio, Deputy Chairman of the NPRC, to stage a "palace coup" that took place on January 16, 1996. At a meeting of NPRC leaders Maada Bio ordered Strasser arrested. There was a fistfight and Strasser was put in handcuffs and flown to Guinea. Maada Bio took over as NPRC head of state.

Maada Bio held informal talks with the RUF on the possibility of peace negotiations, but Foday Sankoh insisted on postponing the elections until formal negotiations were held and a peace settlement reached. Bio rejected this and went ahead with the elections.

Sankoh responded by ordering "Operation Stop the Election", a brutal campaign of amputations and beheadings of civilians. People caught by the RUF were lined up and their fingers, hands, or limbs cut off with matchets and axes. Many victims died from trauma and loss of blood. There were attacks on towns and villages including an attack on Tihun, the Kamajor base in Bonthe District, where hundreds of civilians were killed.

Maada Bio and Foday Sankoh

The elections were held on February 26th and proceeded despite RUF attacks on polling stations. After a run-off for the required 55% of the vote, the SLPP, the party that had been banned during Siaka Steven's one-party regime, came into power with Ahmad Tejan Kabbah, a former employee of the United Nations Development Program and an ethnic Mandingo, elected president. The discredited APC party of Siaka Stevens and Joseph Momoh received only 5.7% of the vote.

Ahmad Tejan Kabbah

The Rebel War: 1991-2002

After the elections the RUF continued their attacks and amputations, still determined to gain power. The attacks forced many people into IDP and refugee camps, and in March there was an appeal by the UN for donor countries to contribute to IDP and refugee relief. The appeal included statistics on refugees and IDPs at the time:

> *The total number of internally displaced and refugee Sierra Leoneans represents 47 percent of the country's pre-war population of 4.47 million persons. Freetown's pre-war population has grown from 731,000 to 1.2 million with 20,000 displaced living in camps. The situation in Bo is even worse with 100,000 of the 230,000 displaced living in camps. The remainder has been absorbed by extended families.*[11]

There were other large IDP centers at Kenema, Blama, Gondama, Masingbi, and Daru.

Mendes in Power, Build-up of Kamajors

With the SLPP elected, the Mendes and smaller allied ethnic groups of the south and east were now in power. In March President Kabbah appointed Chief Samuel Hinga Norman, a Mende, as Deputy Minister of Defense (the president himself held all ministry portfolios so Norman was a "deputy").

Kabbah and Norman's response to the rebel problem was to build up the Kamajors at the expense of the army, who they considered a northern force more loyal to the APC. Hinga Norman had been a Kamajor leader since 1994, and he began an extensive recruitment campaign. A Kamajor Director of War was appointed, a former military commander named Moinina Fofana. Like the RUF and the army, the Kamajors enlisted underage fighters.

Samuel Hinga Norman, Deputy Minister of Defense under Kabbah (Special Court Photo)

Moinina Fofana, Kamajor Director of War (Special Court photo)

Sierra Leone Army soldiers were against the build-up of the Kamajors, afraid they would lose power and be marginalized from their role as the nation's army. President Kabbah and Hinga Norman had legitimate reasons to question the army's performance, and they probably felt the need for a loyal force that could protect them from a coup. However, Kabbah and Norman made no attempt to reconcile with the army or to unite the two forces. The Truth and Reconciliation Commission Report noted that Hinga Norman even made inflammatory remarks against government soldiers that put them at risk of being killed by Kamajors.[12] The situation was becoming more complex with the government and army at odds while the rebels were still trying to take control. The elections, meant to bring democracy, resulted in a return to tribal politics and bigger problems.

Abidjan Peace Accord
With the elections over Foday Sankoh agreed to meet for peace talks, bargaining from a position of relative strength with his troops spread over almost the entire country and only Executive Outcomes fighting them successfully. Talks organized by the UN, OAU, and ECOWAS began on April 22, 1996 in Yamoussoukro, the capital of the Ivory Coast. Foday Sankoh flew to the Ivory Coast and began a six-month stay at luxury hotels. President Kabbah and Foday Sankoh met, and Sankoh made two main demands: a share in power and an end to the use of mercenaries. Sankoh promised to disarm his fighters if the government met his demands.

The war hadn't been widely reported on internationally and Foday Sankoh was mostly unknown to the outside world. A reporter expressed this in a New York Times article in June, also commenting on Sankoh's personal style:

> *Until he emerged from the bush to engage in peace talks here recently, the most frequently asked question about Foday Sankoh, the leader of West Africa's most mysterious guerrilla movement, was whether he really existed at all....Mr Sankoh comes across as a man so blinded by the 'rightness' of his vague calls for social justice and his eclectic assortment of ideological influences that he has become oblivious to the pain his struggle has brought his country. He does not seem especially concerned about the havoc he has caused.* [13]

A two-month ceasefire was agreed on but immediately broken, and fighting continued during the talks. In September and October Executive Outcomes and their troops successfully destroyed Zogoda and other RUF camps, though they weren't able to capture RUF headquarter bases in Kailahun District. Many RUF fighters ran to Liberia where they were given safe haven by Charles Taylor.[14]

The Rebel War: 1991-2002

While President Kabbah was discussing peace with Foday Sankoh, he was also negotiating with the International Monetary Fund on a new loan for 1997. Unrealistically, during unresolved peace talks, the IMF designed a loan agreement that focused on post-conflict demilitarization and reconstruction with a reduction in military spending, including funds spent on Executive Outcomes. This, and criticism from the West on the use of mercenaries, made the removal of Executive Outcomes a viable point for Foday Sankoh to pursue.

Under pressure from foreign countries who hoped an agreement would stop the fighting, the government agreed to Sankoh's demands and the Abidjan Peace Accord (negotiations had moved to the commercial capital of Abidjan) was signed on November 30, 1996. The agreement included demobilization of the RUF and incorporation of RUF troops into the army, the transformation of the RUF into a political party, and the removal of foreign forces from the country. There were jubilant celebrations all over the country.

Foday Sankoh had been persuasive and manipulative, convincing the negotiators that he would become a legitimate politician and winning the removal of Executive Outcomes as a key point in his continuing plan to take control. Sankoh had no intention of ending the war: with the support of Charles Taylor and Qaddafi he had used his time in the Ivory Coast to buy arms, a point stated in the Special Court Judgment on Charles Taylor:

> *The accused [Taylor] instructed Foday Sankoh to participate in the Abidjan peace talks from March to November in 1996 in order to obtain ammunition and material for the RUF. The evidence established that while in Abidjan, Sankoh obtained arms and ammunition for the RUF using funds from Libya.*[15]

Anger in the Army

The Kabbah government began making reductions in the size of the Sierra Leone Army even before the peace agreement was signed, and a number of officers and junior officers were retired. There was also a decrease in rice rations for soldiers. The following facts and figures are from the Truth and Reconciliation Commission Report:

> *In 1994 the size of the army was over 11,000. When Kabbah came to power he ordered a census of the army, at that time the government was giving out approximately 25,000 bags of rice every month. The official size of the army presented to the president was approximately 17,000. The government decided to reduce the size to 7,000 and only 8,000 bags of rice were released to the army every month. Senior officers were thought to be skimming off rice and living well, and this caused resentment by junior officers and rank and file soldiers who blamed the government and senior officers for the reduction.*[16]

The army was angered by the reductions and the simultaneous build-up of the Kamajors. Coup plots were detected and aborted with arrests of suspected plotters. Among those arrested and imprisoned was Sierra Leone Army Major Johnny Paul Koroma, who would become the country's leader the coming year.

1997: Peace Accord breaks down, Sankoh arrested in Nigeria, AFRC coup, AFRC and RUF merge, Hostilities, The two sides prepare to fight

Peace Accord Breaks Down, Sankoh Arrested in Nigeria

The government kept to the terms of the Abidjan Peace Accord and Executive Outcomes left the country in February 1997, but the agreement broke down when the RUF failed to report for demobilization. Hinga Norman ordered the army and Kamajors to resume attacks, and the war continued.

The government took revenge on Foday Sankoh. In March Sankoh traveled to Nigeria and was arrested at Lagos Airport for illegal possession of weapons. President Kabbah asked Nigeria to hold him, and he was put under house arrest in Abuja. With Sankoh out of the picture Mosquito took over as leader of the RUF, and he stayed in close contact with Charles Taylor who gave him instructions and guidance.[17]

At the same time hostilities between government soldiers and Kamajors (and other Civil Defence Forces) increased. There was fighting at Tongo Field in March when army troops tried to take over a diamond mine controlled by Kamajors. In May there were clashes in Kenema and Matotoka. That month the Sierra Leone Web reported that over two hundred army and CDF fighters had died in fighting between the two groups since the beginning of the year.[18]

AFRC Coup, AFRC and RUF Merge

Anger in the army reached a breaking point and a group of junior officers staged a coup d'état in Freetown on the morning of May 25, 1997. They arrested senior officers at Wilberforce Barracks and were joined by other soldiers, and the group proceeded to Pademba Road Prison in central Freetown where they released prisoners including Major Johnny Paul Koroma.

After overcoming ECOMOG troops at the State House the soldiers formed a new government with Johnny Paul Koroma as chairman. The junta called themselves the Armed Forces Revolutionary Council, or AFRC. Around 80 percent of the army joined the AFRC[19] while the others went into hiding or surrendered to ECOMOG. The AFRC suspended the constitution and banned political parties. Soldiers went on a looting and shooting spree and the colonial-era Treasury Building in downtown Freetown was burned. President Kabbah fled the country and set up a government-in-exile in Guinea.

The day after the coup, ECOMOG troops already in the country secured two bases near the city. The first was at Lungi Airport, the international airport across the harbor from the city, and the second was at Hastings Airfield and the nearby town of Jui located on the main highway between Freetown and Waterloo. ECOMOG used Lungi Airport to bring in troops and supplies by air, while at Hastings and Jui ECOMOG troops screened anyone entering or leaving the city along the main highway.

Johnny Paul Koroma (photograph taken when he was CCP Chairman—photo by Peter Andersen)

Upcountry, ECOMOG troops moved to separate camps in the towns and barracks where they were posted. The junta banned the Kamajors and they retreated to their villages or went into hiding, though some stayed around towns in the south and east in an uneasy truce with the army. Most Sierra Leoneans were opposed to the coup, but there were also pro-AFRC demonstrations in Freetown. Politically it was assumed that the northern-based, out-of-power APC party was behind the coup, and northern politicians were accused of backing the junta.

Johnny Paul (as he was generally known) might have thought his junta could remain in power like the previous NPRC military government. However, President Kabbah had signed a new bilateral defense agreement with Nigeria in March and General Sani Abacha, Nigeria's military ruler, pledged to restore him to power. Abacha put General Maxwell Khobe (also a Nigerian) in charge of ECOMOG forces in Sierra Leone, and Khobe moved quickly against the junta.

Two days after the coup four Nigerian frigates docked in Freetown harbor and hundreds of Nigerian soldiers came ashore. Johnny Paul didn't try to stop them. Both he and ECOMOG downplayed their arrival, and they were deployed around the city. Additional ECOMOG troops arrived from Guinea and Ghana.

Then, in an unexpected move, Johnny Paul Koroma phoned Foday Sankoh in Nigeria and asked the RUF rebels to join the AFRC junta. He told the public that the reason was to bring peace by uniting the rebels and the new government, though it was more likely a move to strengthen the defenses of the junta while eliminating the RUF as an enemy.

History

AFRC commander Alex Tamba Brima ("Gullit"). (photo by Peter Andersen, 2008)

AFRC commander Ibrahim Bazzy Kamara ("Bazzy") (photo by Peter Andersen, 2008)

AFRC commander Santigie Borbor Kanu ("Five-Five") (photo by Peter Andersen, 2008)

« *RUF commander Issa Sesay (Special Court photo)*

» *RUF commander Morris Kallon (Special Court photo)*

Foday Sankoh agreed immediately, seeing it as a chance to expand RUF power. A statement from Sankoh was read on state radio ordering RUF fighters to cease hostilities and unite with the AFRC, and RUF fighters left the bush and joined the AFRC junta soldiers in towns and at military barracks. The RUF changed its name to "The People's Army" and entered Freetown with their accustomed looting and violence. In upcountry towns the two forces mingled and harassed civilians for food, lodging, and personal items. The two forces became nominal allies, working together when it was to each other's benefit.

Johnny Paul set up a Supreme Council at Cockerill Military Headquarters in western Freetown that included both AFRC and RUF commanders, with Mosquito in the position directly under him. Others on the council were Alex Tamba Brima (called "Gullit"), Ibrahim Bazzy Kamara (known as "Bazzy"), and Santigie Borbor Kanu ("Five-Five") from the AFRC. From the RUF, in addition to Mosquito, were Issa Sesay and Morris Kallon. SAJ Musa, the former NPRC deputy chairman, returned from Britain and became a member of the council for the AFRC.

The Sierra Leone Web quoted Johnny Paul as saying:

They [the RUF] are tired of fighting. We too are tired of fighting. We need peace and we want it now, and we are going to get peace....Our intention is to form a broad based government of national unity fully incorporating the RUF to restore everlasting peace and sanity throughout the country.

President Kabbah replied from Guinea:

The coup really was a miscalculation on the part of the soldiers. They thought that bringing in the RUF would bring control and they would become chummy, but they were naive in that respect. Instead the RUF has unleashed a terror that went completely out of control.[20]

The AFRC coup changed the configuration of the war. Now three groups—the RUF under Sankoh and Mosquito, the AFRC under Johnny Paul and SAJ Musa, and the elected government under President Kabbah and Hinga Norman—were fighting for control of the country. Not all government soldiers joined the AFRC. Some remained loyal and fought on the side of the government. However, the majority of the army followed the AFRC leaders through the upcoming battles and campaigns where they used the same cruel tactics as the RUF, hoping like the rebels to win through intimidation and fear; and despite their extreme violence, many AFRC soldiers believed to the end of the war that they were fighting to regain their rightful position as the country's army.

Hostilities

On June 2nd Nigerian ships shelled the western side of Freetown aiming at Cockerill Military Headquarters, but some shells landed off target and killed civilians which resulted in harsh criticism of ECOMOG.

The same day AFRC/RUF troops (the combined AFRC junta and RUF rebels) attacked ECOMOG soldiers who were evacuating foreigners at the Mammy Yoko Hotel in Aberdeen. They caused extensive damage to the hotel with machine guns, mortars, and RPGs while the Nigerians and foreigners took refuge in the basement.

The siege ended through mediation by the International Committee of the Red Cross and the civilians were evacuated. The AFRC/RUF took three hundred Nigerian soldiers hostage and held them at Wilberforce Barracks until Johnny Paul ordered them released. ECOMOG continued shelling military targets and there were clashes between ECOMOG and the AFRC/RUF at Jui and Lungi Airport.

The Organization of African Unity condemned the coup and gave ECOWAS a mandate to restore the elected government through negotiations, sanctions, or use of force. The Commonwealth suspended Sierra Leone and the UN Security Council expressed support for the restoration of the civilian government. In July there were peace talks in Abidjan, but the negotiations failed when Johnny Paul announced that he would stay in power for up to four more years.

This led to a blockade of Freetown harbor to stop weapons and petroleum from entering the country. Humanitarian aid was also blocked and there were shortages of rice and other commodities. Britain helped the Kabbah government-in-exile set up radio station 98.1 FM at Lungi to make broadcasts against the AFRC junta to the residents of Freetown.

The AFRC/RUF partnership faced immediate difficulties. The new allies had been enemies since 1991 and both wanted control of the country. The RUF refused to submit to AFRC authority and there were conflicts over command structure and the behavior of RUF troops in the capital.

Mosquito left Freetown and returned to the east after disputes with Johnny Paul, and Issa Sesay went to Makeni when he was accused of involvement in looting the Iranian Embassy. Upcountry, RUF fighters returned to the bush and attacked Kamajor and ECOMOG positions and took control of diamond mining in Kono and Tongo Field, with increased trade in diamonds for arms with Charles Taylor.[21]

The AFRC reacted brutally against its Kamajor and SLPP adversaries. In Bo and Kenema the AFRC arrested, tortured, and killed supporters of the SLPP. In Bo, AFRC soldiers attacked and killed Kamajors and murdered a prominent Paramount Chief. Villages in the south and east suspected of harboring Kamajors were attacked and burned, and suspected Kamajors were harassed and killed at roadblocks. Student demonstrations against the coup were violently suppressed in Freetown and Bo. Amnesty International described abuses by the AFRC in a 1998 report:

> *The period from 25 May 1997 until 12 February 1998 was marked by a total disregard for the rule of law and demands from the international community to respect international humanitarian and human rights law. The rule of law completely collapsed and violence engulfed the country. Hundreds of people who were associated with the government of President Kabbah or his political party, the Sierra Leone People's Party (SLPP), or who*

were perceived to be opposed to the AFRC were detained without charge or trial, torture and ill-treatment were systematic, and many of those perceived to be political opponents of the AFRC were extra judicially executed. ...The victims included those associated with the government of President Kabbah, journalists, students and human rights activists.[22]

The Two Sides Prepare to Fight
The Kabbah government-in-exile began making plans for a military action to overthrow the AFRC and return to power, and in the second half of 1997 Hinga Norman increased recruitment of Kamajors. An operational plan was developed whereby ECOMOG troops in Freetown would oust the AFRC/RUF from the capital while Kamajors would sweep in from the Liberian border and Bonthe District and drive them out of Kenema and Bo, supported by additional ECOMOG forces from the Liberian border.

Hinga Norman set up a Kamajor headquarters at the ECOMOG base in Liberia and trained a contingent of Kamajors for the attacks on Kenema and Bo. In Bonthe, Kamajors gathered at Base Zero, which had been moved from Tihun to a more secure location further south at Talia. Allieu Kondowai and his assistants Kamoh Brima and Kamoh Lahai initiated large numbers of men and boys into the Kamajor forces, a process that made them wealthy as recruits had to pay to be initiated. Civilians in the south and east supported the Kamajors by providing food, helping them send messages, and attending AFRC meetings undercover.

President Kabbah was concerned about balancing the Kamajors with Civil Defense Forces from the north, and he assigned M.S. Dumbuya, the former head of the Special Security Division, as Northern Commander of the CDF. However, Hinga Norman gave Dumbuya few resources and ignored the north in his plans. Norman didn't trust the northern tribes who could be allied with the AFRC.

At the same time, Charles Taylor was arranging shipments of arms for the AFRC/RUF. After years of fighting and negotiations Taylor became President of Liberia on August 2, 1997, and his new position gave him improved logistics to buy and smuggle arms. In September he attended a charity dinner in South Africa hosted by Nelson Mandela where he befriended model Naomi Campbell, and that night he sent her a small package of uncut diamonds. The gesture resulted in Campbell being called to testify at the Special Court trial of Charles Taylor at The Hague in 2010.

The prosecution tried to link the diamonds to shipments of arms Taylor had purchased in South Africa and shipped to the AFRC/RUF in 1997. Campbell's testimony couldn't prove the link, though it confirmed that Taylor had been in possession of rough diamonds, a point he had previously denied, and this helped establish him as an unreliable witness which the prosecution used to discredit future testimony. The prosecution used other testimony to prove that Taylor had made the shipments, and the Taylor Judgment states:

> *The Accused [Taylor] facilitated two large shipments of ammunition. The first occurred in late 1997. In around September 1997, the Accused sent Ibrahim Bah [an intermediary] to Freetown to meet with Sam Bockarie [Mosquito] and Johnny Paul Koroma to make arrangements for the procurement of arms and ammunition. Bah was given 90 carats of diamonds and $USD 90,000 to pay for the shipment. This shipment of arms and ammunition was delivered by plane to Magburaka in Sierra Leone sometime between September and December 1997 and was distributed amongst members of the AFRC/RUF Junta.*[23]

Fighting seemed inevitable but a final attempt was made for a negotiated settlement, and the Conakry Peace Plan was signed on October 23rd, the AFRC agreeing to step down and disarm in six months. However, when Johnny Paul stated that he would delay his handover, a decision was made to proceed with the military action.

At this point a scandal erupted in Britain over arms for the fighting. In October the UN Security Council imposed an oil and arms embargo on Sierra Leone. The Kabbah government, searching for arms to fight the AFRC, contacted Sandline, a private security company with ties to Executive Outcomes and Branch Energy. An arrangement was made for Sandline to provide military equipment which was sent to Lungi Airport in breach of the arms embargo. The equipment was discovered and confiscated, and there was much debate in Britain over whether the British Ambassador to Sierra Leone was involved in the agreement with Sandline.

In Liberia, Charles Taylor wasn't happy that troops were being trained on his territory to fight his RUF/AFRC allies and he ordered Hinga Norman and the Kamajor fighters to leave. They moved to the border area and established a new base at Gendema on the Sierra Leone side of the Mano River Bridge. Kamajors assembled there and began fighting the AFRC/RUF at the bridge and in the nearby town of Zimmi.

Fighting in Zimmi was intense and the AFRC/RUF soldiers holding the town had to be supplied with ammunition and food by helicopter until they were finally forced out. Kamajors also made repeated assaults on a military barracks at Koribundu in Bo District where AFRC and RUF troops were based, and there was fighting at Tongo Field over control of diamond mines.

Late in the year the Kamajors began a series of attacks on the AFRC/RUF called "Operation Black December". They set up checkpoints on roads in the south and east and carried out torture and summary killing of suspected AFRC and RUF fighters and supporters. The Special Court Trial Judgment of Kamajor leaders describes an incident at Panguma, Kenema District, that took place after a failed attack on Tongo Field. Kamajors fighters captured a large group of civilians fleeing the fighting and ordered them to line up by tribe. The Kamajor commander then ordered his fighters to use their matchets to kill all the northerners, and a total of one hundred and fifty Temne, Limba, and Loko civilians were massacred.[24] Because of this and other abuses Kamajor leaders were indicted by the Special Court in 2003.

1998: Intervention, AFRC/RUF retreat to the north and east, Repercussions, Operation No Living Thing, ECOMOG and Kamajors move into the north and east, Events in Freetown, Treason trials, AFRC/RUF move to attack Freetown

Intervention, AFRC/RUF Retreat to the North and East

In February 1998, ECOMOG began its military operations to expel the AFRC/RUF from Freetown, Kenema, and Bo. There were approximately 10,000 ECOMOG troops in Freetown stationed at Lungi Airport and Jui/Hastings Airfield, and to avoid heavy fighting in the capital ECOMOG's plan was to enter Freetown from the east and push the AFRC/RUF out the western side of the city and down the peninsula road along the coast. ECOMOG forces were supported by Sierra Leone Army troops loyal to the Kabbah government, and Kamajors were brought from Base Zero and stationed at the Brookfields Hotel in the capital. This operation, along with the actions in Bo and Kenema, are known locally as the "Intervention".

On February 2nd ECOMOG and allied fighters were airlifted to Hastings Airfield, and on February 7th they began to move into the city along two routes—the main highway from upcountry and the road to the south of the Freetown mountains that passes through Grafton and Regent. They met heavy resistance but on February 13th they reached the city center and took control of the State House, then continued pushing the AFRC/RUF to the west and out of the city.

The AFRC/RUF fighters retreated as planned via the peninsula road passing through Lumley, Goderich, and York. At the bottom of the peninsula, at the

History

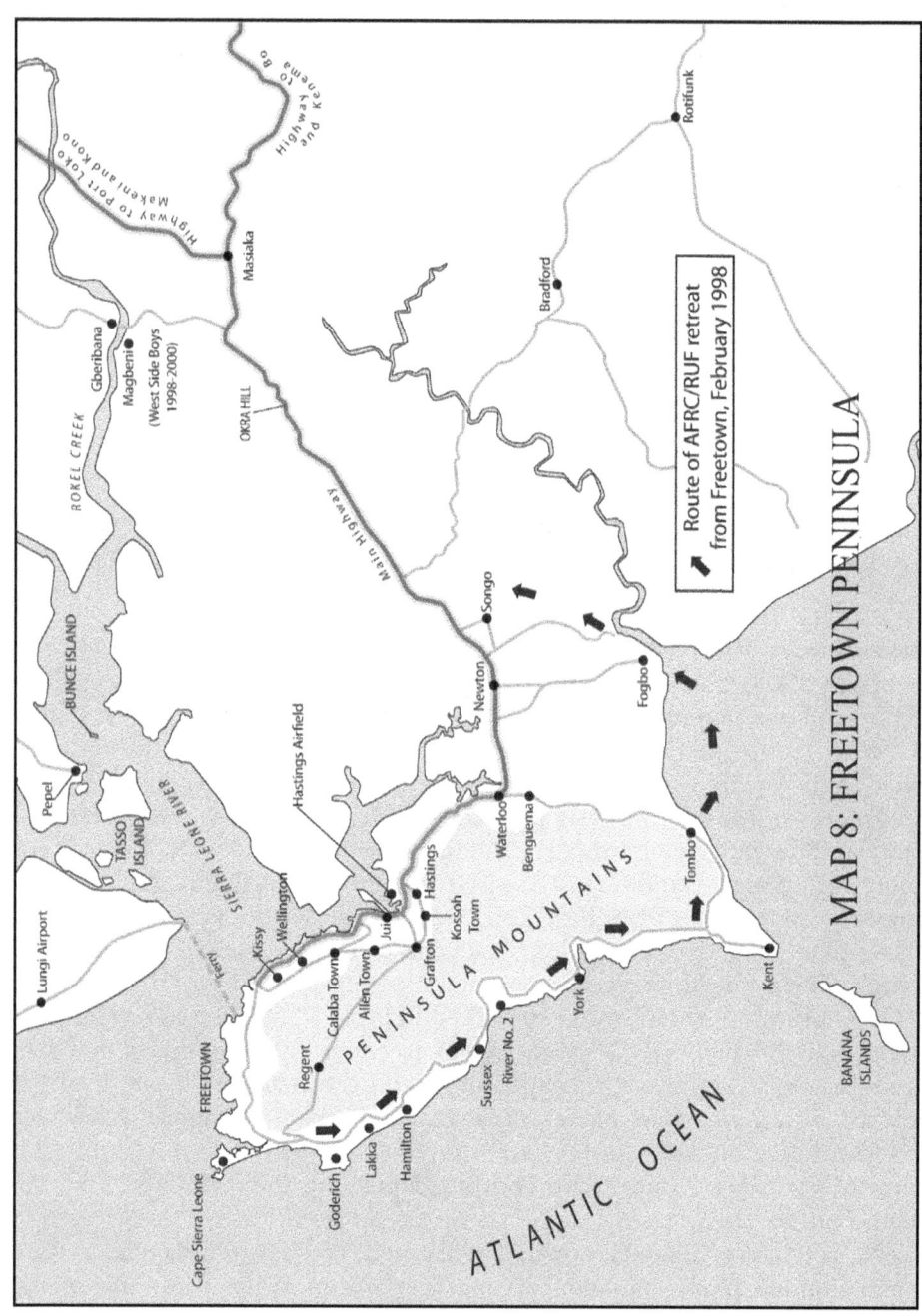

Map 8: *The Freetown Peninsula, with route of the AFRC/RUF retreat during the Intervention*

fishing village of Tombo, they commandeered boats from local fishermen and crossed to Fogbo on the opposite shore to evade the ECOMOG troops stationed at Waterloo and Jui.

They regrouped at Newton, Songo, and Masiaka and split into groups. A smaller group traveled south to attack Bo while the majority of the fighters moved into the northern districts. Other fighters stayed nearer Freetown between Waterloo and Masiaka and made camps in the Okra Hill area which later became a mixed AFRC/RUF camp called West Side Base. From their positions they attacked vehicles on the highway and fought ECOMOG troops moving upcountry from Freetown.

Johnny Paul Koroma, who was with the northern group, used the BBC to announce "Operation Pay Yourself" stating that because he was unable to pay his AFRC fighters he was giving them freedom to loot, and the announcement resulted in widespread violence against civilians. (The AFRC couldn't pay its troops because it no longer had access to the country's treasury.)

Tombo, the fishing village at the bottom of the peninsula where the rebels and AFRC escaped to the opposite shore

Continuing the Intervention, Kamajors moved in from the Liberian border and Base Zero. They forced the AFRC/RUF out of Kenema and Bo on February 15th and proceeded to loot both towns. Three days later a contingent of AFRC/RUF fighters re-entered Bo disguised in Kamajor uniforms. They fought off the Kamajors and recaptured the town with looting and reprisals against Kamajor supporters.

The ECOMOG troops at the Liberian border moved in behind the Kamajors with tanks and heavy weapons. They arrived in Kenema on February 19th and in Bo on February 22nd and took over the fighting, ending the looting by Kamajors in Kenema and finally forcing the AFRC/RUF out of Bo.

ECOMOG and the Kamajors then captured Mile 91 which left the south mostly free of AFRC/RUF. This was the end of the Intervention. The AFRC junta and RUF rebels had been forced out of Freetown, Bo, and Kenema after nine months in power, but problems were to continue in the north and east where they had retreated.

Repercussions

Repercussions by the victors were severe. In Freetown, ECOMOG troops and Kamajors searched for suspected AFRC/RUF fighters and executed those they caught. Known supporters of the AFRC and RUF were arrested, including former president Joseph Momoh who had joined the junta.

There were revenge attacks against civilian collaborators and suspected collaborators. Victims were arrested, beaten, and burned to death with petrol or kerosene-filled tires around their necks. Radio 98.1 broadcast the names of supposed collaborators who could be harassed or killed. Hundreds of people were imprisoned at Pademba Road Prison where many died from torture and inhumane conditions.

Upcountry in Bo and Kenema there were killings of AFRC and RUF fighters, collaborators, and supporters. Kamajors captured the army barracks at Koribundu and destroyed the town, committing atrocities against local civilians in revenge for their presumed support of the army. The Truth and Reconciliation Commission Report states that Hinga Norman ordered the Kamajors to destroy the town and later gave a speech congratulating them for the destruction.[25]

In Kono District, when word reached Koidu that the Intervention had taken place, local youths chased the AFRC/RUF out of town and asked Civil Defense Forces to secure the area. CDF fighters took control of Koidu and fought the AFRC/RUF in the bush surrounding the town.

President Kabbah returned to the country in March and put General Maxwell Khobe in charge of national security. A British warship arrived to provide assistance and aid and it was announced that the old Sierra Leone Army, which was mostly the expelled AFRC, would be disbanded and a new army formed.

Operation No Living Thing

A new phase of the war began with Freetown and the south back in government hands and the AFRC/RUF retreating into the north and east where they would regroup and prepare for an attack on Freetown.

Makeni was the first major town the main group of AFRC/RUF reached in their retreat from the capital, and when they entered the city there was chaos and looting and the civilians fled to rural areas. Top AFRC and RUF leaders assembled and held a meeting to plan their strategy. Those attending included, from the RUF: Issa Sesay, Morris Kallon, and Dennis Mingo (Superman); and from the AFRC: Johnny Paul Koroma, SAJ Musa, Alex Tamba Brima (Gullit), Ibrahim Bazzy Kamara (Bazzy), and Santigie Borbor Kanu (Five-Five). Mosquito was elsewhere and didn't attend.

There was immediate conflict between the AFRC and RUF leaders when the RUF tried to take charge. AFRC commander SAJ Musa refused to submit to the RUF, and he broke away and established his own headquarters in Koinadugu District to the northeast of Makeni. SAJ Musa became the main commander of the mixed AFRC/RUF forces in the north, and he assembled fighters and began to develop a plan to attack Freetown.

A few days later a large contingent of AFRC/RUF commanders and fighters left Makeni and moved east to take over Kono District. They captured and burned the town of Njaiama Sewafe on the Sewa River, then captured Koidu on around March 1st and executed many of the local youth who had chased their fighters out of the town after the Intervention.

At this point the AFRC/RUF began a new campaign of terror to revenge their ouster from government and to show the country they meant business. AFRC leader Johnny Paul Koroma ordered his troops to clear Koidu town of civilians and burn the houses of government supporters. Mosquito announced "Operation No Living Thing" on the BBC. This was a viscous campaign of terror against civilians with abductions, killings, rapes, and amputations in Kono and the north. AFRC/RUF troops burned people alive in houses and coerced boys to take part in murdering, torturing, and amputating civilians. In one incident AFRC commander Gullit ordered an attack on Tombodu, a small mining town near Koidu, and a fighter named Savage led a massacre in the town, beheading civilians and throwing their bodies into a flooded mining pit.

From Koidu, AFRC/RUF troops moved south to the RUF headquarters at Buedu in Kailahun District, passing through Gandorhun and fighting off attacks from Kamajors guarding the road. In Buedu they were under the command of Mosquito, the top RUF commander, and Issa Sesay, second in command.

History

Buedu, site of RUF headquarters and landing strip (at left), Kailahun District

Johnny Paul Koroma also traveled from Koidu to Buedu with packets of diamonds and plans to talk to Charles Taylor in Monrovia. However, Mosquito had him arrested and put in detention, and he remained under arrest for the next eighteen months. With Johnny Paul out of the way the RUF had control of the mixed AFRC/RUF troops in the east. Mosquito and Issa Sesay worked with Charles Taylor to plan an attack on Freetown, at odds with AFRC commander SAJ Musa in the north who was also planning an attack.

Civilians in Kono District and the north were plagued by extreme violence in 1998. Thousands of civilians fled to Guinea and entered refugee camps. At the end of the year the chairman of the United Nations Security Council Sanctions Committee reported that more than 4,000 people were mutilated or murdered after the Intervention.[26]

ECOMOG and Kamajors Move into the North and East
In March, with Freetown secure, ECOMOG troops backed by loyal government soldiers and Kamajors followed the AFRC/RUF into the north. They took back major towns including Masiaka, Lunsar, Port Loko, Kamakwie, Kabala, Kambia, and Makeni. The AFRC/RUF fighters retreated into the countryside where they attacked villages and ambushed vehicles. In the liberated towns there were killings of suspected rebels and AFRC.

After securing Makeni ECOMOG continued to Kono District and established their headquarters at Koakoyima, a suburb on the western edge of Koidu. There was heavy fighting and ECOMOG took over Koidu early in

May with the AFRC/RUF destroying the town as they retreated. From Koidu, a contingent of ECOMOG troops and Kamajors continued south to Gandorhun to strengthen defenses along the road to Kailahun, hoping to stop the AFRC/RUF from using the road to reattack Kono.

The AFRC/RUF were forced out of Koidu but they didn't leave Kono District. They established camps with names like Superman Ground, Gandorhun Highway, and Sewafe Bypass and attacked towns around the district, especially those with diamonds such as Motema, Bumpeh, and Njaiama Nimikoro. They made attacks on Koidu but failed to retake it. All three groups, the AFRC/RUF, ECOMOG, and Kamajors settled into areas of control and mined diamonds when they weren't fighting.

AFRC commander Gullit was around Koidu, and when he learned that his leader, Johnny Paul Koroma, had been arrested and detained by Mosquito, he and a group of fellow AFRC fighters left Kono and joined SAJ Musa in Koinadugu District, strengthening the AFRC forces in the north. To build up the northern forces SAJ Musa set up a camp at Rosos in Bombali District to train newly conscripted fighters. Some northern villagers gave them support, considering them their brothers from the same tribes.

The northern fighters committed numerous atrocities. They made repeated attacks on the town of Kabala in Koinadugu District, and, among other brutal acts, they murdered a group of men assembled in a mosque for prayers in the town of Karina in Bombali District. A notorious female fighter named Adama Cut Hand traveled around the north amputating hands.

In July ECOMOG attacked Kailahun District in an attempt to destroy the RUF headquarters. They captured Koindu, Buedu, and Kailahun town, and from September to November they bombed RUF bases and camps, but they weren't able to capture the district and the RUF retook their headquarter towns.

Despite the attacks from ECOMOG, Mosquito and Issa Sesay continued to build up their forces in Kailahun with the help of Charles Taylor, who had Sierra Leonean deserters and refugees rounded up in Liberia and sent to Kailahun to fight for the RUF. Taylor was aided in this effort by his US-born son Chuckie Taylor who, when he was twenty years old, had traveled to Liberia and become the head of the Anti-Terrorist Unit, Charles Taylor's personal security force that tortured and murdered his political enemies. Chuckie Taylor and the Anti-Terrorist Unit searched for Sierra Leoneans in Liberia and forced them to fight for the RUF, or tortured and killed them if they refused to go.

Events in Freetown, Treason Trials
Other events were taking place in Freetown where President Kabbah was back in control. The government offered amnesty to all AFRC and RUF fighters

and began to rebuild the national army. ECOMOG screened candidates and recruited and trained 5,000 soldiers including 1,500 surrendered AFRC fighters. ECOMOG was careful about the screening process, as there had been problems during the Intervention when soldiers they thought were loyal to the government turned on them and fought on the side of the AFRC.

On June 8, 1998 Sani Abacha died and the new military ruler of Nigeria, General Abdusalam Abubakar, stated that he would continue Nigeria's commitment to Sierra Leone. In July the UN Security Council established a mission under the acronym UNOMSIL (United Nations Observer Mission to Sierra Leone) to monitor the military and security situation, the demobilization of combatants, and violations of international humanitarian law, though the country was still at war and not ready for demobilization.

In July, U.S. President Bill Clinton sent the Rev. Jesse Jackson as Special Envoy to West Africa to meet with Presidents Kabbah and Taylor. After discussions the two presidents agreed to a non-aggression pact and cooperation on security issues, though the promises by Charles Taylor were a complete sham. Jesse Jackson apparently believed that he and Taylor had a personal, trusting bond based on their shared Baptist religion. (Jackson also believed that Foday Sankoh was a true revolutionary and later outraged Sierra Leoneans by comparing Sankoh to Nelson Mandela.)

Foday Sankoh had been in detention in Nigeria for over a year, and on July 25th he was brought to Freetown to stand trial for treason. He appeared on television and urged his followers to put down their weapons. He brushed aside questions about RUF violence against civilians, saying it had happened because he was out of the country.

Before Sankoh's trial began, there was a treason trial for thirty-seven soldiers who had taken part in the AFRC coup. Of that number thirty-four were given death sentences, and twenty-four, including one woman, were executed by firing squad at Goderich Beach on October 19th despite appeals from the international community and human rights groups. The execution of their colleagues infuriated the AFRC and they threatened to attack Freetown in revenge.

Foday Sankoh came to trial in September and was found guilty of treason. He was given a death sentence and held at a secure location. Mosquito threatened genocide if Sankoh wasn't released. On November 4th, in a trial of civilians, sixteen were convicted of treason and conspiracy for collaborating with the AFRC, including former president Joseph Momoh and Hilton Fyle, a former reporter for the BBC who had set up a radio station for the RUF in Kailahun. They were imprisoned at Pademba Road, though none from this group nor the remaining ten prisoners from the previous trial were executed and all were given amnesty after the 1999 Lomé Peace Accord.

Pademba Road Prison, located near the center of Freetown, was built by the British early in the century. One of the prisoners arrested for treason gave the following testimony to the Truth and Reconciliation Commission about conditions at the prison:

[The conditions were] abysmal, awful, hopeless, useless, degrading, wretched, oppressive, abhorrent and all such vices most inhumane. I and many others were selectively tortured. Pademba Road prisons were designed for about four hundred inmates. The period following the restoration of the Kabbah government in 1998 saw an unprecedented large number of children of all ages stuffed into very untidy cells at Pademba Road. Whilst I and many others were charged for treason, the bulk of our unfortunate compatriots were dying by the hour in the cells at Pademba Road prisons. Our human rights were grossly abused.[27]

Pademba Road Prison, located in central Freetown

AFRC/RUF Move to Attack Freetown

While the treason trials were taking place, Charles Taylor, Mosquito, and Issa Sesay continued their preparations for the attack on Freetown. Diamonds mined in Kono and Tongo Field were sent to Mosquito, then to Charles Taylor who made arrangements for deliveries of arms and other military equipment. Taylor kept a guest house for the rebels in Monrovia for the delivery of diamonds and a logistics base to plan and monitor the upcoming attacks. Taylor also sent Liberian troops and white mercenaries to Kailahun, and he had Mosquito build a landing strip at Buedu for the direct shipment of arms.

In planning the attack Taylor advised Mosquito to capture Kono and Kenema first to secure the diamond fields and to pin down ECOMOG at Moa Barracks, then to move on Freetown in an operation that was "fearful", meaning an attack with extreme violence. The Taylor Judgment states:

> In November/December 1998, when Bockarie [Mosquito] met with the Accused [Taylor] in Monrovia, the Accused jointly designed with Bockarie the two-pronged attack on Kono, Kenema and Freetown outlined by Bockarie to his commanders in a meeting at Waterworks [in Kailahun District] on his return to Sierra Leone. Although the idea to advance toward Freetown was already in discussion when Bockarie went to Monrovia, the Accused emphasized to Bockarie the need to first attack Kono District and told Bockarie to make the operation 'fearful' in order to pressure the Government of Sierra Leone into negotiations on the release of Foday Sankoh from prison, as well as to use 'all means' to get to Freetown.[28]

The overall plan was for SAJ Musa, who was in the north and nearer Freetown, to clear the way to the capital while Mosquito's forces were taking over Kenema and Kono, after which the two forces would join to attack the capital. However, SAJ Musa had his own plan to capture Freetown first and put the army back in control before the RUF reached the city. Mosquito ordered SAJ Musa to follow the overall plan, but Musa ignored the order and began his move to attack Freetown.

In October SAJ Musa and second-in-command Gullit formed their attack force, which included the new fighters trained at Rosos. They began by making attacks in Kambia District near the Guinean border to capture arms, but Guinean troops fought them back. They moved south through Kambia District and attacked the town of Mange to take control of a main bridge, then moved nearer Freetown and set up bases. In early December they again moved north and attacked towns and junctions, and around December 10th they regrouped at their bases near Freetown. During these operations they committed numerous atrocities and abducted large numbers of civilians who they brought to the bases.

Mosquito announced that there would be an attack on Freetown. On December 22nd SAJ Musa's troops attacked and looted Waterloo, then moved into the capital as far as Wellington before they were repulsed by ECOMOG. The Minister of Information, Dr. Julius Spencer, denied on the radio that the security situation was deteriorating, and President Kabbah assured the Freetown population that ECOMOG was in control.

Back in Kailahun, Mosquito and Issa Sesay began their attacks on Kenema and Kono. A group of fighters moved to attack Segbwema, Daru, Moa Barracks, and Kenema, while another group headed for Kono under command of Issa and Akim Turay, a well-known fighter. The first group captured Segbwema but failed to take Kenema. The Kono group was more successful. As they moved toward Koidu, the ECOMOG troops and Kamajors guarding the road were overwhelmed and forced to retreat to Kenema. The fighters attacked Koidu on December 16th, captured the city, and seized stockpiles of arms and ammunition abandoned by ECOMOG as they retreated down the highway to Makeni. Thousands of civilians fled Koidu, following ECOMOG along the highway or escaping through the bush.

After securing Koidu, Issa and his troops followed ECOMOG down the highway and captured Magburaka, then forced ECOMOG out of Makeni and looted their arms and ammunition. Mosquito, who remained at the Buedu headquarters, was active on his satellite phone receiving reports and discussing operations with Charles Taylor. Mosquito also had an open line to the BBC to broadcast threats and fake progress reports, while claiming he was involved in the fighting.

Near Freetown, SAJ Musa and his troops fought for Waterloo and attacked the military base at Benguema a few miles to the south. On December 22nd the fighters looted the armory at Benguema. A shell exploded and killed SAJ Musa, ending his move to take over the government. The cause of SAJ Musa's sudden death became a point of debate: most people agree with the reports that he was killed in an explosion, but others believe that he was murdered by the RUF to keep him from taking power.

Gullit took over command. He called Mosquito and they agreed to follow the original attack plan and coordinate the capture of the capital. Issa and his troops left Makeni to reinforce Gullit, but they met resistance from ECOMOG in Port Loko District which slowed them down. Gullit's forces moved toward the capital, and at the end of the year were battling ECOMOG and Kamajors along the highway between Waterloo and Hastings.

1999: Attack on Freetown, A stalemate, Lomé Peace Accord, AFRC commanders move to West Side Base, RUF fights for Taylor, Sankoh and Johnny Paul join the government, AFRC/RUF alliance breaks down, Peacekeepers and problems with disarmament, Mosquito leaves

Attack on Freetown
The attack forces included AFRC fighters and a smaller number of RUF and Liberians. (The majority of the force was AFRC and not RUF, though they were lumped together as "rebels" in news reports.) When Gullit observed ECOMOG troops being airlifted into Hastings Airfield he decided to attack

History

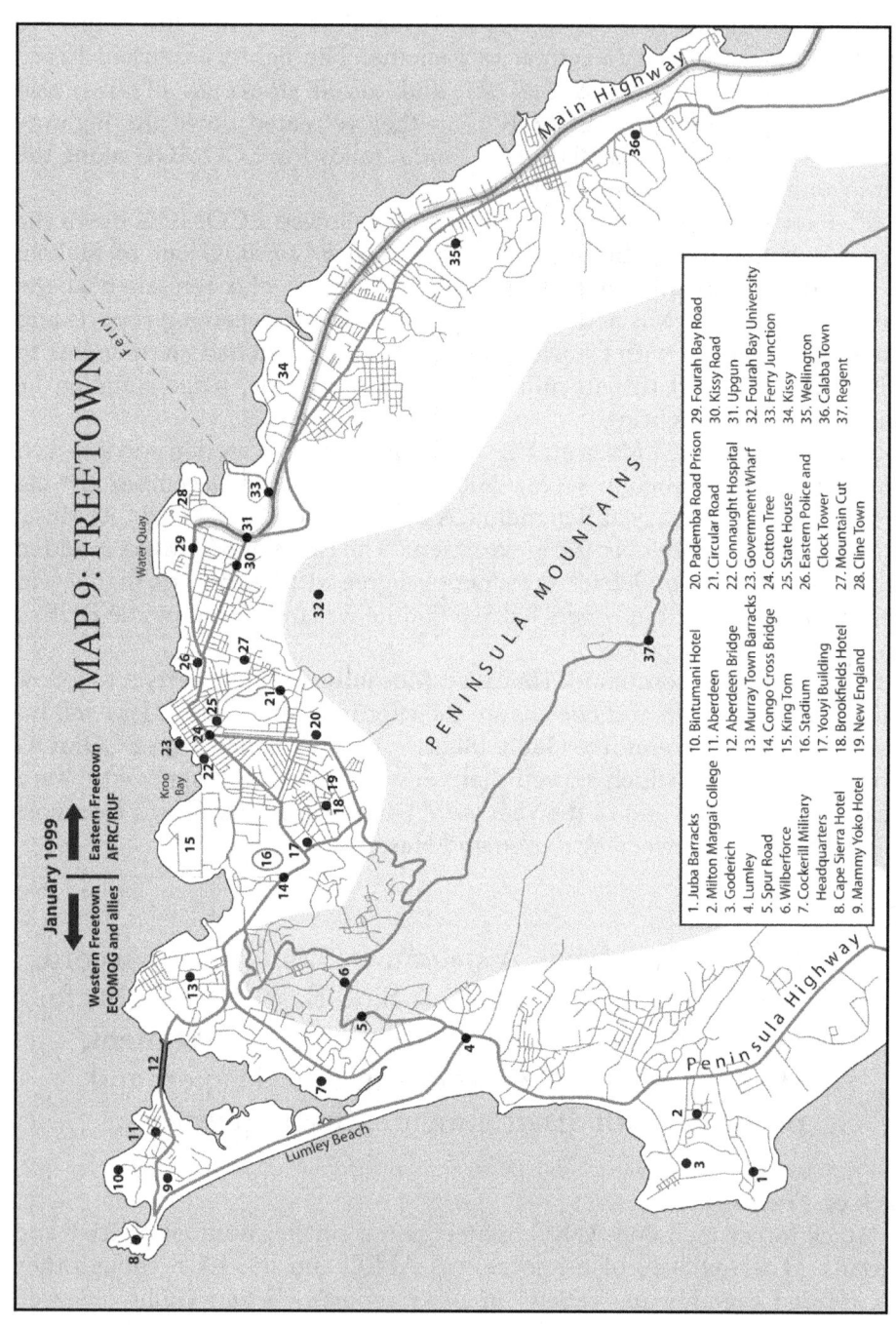

Map 9: Freetown, including route from upcountry, eastern and western Freetown and the furthest point the rebels reached, with locations mentioned in the text

Freetown immediately without waiting for the reinforcements. There were ECOMOG troops stationed from Hastings through the main junctions in eastern Freetown and at the State House in central Freetown.

There was heavy fighting and the attackers took control of Hastings and Kossoh Town, and on January 4th captured Jui and Allen Town. The next day they took over Calaba Town and headed down Bai Bureh Road (the main highway) into the city. Many of the AFRC/RUF wore civilian clothing so they could hide among the civilians fleeing toward the city center, and they used civilians as human shields which made it difficult for ECOMOG to fire on them. They began committing atrocities immediately on entering eastern Freetown.

On the morning of January 6th the attack force reached Ferry Junction and Upgun and fought off the defenders. They moved down Kissy Road and Fourah Bay Road to the Clock Tower and burned the Eastern Police Station, then continued to the State House and Pademba Road Prison. They shot open the prison doors with an RPG and released the prisoners, though they weren't able to find Foday Sankoh who was being held by the government in a secret location.

During the fighting Gullit was in contact with Mosquito by satellite phone. Mosquito announced on Radio France International that Freetown had been taken, then announced on the BBC that he was sending reinforcements and that government buildings in Freetown should be burned. At the State House the AFRC/RUF rounded up a large group of Nigerian civilians and killed them in revenge for Nigeria's role in ECOMOG.

The Clock Tower in eastern Freetown

History

Thousands of civilians took refuge at the stadium, and the main ECOMOG forces retreated to western Freetown where three army barracks are located at Murray Town, Wilberforce, and Juba. The invaders then walked through the streets of central Freetown asking the public to join them, though they received little support, and the fighting resumed.

Congo Cross Bridge looking east—where the attackers were turned back

The attackers fought their way toward western Freetown, but were stopped at Congo Cross Bridge by a well-armed force of ECOMOG, army soldiers, and Kamajors. There was a fierce battle at the bridge and on January 10th the fighting turned and the defenders began pushing the AFRC/RUF back toward the city center. As they were being pushed back they committed serious atrocities against civilians—burning people in houses, rape, amputations, and murder. Hundreds of houses and local landmarks were burned.

After a week of street-to-street fighting ECOMOG and its allies pushed the attack force back to the eastern side of the city and took control of the city center, Cline Town, Water Quay, and Fourah Bay College. A week later most of Freetown was clear, and checkpoints were set up and young men suspected of being junta soldiers or rebels were taken away and killed.

The invading forces retreated to Waterloo where they met the reinforcements sent by Mosquito. The two forces attempted another attack on the city but were repulsed. ECOMOG cleared the peninsula and on February 24th announced that they had control of Freetown and the Western Area.

It is estimated that 5,000 people died in the Freetown attack and many more were raped, abducted, or mutilated. The attack was widely reported in the international press and brought the world's attention to the Sierra Leone conflict. The extreme violence led many in the West to call for a stop to the war. Human Rights Watch wrote:

> *The battle for Freetown and ensuing three week rebel occupation of the capital was characterized by the systematic and widespread perpetration of all classes of atrocities against the civilian population, and marked the most intensive and concentrated period of human rights violations in Sierra Leone's [up to then] eight-year civil war. Government and ECOMOG forces also carried out serious abuses, including over 180 summary executions of rebels and their suspected collaborators.*[29]

A Stalemate

The AFRC/RUF were still in control of Makeni, and after the attack on Freetown ECOMOG attacked and bombed the town but weren't able retake it. In March and April, after securing Freetown, ECOMOG moved into the north and captured a number of northern towns including Masiaka, Mile 91, Lunsar, and Rogbere Junction, but they were stretched thin and couldn't go further, and the AFRC/RUF remained in control of Makeni, rural areas of the north, and Kono and Kailahun Districts.

The AFRC/RUF again rebuilt their forces. A contingent of fighters led by RUF commander Komba Gbondema established a training base at Gbunumbu in Bombali District to train new recruits and abductees. They attacked and took over Kambia District and raided the Guinean border. The Guinean army retaliated by bombing their positions in Kambia. In Kono the AFRC/RUF set up a training camp in the town of Yengema, near Koidu, to train new fighters, and intensive diamond mining resumed in Kono and Tongo Field.

The war became a stalemate. The government and the AFRC/RUF each controlled about half the country. The Kabbah government didn't have the military strength to fight the AFRC/RUF, and worse, it was losing the support of Nigeria. After ten years of military rule Nigeria was holding democratic elections and both major candidates had made campaign promises to withdraw Nigerian troops from Sierra Leone.

No country except Guinea would support the Kabbah government. Britain and the U.S. were involved in Kosovo, and Sierra Leone had no strategic importance to them. In addition, the killing of peacekeepers in Somalia in 1993 and in Rwanda in 1994 had turned the British and American public against sending troops to Africa. President Kabbah was forced to negotiate with the RUF.

Lomé Peace Accord

At the insistence of foreign governments, Foday Sankoh was released from detention to travel to Lomé, the capital of Togo, for peace talks. Jesse Jackson attended the talks as Clinton's Special Envoy and helped negotiate a ceasefire between President Kabbah and Foday Sankoh that was signed on May 18, 1999. Formal talks then began between the government and the RUF. The AFRC sent a representative, a fighter named Idrissa Kamara (known as "Leatherboot"), but he didn't take part in the negotiations.

The Lomé Peace Accord was signed on July 7, 1999. The agreement included the transformation of the RUF into a political party with a share of cabinet positions, a position for Foday Sankoh in the government with the status of vice president, disarmament of all combatants by a neutral peacekeeping force, and the establishment of a truth and reconciliation commission. The AFRC wasn't mentioned in the agreement.

Kabbah's weak position had resulted in Foday Sankoh joining the government despite the brutality of his troops and his long history of lies and deception. Again, the agreement was encouraged and supported by Western countries in the hope that a signed agreement would bring peace, though there was also criticism of Bill Clinton, Jesse Jackson and others for supporting a stopgap agreement that brought Sankoh into the government when it was becoming well known that he was supported by Taylor and Qaddafi.

The RUF also negotiated a clause that pardoned all combatants and collaborators who had committed war crimes. There was international condemnation of the clause and UN Secretary General Kofi Annan refused to accept it. A notation was made on the accord by UN representative Francis G. Okelo that the amnesty did not apply to "gross violations of human rights,... international crimes of genocide, crimes against humanity, war crimes, and other serious violations of international humanitarian law."[30]

In Sierra Leone there was jubilation at the signing of the accord. Upcountry, thousands of civilians emerged from the bush in need of food and medicine. The country had been devastated. On both the Human Development Index and World Health Organization life expectancy reports for 1999 Sierra Leone ranked last in the world (with 25.9 years life expectancy).[31, 32]

For Charles Taylor the peace agreement didn't mean an end to his support for the RUF, as there was still a chance that Foday Sankoh could take over the government. Taylor was also having problems with an insurgent force preparing to attack him from Guinea, and he needed the RUF to help fight them. Charles Taylor was present at the negotiations and signing of the Lomé Accord, and the Taylor Judgment states that:

> ...the Accused [Taylor] was engaged in arms transactions at the same time that he was involved in the peace negotiations in Lomé, publicly promoting peace at the Lomé negotiations while privately providing arms and ammunition to the RUF.[33]

After the signing, Foday Sankoh didn't return to Sierra Leone for three months. He went to Libya where he held meetings with Muammar Qaddifi, and to Liberia where he met with Charles Taylor and Mosquito.

AFRC Commanders Move to West Side Base
Relations between the AFRC and RUF had never been smooth but after the Lomé Accord they fell apart completely. The AFRC commanders and troops, all former government soldiers, weren't satisfied with the agreement. They had been excluded from the negotiations, the RUF still had their leader, Johnny Paul Koroma, in detention in Kailahun, and their status as soldiers hadn't been addressed by the government.

The AFRC and RUF still held the major town of Makeni and used it as a gateway to Kono and Kailahun. In April RUF commander Issa Sesay challenged Superman over supporting the AFRC, and a fighter named Boston Flomo (known as "RUF Rambo") was killed in a shootout. This caused the AFRC/RUF alliance to break down further.

Around the time of the Lomé Accord two AFRC commanders, Bazzy and Hassan Papa Bangura (known as "Bomblast"), left Makeni and established the West Side Base to campaign for recognition and reinstatement into the army. The base was located at Magbeni on Rokel Creek around 45 miles from Freetown. It was in a strategic location where they could attack the main Freetown highway, and it had access to the small towns and villages north of the river for food finding and looting. Hundreds of fighters stayed at West Side Base and were known as the West Side Boys or West Side Junglers.

The casual use of terror in the Sierra Leone war can be seen in this testimony from the Taylor trial, where a witness describes to the prosecutor how Bazzy and his fighters moved across Rokel Creek from Magbeni to take over the town of Gberibana on the opposite bank:

> *Wit: Bazzy ordered Keforkeh to cross the river [Rokel Creek]. You had to cross in a boat to Gberibana. He said they should execute any civilians in Gberibana so that no one would know where we [were] based. Keforkeh moved there with more than 50 men.*
> *Pros: How do you know about this order?*
> *Wit: This reorganization was done in our presence. The order was also made in our presence.*

> *Pros: What was the composition of Keforkeh's group that went to Gberibana?*
> *Wit: SLAs [Sierra Leone Army/AFRC],...RUFs,..., former NPFL fighters. All of them were in that Lion Battalion.*
> *Pros: What happened when the Lion Battalion crossed to Gberibana?*
> *Wit: Keforkeh sent [word] that he captured the group and had made the ground fearful. When we also crossed, we saw the bodies of about 15 civilians who had been killed. The force killed them and displayed their corpses on the road.*
> *Pros: How did you get to Gberiebana?*
> *Wit: The troop started moving together with the family members. I moved with Hassan Papa Bangura and Bazzy. I saw the display of these corpses at Gberibana.*
> *Pros: Did Bazzy react when he saw this display?*
> *Wit: He just said, 'job well done...'* [34]

On the Freetown highway near West Side Base is a long hill called Okra Hill. The West Side Boys used the bottom of the hill as a point to ambush vehicles and loot passengers. They didn't do it to every vehicle. ECOMOG had a checkpoint nearby at Masiaka and they didn't want to attract reprisals.

In early August the West Side Boys kidnapped a contingent of ECOMOG troops, UNOMSIL officials, journalists, and a priest visiting West Side Base on a ruse set up by Bazzy to hand over child combatants. In return for the release of the hostages Bazzy demanded a meeting with Johnny Paul Koroma who was still under RUF detention. Charles Taylor intervened and arranged for helicopters to take Johnny Paul and a group of West Side Boys to Monrovia—Johnny Paul from Kailahun and the West Side Boys from Freetown.

The group met and the AFRC issued their grievances and asked to be reinstated into the national army. There was no response from the government, and at the end of the month the West Side Boys attacked and kidnapped an RUF delegation heading upcountry. At the end of the year they held a demonstration in Freetown demanding to be reinstated into the army and, incredibly, to be given back pay dating to the Intervention. (President Kabbah agreed but never gave them the money.)

RUF Fights for Taylor
In April 1999 the anti-Taylor forces in Guinea began making attacks on Liberia to overthrow Charles Taylor. The forces, named LURD (Liberians United for Reconciliation and Democracy), were supported by Guinean president Lansana Conté who was suspicious of Charles Taylor's regional ambitions. The

attacks were the beginning of a four-year conflict known as the Second Liberian Civil War. For the next year and a half the RUF stalled disarmament to help Taylor fight LURD, and to allow Sankoh to continue his attempts to take over the government.

LURD's bases were in southeastern Guinea near the border of Lofa County in Liberia and Kono and Kailahun Districts in Sierra Leone. In August Charles Taylor ordered Mosquito to send RUF troops from Kailahun into Lofa County to help the Liberian army (Taylor's official troops) repel a LURD group headed by a commander named Mosquito Spray. RUF fighters, including Mosquito and Issa Sesay, went to Liberia and were victorious over Mosquito Spray and his squad, pushing them back into Guinea.

In September, in the north, the RUF attacked a contingent of Guinean ECOMOG troops in Kambia District and seized their arms and armored vehicles. In retaliation Guinea attacked the RUF and bombed their positions in Kambia. In January 2000, Foday Sankoh ordered the RUF to return the arms and vehicles, four months after they had been seized, and the fighting stopped.

Sankoh and Johnny Paul Join the Government, AFRC/RUF Alliance Breaks Down

Foday Sankoh arrived in Freetown on October 3rd, and on October 23rd the RUF officially joined the government. Sankoh was given the position of Chairman of the Commission for the Management of Strategic Resources, National Reconstruction, and Development which gave him power over all mining in the country. Three ministries were given to the RUF including the Ministry of Trade and Industry which was headed by Mike Lamin, one of the original fighters trained in Liberia, while the AFRC was given the Ministry of Tourism.

President Kabbah also gave AFRC leader Johnny Paul Koroma a position in the government. He was named head of the Committee for the Consolidation of Peace, or CPP, the agency charged with implementing the Lomé Accord including the demobilization of combatants.

The AFRC and RUF had been holding the northern town of Makeni since the attack on Freetown, but confrontations continued between the two factions. In mid-October Issa Sesay and a large force of RUF fighters traveled from Kailahun to Makeni and forced the AFRC out of the town. Sankoh later admitted that he had ordered the attack, giving the excuse that the AFRC troops weren't disarming, though it was clearly a move by the RUF to control Makeni free of the AFRC.

As new members of the government Foday Sankoh and Johnny Paul set up "lodges" in Freetown—large mansions where they lived with their staff, extended families, and bodyguards. Sankoh's lodge was on Spur Road, half way up the hill between Lumley and Wilberforce. Sankoh chose his bodyguards from Kailahun and brought thirty fighters to his lodge.

Johnny Paul, whose lodge was at Juba Hill near Goderich, had a force of around fifty bodyguards, mostly from West Side Base including West Side commanders Gullit and Bazzy. When these commanders left, there was fighting over who would be the new commander of the West Side Boys, and the toughest of the group, Corporal Foday Kallay, became the new leader.

Peacekeepers and Problems with Disarmament

With the new government in place an effort was made to disarm the combatants. On October 22nd the UN Security Council approved a new peacekeeping mission to replace UNOMSIL with the similar acronym of UNAMSIL (United Nations Mission in Sierra Leone) with an initial force of 6,000 peacekeepers. There were around 45,000 combatants to be disarmed including RUF, AFRC, and Kamajors and other Civil Defense Forces. On November 4th the Disarmament, Demobilization and Reintegration (DDR) program began. ECOMOG troops acted as peacekeepers until the UNAMSIL troops started arriving in December.

The factions were slow to disarm. On November 10th Foday Sankoh traveled to Segbwema and told his RUF fighters to disarm, though many Sierra Leoneans believe he told them not to disarm in the Mende language, which UN personnel couldn't understand. Some fighters and child combatants handed in their weapons at the West Side Base, and Caritas, a Catholic organization, rescued a large number of abducted children and reunited them with their families or gave them school lessons in camps. In early December Johnny Paul went to Kabala to disarm a group of AFRC troops, but by December 15th, the target date for completion, only 9,000 fighters had demobilized.

Mosquito Leaves

When disarmament began, a rift developed between Foday Sankoh and Mosquito who was still at RUF headquarters in Kailahun. Sankoh wanted to make it appear that the RUF was disarming while Mosquito, who was losing power as Sankoh moved into the government, was voicing strong opinions about keeping an active fighting force. The hot-headed Mosquito became belligerent and in November he executed a group of RUF fighters who wanted to disarm. In December he abducted two Médicins Sans Frontières workers, declaring that Sankoh was trying to kill him. He went to Segbwema with a group of his supporters to attack RUF troops undergoing disarmament, but the troops persuaded them not to attack.

Mosquito then executed a group of eight RUF officers and fled to Liberia. On December 21, 1999 he met in Monrovia with Charles Taylor, Foday Sankoh, and Olusegun Obasanjo, the new president of Nigeria, and they convinced him not to return to Sierra Leone. Mosquito remained in Liberia and fought for Charles Taylor against LURD.

The year had been long and eventful. The attack on Freetown and the documentary "Cry Freetown" brought widespread awareness of the brutality of the war, and conflict diamonds became an international issue. In October British Foreign Secretary Robin Cook proposed controls on the sale of uncut diamonds, and a movement began to certify diamonds which ultimately became the Kimberly Process. It was a difficult year for journalists in the country: ten reporters died including one under detention at Pademba Road who didn't receive medical care.

2000: ECOMOG withdraws, RUF fighters abduct peacekeepers and advance on Freetown, Demonstrations and arrests, Britain enters the war, Sankoh arrested, Issa becomes leader of the RUF, Pressure on Charles Taylor, West Side Boys abduct British soldiers, Fighting in Guinea, Abuja Ceasefire

ECOMOG Withdraws

UNAMSIL, the disarmament and peacekeeping force, began arriving at the end of 1999 and by the beginning of February there were 11,000 peacekeepers in the country from Bangladesh, Pakistan, India, Ethiopia, and many other countries, with the U.S. and Britain contributing funds. The peacekeepers were deployed in the south at Bo, in the east at Kenema and Moa Barracks, and in the north at Makeni and Magburaka. The RUF wouldn't allow them into Kono District.

ECOMOG withdrew and the country was left with a lightly-armed peace-keeping force. ECOMOG had been involved in the war for ten years and the Truth and Reconciliation Commission Report praised its contribution as follows:

> *The Commission finds that it was ECOMOG that ultimately prevented the RUF from occupying the entire country. Sierra Leone owes a debt of gratitude to those that comprised the ECOMOG peacekeeping forces, in particular, the Nigerian troops who comprised the majority of the force.* [35]

The number of ECOMOG soldiers who died in the war hasn't been released.

Foday Sankoh was now part of the government, and as Chairman for the Management of Strategic Resources he made statements about controlling diamond mining while allowing his RUF troops to continue their mining operations in Kono and Tongo Field. In February he traveled to Ghana, supposedly for medical reasons, but continued to South Africa where he was expelled for trading in diamonds. In March he refused to meet with the Sierra Leone Parliament to explain why the RUF wasn't disarming. There were demonstrations in Freetown against the slow pace of demobilization. People were convinced that Foday Sankoh was maneuvering for a takeover.

Johnny Paul Koroma was also in the government as head of the CPP. Late in February he announced that he and his AFRC forces were ending their association with the RUF and were now on the side of the government, and that armed AFRC fighters would remain at the West Side Base to protect Freetown from another RUF attack. The West Side Boys stayed at their base but continued their renegade activities, attacking vehicles and harassing civilians. President Kabbah announced that AFRC soldiers would be screened and allowed into the new army.

RUF Fighters Abduct Peacekeepers and Advance on Freetown, Demonstrations and Arrests

In late April events took a critical turn. RUF troops in Magburaka forced UNAMSIL peacekeepers to dismantle a disarmament center that had been set up in the town. Then on May 1st, RUF fighters led by commanders Augustine Gbao and Morris Kallon attacked a disarmament center in Makeni when peacekeepers refused to return ten RUF fighters who had reported for disarmament. Four Kenyan peacekeepers were killed and around fifty were taken hostage.

This was followed by abductions of UNAMSIL peacekeepers in other districts. In Kailahun, RUF fighters surrounded a group of Indian peacekeepers and held them under siege. Others were taken in the north and within a few days the RUF had seized over five hundred peacekeepers. Foday Sankoh blamed UNAMSIL, saying that the peacekeepers were forcing rebels to disarm. He didn't order the RUF to release the hostages.

While seizing the peacekeepers, the RUF also captured weapons and armored personnel carriers and began moving toward Freetown in what appeared to be a new attack on the capital. They captured Lunsar on May 6th and moved further to Masiaka, nearing the

RUF commander Augustine Gbao (photo by Peter Andersen, 2001)

capital. Britain, alarmed that there could be another attack on the city, sent troops to evacuate foreign nationals.

Events unfolded quickly. Rumors spread that Foday Sankoh was planning a coup and the government put him under house arrest at his lodge on Spur Road. A demonstration was held at Sankoh's lodge on May 6th by women demanding peace, but Sankoh refused to talk to them.

On May 7th Johnny Paul Koroma held what he called a "Peace Rally" at the national stadium attended by thousands of civilians, soldiers, and Kamajors. Johnny Paul called on the crowd to defend Freetown from the RUF, and that evening he organized a "task force" that spent the night arresting RUF politicians and looting their houses. He stated on the radio that the rebels were planning a coup and that President Kabbah supported the arrests. There was one death: Susan Lahai, RUF Deputy Minister for Transport and Communications, was raped and killed at her home. Foday Sankoh wasn't arrested but remained at Spur Road with family members, staff, and armed bodyguards.

The next day, May 8th, there was a demonstration at Sankoh's lodge organized by the Sierra Leone Parliament and civil society groups. A large group of civilians met at Victoria Park in downtown Freetown and walked to Spur Road, singing and carrying placards. There were around thirty UNAMSIL troops guarding Sankoh's lodge, and armed Kamajors joined the demonstrators as they reached the lodge.

The crowd tried to force the gate open, a UNAMSIL soldier fired into the air as a warning, and Sankoh's bodyguards and Kamajors began exchanging fire. There was a gun battle and a rocket-propelled grenade was fired into the crowd by an RUF bodyguard. Sankoh and some of his followers escaped through the back while others were killed, and the crowd looted Sankoh's compound. Around forty people died including nineteen demonstrators. It was announced that documents were found at Sankoh's lodge that proved he was trading diamonds for arms. (The documents were later used in Charles Taylor's Special Court trial.)

The same day the RUF fighters continued their advance on Freetown. They captured Masiaka but were brought to a halt by a coalition of army troops, Kamajors, and West Side Boys and forced back to Lunsar, where fighting continued.

Britain Enters the War, Sankoh Arrested
British troops arrived the same day and, in an action codenamed "Operation Palliser", secured Lungi Airport and the Mammy Yoko Hotel which would again be the staging point for evacuations. On May 13th British ships arrived in Freetown carrying 1,000 royal marines. The leader of the British forces, General David Richards, made the decision to expand his mandate from evacuating

foreign nationals to helping the government stop the RUF. Richards later said in an interview:

> *The military activities we needed to do to facilitate an evacuation operation were remarkably similar to what I was intending to do for a different purpose, which was to stop the RUF advance, because we had to do that to allow the evacuation…I had to get to the next level up, really to Tony Blair.*[36]

Tony Blair backed Richards' plan despite criticism from the British Parliament and public for "mission creep". To demonstrate their formidable power the British staged helicopter attacks and an amphibious landing at Lumley Beach that were viewed by President Kabbah and other officials. Richards and his advisors joined planning meetings with UNAMSIL and the army to help bring cohesion to military actions against the RUF, and British troops defended Lungi Airport and patrolled Freetown. The British supplied weapons and training to government troops and transported them by helicopter to combat areas around Lunsar where they fought with and eventually defeated the RUF fighters who had moved to attack the capital.

On May 17th Foday Sankoh emerged from his hiding place in the hills above Freetown. He was captured, paraded through the streets naked, and put under custody. The same day RUF troops attacked Lungi Airport but were thoroughly beaten by the British forces. Late in May President Kabbah announced that Sankoh would stand trial for crimes committed since the signing of the Lomé Peace Accord.

The UNAMSIL peacekeepers were still being held by the RUF, and ECOWAS asked Charles Taylor to negotiate their release. Taylor met with the RUF and, beginning in mid-May, groups of peacekeepers were released to Lofa County in Liberia, leaving only the Indian peacekeepers under siege in Kailahun. In his Special Court trial Taylor tried to use these negotiations to show that he hadn't supported the RUF but had only been a peacemaker, though to many the success of the negotiations was proof that he controlled the RUF.

On July 15th an operation to rescue the Indian peacekeepers codenamed "Operation Khukri" was mounted by UNAMSIL Indian forces backed by British helicopters. They staged a surprise helicopter attack on Kailahun town and rescued a group of injured and ill peacekeepers, while other forces traveled in vehicles from Moa Barracks and rescued the remaining troops, overcoming the RUF in a battle at Pendembu and sniper attacks along the road as they made their way back to the barracks. The operation was a success and gave a boost to the morale of UNAMSIL forces.

The Rebel War: 1991-2002

Issa Becomes Leader of the RUF, Pressure on Charles Taylor

The war seemed to be over in the capital but problems persisted upcountry. With Sankoh in detention and Mosquito in Liberia, the rebels were without a leader. In July ECOWAS heads of state met in Monrovia and approved Issa Sesay, who had been third in command after Sankoh and Mosquito, as interim RUF leader. Issa Sesay was in Monrovia for the meeting and Charles Taylor used the occasion to discuss other plans with him, as the Taylor Judgment states:

> *In July 2000, a meeting was convened in Monrovia to discuss the selection of new leadership for the RUF following Sankoh's imprisonment. The meeting was attended by all of the ECOWAS heads of state and an RUF delegation led by Issa Sesay where it was proposed that Sesay take over as Interim Leader of the RUF. In another meeting late that night, the Accused [Taylor] privately advised Issa Sesay to say that he would disarm but 'not do it in reality'. At that time, the Accused was supplying Sesay with arms and ammunition, and also calling on the RUF to send forces to help him fight his own enemies together with the AFL [Armed Forces of Liberia] in Liberia and in Guinea.*[37]

Taylor was instructing Issa Sesay to delay disarmament so the RUF could continue fighting for him against LURD.

Rebels at Masingbi, a town east of Makeni held by the RUF during this period (photo by Peter Andersen, 2001)

It was evident to the UN and Western countries that Charles Taylor was keeping the RUF armed and that diamonds were the main source of funds, and they began to put pressure on Taylor. On July 5th the UN Security Council adopted a resolution that imposed an embargo on the sale of uncut diamonds from Sierra Leone. The resolution made it illegal to trade in Sierra Leone diamonds without a certificate of origin from the government, and because the government had no certification system in place, any trading in diamonds was illegal.

Britain and the U.S. also criticized Taylor directly. On August 1, 2000 the New York Times reported on accusations by British and American diplomats at the UN that Charles Taylor and Blaise Compaoré, the president of Burkina Faso, were violating the embargo on diamonds, that Taylor "had personally taken command of rebel forces", and that Compaoré was allowing the transshipment of weapons from the Ukraine through his country to the RUF. The same article reported on a meeting in Monrovia in July where Thomas R. Pickering, U.S. Under Secretary of State for Political Affairs, told Taylor that the United States would invoke sanctions on Liberian officials unless they stopped supporting the rebels.[38]

West Side Boys Abduct British Soldiers
Late in August there was a crisis that gave the British troops a chance to use their fighting skills. To the east of Freetown the West Side Boys were still based in the villages of Gberibana and Magbeni on Rokel Creek with Foday Kallay, now a self-promoted colonel, as their leader. During the recent RUF move to attack Freetown the West Side Boys had cooperated with the government to fight off the attackers, but after the fighting they returned to their base and continued their renegade and violent activities. They set up roadblocks on the highway and in July clashed with UNAMSIL troops. In mid-August Foday Kallay executed a group of his fighters who tried to disarm.

On August 25th a group of eleven British soldiers and one Sierra Leonean liaison officer, Lieutenant Musa Bangura, were returning to Freetown from a patrol at Masiaka when they deviated from their planned course and turned onto the dirt road leading to Magbeni in West Side Boys territory, the commander in charge not understanding how dangerous the West Side Boys were. They were captured and taken across the river to Gberibana where Kallay and his fighters treated them brutally with beatings and mock executions. Lieutenant Bangura was given harsher treatment. He was tied up and put in a "jo-jo", or dungeon, a pit covered with metal sheets. He remained there, lying in mud and urine, and was taken out for frequent beatings.

After negotiations the West Side Boys released five of the captives in exchange for medical supplies and a satellite phone, and when they made a call on the phone the British used the signal to pinpoint their location. Special Forces arrived from Britain and staged an intervention to rescue the hostages, codenamed "Operation Barras".

British observation teams were moved by boat to Gberibana where they hid in the bush and reconnoitered the base. In the early morning of September 10th British forces staged a surprise helicopter assault. The observation teams attacked first while the main force slid down ropes from the helicopters. There was heavy fighting and the British troops rescued all the captives and killed a large number of West Side Boys (the exact number is disputed). One British soldier was killed. Foday Kallay was arrested and sentenced to ten years for conspiracy.

Fighting in Guinea, Abuja Ceasefire
The war began its final stage. In Liberia, Charles Taylor's conflict with LURD intensified and Taylor ordered the RUF to attack Guinea on two fronts—in the north from Kambia District and in the east from Kono and Kailahun Districts and Lofa County in Liberia. In the north, beginning in September, the RUF made attacks on the Guinean town of Pamalap, located at the crossing point between the two countries, and advanced part way to Conakry. The Guinean army pushed them back, then shelled and bombed Kambia District.

In the east, LURD attacked Lofa Country in July, and in September Taylor's army and the RUF attacked Guinea from Lofa County and Kono District. They captured the Guinean towns of Macenta and Gueckedou in December and moved toward Kissidougou, battling a coalition of LURD, the Guinean army, and Sierra Leonean fighters, including Kamajors, who had gone to Guinea to fight. Thousands of refugees and civilians fled the fighting and many were killed.

As the fighting continued in Guinea, ECOWAS organized a meeting in Abuja to forge a stronger agreement on disarmament. The Abuja Ceasefire Agreement was signed on November 10, 2000 with the RUF again agreeing to a ceasefire and total disarmament.

Two days later a British naval task force arrived in Freetown to reinforce Britain's support for the government. British troops put on a show of force including another amphibious landing and jungle training with live ammunition. Later in December Issa Sesay met with UNAMSIL in Makeni to discuss the deployment of peacekeepers, but at the end of the year the rebels were still fighting for Taylor.

2001: Sanctions on Taylor, RUF defeated, End of hostilities, Disarmament

Sanctions on Taylor, RUF Defeated
At the beginning of 2001 Britain announced that it would maintain its military presence in Sierra Leone until the war was resolved, and in another show of

force British troops held a rapid deployment parachute exercise at Lungi and a demonstration of firepower from a warship.

The fighting on the border continued for a few more months but gradually came to an end. In Kambia district and along the northern border Guinean forces crossed into Sierra Leone to pursue RUF fighters and continued shelling and bombing Kambia district.

In the east there was heavy fighting around Gueckedou and the UNHCR was forced to withdraw from refugee camps, which left thousands of refugees without food and other aid. In February the Guinean army, LURD, and Sierra Leonean fighters began to overpower the RUF and Taylor's army with artillery and air strikes, forcing them back into Sierra Leone and Liberia and thoroughly overwhelming them. Important RUF commanders Superman and Komba Gbondema were killed in the fighting.

At the same time the UN increased its pressure on Charles Taylor, imposing sanctions on Liberia in January and strengthening an arms embargo in March, while the Security Council increased the number of UNAMSIL peacekeepers to 17,500. Fighting finally ended in April, and the RUF agreed to the deployment of peacekeepers throughout the country.

Additional sanctions were put in place in May, including an embargo on diamonds from Liberia and an international travel ban on Liberian leaders, and Charles Taylor ended his support of the RUF. The war was over, though skirmishes continued in Kono District between the RUF and Kamajors.

*A rebel commander and his wife in Koidu, Kono District
(photo by Peter Andersen, 2001)*

End of Hostilities, Disarmament

An agreement to end hostilities was signed between the government and the RUF on May 14, 2001 that included a process and timetable for disarmament. It was decided that the districts would disarm in pairs—one district controlled by the RUF paired with one controlled by the army and Kamajors. Kambia and Port Loko Districts would be the first to disarm followed by Kono and Bonthe, Koinadugu and Moyamba, Bombali and Bo, Tonkolili and Pujehun, and finally Kailahun and Kenema.

Sporadic fighting continued in Kono until August when peacekeepers were deployed in the district. On September 3rd a public meeting was held in Koidu with Presidents Kabbah, Obasanjo, and Alpha Oumar Konaré of Mali attending. They praised Issa Sesay for his leadership and willingness to disarm. (Issa was later convicted of war crimes by the Special Court.)

On September 11, 2001 the Sierra Leone Web reported that 60 percent of the combatants had demobilized.[39] The total at the end of the year was 47,781 fighters disarmed including over 19,000 RUF and 28,000 Kamajors and other CDF. More than 4,000 underage fighters were disarmed, around eight percent of the total. Over 25,000 weapons were destroyed.[40]

The Disarmament, Demobilization and Rehabilitation program in Sierra Leone was considered a success, though there were complaints from ex-combatants about the quality of skills training and the meager amount of money they received. There were also concerns that many female fighters, including underage girls, had not taken part in DDR because of the greater emphasis given to disarming male fighters, and the shame women and girls would experience if they returned to their homes as documented combatants. The Truth and Reconciliation Commission found that:

> *Men and boys were favoured over women and girls in the disarmament and reintegration processes. Little effort was made to recognise the experiences of women in the war. Most former female combatants and those who played a supporting role in the war were not able to access the necessary assistance to reintegrate into their communities.*[41]

A final conflict took place in Kono District in December 2001. Known as the Cutlass War, it erupted when ethnic Kono activists tried to force non-Kono miners, mainly former fighters, out of diamond fields in Koidu. The two groups fought with clubs, knives, matchets and axes (they had been disarmed), and seven people died before Pakistani peacekeepers stopped the fighting.

2002: Final Ceremony

With disarmament concluded a ceremony was held on January 18, 2002 at Lungi to formally mark the end of the war. All factions were represented and President Kabbah was joined by international leaders. The program included a ceremonial burning of 3,000 weapons. Foday Sankoh, the RUF leader whose plans to take over the country had caused the deaths of an estimated 50,000 people, was in prison awaiting trial, while Charles Taylor was still fighting to stay in power in Liberia.

AFTER THE WAR

Following are events related to the war that took place after the January 18, 2002 ceremony:

March 2002: Sankoh in Court
On March 4, 2002 Foday Sankoh was arraigned at a Freetown Magistrate's Court and charged with murder and other offences. Sankoh had deteriorated physically since his arrest and he appeared frail and wore his long, gray hair in dreadlocks. The government was bringing his case to trial so it could continue holding him in prison, and he was eventually indicted by the Special Court. Six months later, in September, Sankoh suffered a stroke and in his final appearance in court he was in a wheelchair and unable to speak.

May 2002: Kabbah Re-elected
President Ahmad Tejan Kabbah was re-elected in May 2002. The party formed by the rebels, the RUFP, ran a candidate but received only 2 percent of the vote.

January 2003: Johnny Paul Coup Attempt and Assumed Death
On January 13, 2003 armed men attempted to break into a military depot in Wellington, possibly attempting to overthrow the government. The group was arrested and former AFRC leader Johnny Paul Koroma was linked to the break-in. He disappeared and it is assumed that he fled to Liberia and died there, though his body has never been found. At the time the Special Court was preparing its indictments and Koroma would have been tried with other top AFRC commanders, and many people believe his killing was ordered by Charles Taylor to cover up evidence of Taylor's involvement.

March 2003: Special Court Indictments
The Special Court for Sierra Leone was formally established in January 2002 by an agreement between the United Nations and the Sierra Leone government. The court had jurisdiction to try the persons bearing the most responsibility for war crimes and crimes against humanity that had occurred after the signing of the Abidjan Peace Accord on November 30, 1996. The court included both Sierra Leonean and international judges and staff. Its facilities were located in the New England section of Freetown and consisted of a court building, offices, and a prison.

Indictments were handed down beginning in March 2003. Those indicted from the RUF were Foday Sankoh and commanders Sam Bockarie (Mosquito), Issa Sesay, Morris Kallon, and Augustine Gbao. From the AFRC were Johnny Paul Koroma and commanders Alex Tamba Brima (Gullit), Ibrahim Bazzy Kamara, and Santigie Borbor Kanu (Five-Five). From the Civil Defense Forces were Samuel Hinga Norman, Allieu Kondowai, and Moinina Fofana. Charles Taylor was indicted, but his indictment was kept sealed until June 4, 2003 when it was opened and a warrant was issued for his arrest while he was on a visit to Accra for Liberian peace negotiations.

The indictment of Hinga Norman and other Kamajors was controversial because they had supported the elected government in the fighting, and it was assumed that President Kabbah had ordered their military actions. The two Kamajor leaders who eventually went to prison received lighter sentences than the RUF and AFRC leaders, though it was because the Kamajors had committed fewer atrocities, and not because they had fought on the side of the government.

April 2003: Truth and Reconciliation Commission
The Truth and Reconciliation Commission, which had been mandated by the Lomé Accord, began public hearings in April 2003 with the stated goal of "healing the nation by investigating the motives of the combatants and the effects of the war on civilians". The commission produced a report of over 1,800 pages that included the historical build-up to the war, the progression of the conflict, recommendations for reconciliation, ways to prevent another war, and a national vision for the country.

The report assigned blame for human rights abuses based on statistics gathered from interviews, and concluded that the RUF had committed the highest number of atrocities while the AFRC committed the second highest, followed by the Kamajors. ECOMOG committed the smallest number of atrocities. The report faulted the Kabbah government for failing to stop or speak out against abuses by the Kamajors and other CDF groups.

The commission held sensitization sessions in towns and villages that included emotional scenes of perpetrators acknowledging their role in atrocities and asking for forgiveness. Sierra Leoneans generally accepted that civilians and ex-combatants had to live together and continue with their lives.

May 2003: Death of Mosquito
Mosquito (Sam Bockarie) had been fighting for Charles Taylor in Liberia since he left Sierra Leone in December 1999. He, his wife, and two children were shot and killed in Liberia in May 2003. It was suspected that Charles Taylor

ordered the killings so Mosquito couldn't testify on Taylor's collaboration with the RUF.

July 2003: Death of Foday Sankoh
Foday Sankoh died at the age of 66 on July 29, 2003 at Choithram Hospital in Freetown while waiting trial by the Special Court. The cause of death was cited as pulmonary pneumonia.

2007-2012: Special Court Convictions
Convictions by the Special Court began in June 2007. Those convicted were found guilty of some or all of the following: war crimes including acts of terrorism, collective punishments, extermination, murder, rape, outrages upon personal dignity, conscripting or enlisting children under the age of fifteen into armed forces, enslavement, and pillage. Appeals were rejected.

Those convicted are serving their sentences at Mpanga Prison in Rwanda, an international standard prison built to hold prisoners convicted at the Rwanda War Crimes Trials. The Sierra Leone Special Court was the first international court that brought convictions for the conscription of children. Following are the sentences:

- Issa Sesay (RUF): 52 years
- Morris Kallon (RUF): 40 years
- Augustine Gbao (RUF): 25 years
- Alex Tamba Brima (AFRC): 50 years
- Santigie Borbor Kanu (AFRC): 50 years
- Ibrahim Bazzy Kamara (AFRC): 45 years
- Allieu Kondowai (CDF): 20 years
- Moinina Fofana (CDF): 15 years (Fofana was released in 2015 and is required to stay in the town of Bo under monitoring for the remaining three years of his sentence.)

Four others were either dead or missing:
- Foday Sankoh (RUF): deceased, indictment withdrawn
- Samuel Bockarie (RUF): deceased, indictment withdrawn
- Samuel Hinga Norman (CDF): died February 22, 2007 before judgment, proceedings terminated (Norman died while undergoing medical treatment in Senegal.)
- Johnny Paul Koroma (AFRC): reported deceased, fate unknown

In September 2012 Ibrahim Bazzy Kamara and Santigie Borbor Kanu received additional sentences of one year and fifty weeks for contempt of court for attempting to bribe a Special Court witness or for otherwise attempting to induce a witness to recant testimony during Charles Taylor's trial.

2008: Chuckie Taylor Arrest and Conviction

Chuckie Taylor (original name Charles McArthur Emmanuel, legally changed to Roy Belfast, Jr.) was Charles Taylor's son, born in Boston in 1977 and raised in Florida by his American mother. When Chuckie was twenty years old he went to Liberia, and his father, who was then President of Liberia, made him head of the Anti-Terrorist Unit, Charles Taylor's personal security force. Chuckie became notorious for torturing and killing his father's enemies and became one of the most feared people in the country. He was involved in the Sierra Leone war in 1998 when he tortured and killed Sierra Leonean refugees and deserters who refused to be sent back to Sierra Leone to fight for the RUF.

U.S. officials had been watching Chuckie Taylor, and in 2006 he was arrested at the Miami airport for entering the U.S. on a passport he had applied for using a false name for his father. A case was brought against him under a 1994 federal law that allows for the prosecution of anyone in the U.S. suspected of committing torture abroad, whether the person is a citizen, legal resident, or just present in the country. Liberian and Sierra Leonean victims were brought to testify and on October 30, 2008 Chuckie Taylor was convicted of torture and other counts. He is serving a 97-year sentence at a federal prison in Florida.

2001-2012: Liberian War, Trial and Conviction of Charles Taylor

After the war ended in Sierra Leone the anti-Taylor LURD fighters, who had helped defeat the RUF, continued their attacks on Lofa County and by February 2002 were nearing Monrovia. In early 2003 another anti-Taylor group, MODEL (Movement for Democracy in Liberia), attacked from the Ivory Coast, and by the middle of 2003 Taylor controlled only a third of the country. In June both insurgent groups began a siege of Monrovia in which hundreds of civilians died. The siege ended in August and U.S. and Nigerian forces took control of the city.

ECOWAS convened peace talks in Accra in June 2003. While Taylor was in Accra the Special Court for Sierra Leone unsealed his indictment and Taylor fled to Liberia. After international pressure, including a phone call from U.S. President George W. Bush, Charles Taylor resigned from the presidency in August 2003. A peace agreement was signed by Moses Blah, his successor, and Taylor went into exile in Nigeria. Nigeria refused to extradite him to the Special Court without a formal request from the Liberia government.

Ellen Johnson Sirleaf was elected president of Liberia in 2005. In March 2006, after international pressure and negotiations, she agreed to ask Nigeria to surrender Charles Taylor to the Special Court under the condition that his trial be held outside of West Africa, because of security issues owing to Taylor's continued popularity in Liberia. Taylor tried to escape and was captured at the Nigeria-Cameroon border.

Charles Taylor's trial began at The Hague in January 2008, and on April 26, 2012 he was found guilty of eleven counts of war crimes, crimes against humanity, and other serious violations of international humanitarian law. Taylor was sentenced to a 50-year prison term. He lost his appeal and is now serving his sentence at a British prison. Taylor's wars in Liberia were bloodier than the war in Sierra Leone. An estimated 250,000 people were killed in Liberia between 1989 and 2003.

Taylor on trial at The Hague (photo by Evert-Jan Daniels)

PART 2: NARRATIVES

THE EAST: REBEL TERRITORY

The two eastern districts of Kenema and Kailahun are located in the far east of the country on the Liberian border. The "parrot's beak" of Kailahun District also shares a border with Guinea. The district headquarter towns have the same names as the districts—Kenema and Kailahun.

Kailahun District was the rebels' headquarters for the entire war. Located near Charles Taylor's main base at Gbarnga in Liberia, it was the point where arms were brought into the country. The main Sierra Leone Army base in the area is Moa Barracks on the Moa River, across from the town of Daru.

Kenema District is located to the west of Kailahun District and is one of the main diamond districts of the country. The diamond mining area of Tongo Field in the north of the district was an important target that the rebels, army, and Kamajors all tried to control. In 1993, at the start of their guerrilla war operations, the rebels established two bases in the district which they used to spread through the country—Peyama Camp near Tongo Field and Zogoda Camp in a remote area in the far south of the district.

During the war the RUF fought the army and Kamajors continuously in the two districts. After the AFRC coup in 1997 the RUF became the allies of the army, and when they were forced out of Freetown in 1998 many of them retreated to Kailahun District where they made plans to attack Freetown.

Kailahun district saw heavy action again during the fighting on the Guinean border in 2000-2001.

Today, rural areas of both districts are depopulated. Kailahun town is economically depressed with little employment for the large number of ex-fighters who live there. The town of Segbwema, located near Moa Barracks, was devastated from frequent fighting, and a nearby college at Bunumbu was completely destroyed.

The narrators are from the two districts and include civilians, RUF fighters, and a Sierra Leone Army soldier. The events they describe are arranged in the approximate order they took place, with some narrators describing single incidents and others covering the entire war.

1. Sheku
   They Called Themselves Freedom Fighters
   Civilian

Sheku is from Bomaru, the first town the RUF attacked. He explains the initial attack and repercussions from Sierra Leone Army troops.

I'm now twenty-eight years old but I'm not sure of my real age. Before all of this I was in Liberia studying Arabic, sent by my parents. When war broke out in Liberia I moved back to Bomaru and was there when the first attack happened on March 23, 1991.

The East: Rebel Territory

Bomaru town center and road to Baiwala, in 2012

There was a refugee camp inside Sierra Leone for Liberian refugees from the war. What the rebels did, they based themselves in the camp and wrote a letter saying they wanted to play a football match with Bomaru civilians. So they came and played the game. Bomaru defeated them two to one. That night there was big dance in the town and the following morning they attacked.

They entered in three groups. It was early in the morning when we heard the firing. We ran into a big house but it was hit with heavy weapons fire that killed some people and injured others. The rebels resembled civilians but some were dressed with nets over their heads to disguise themselves. Some also painted their faces with colors so they couldn't be recognized. They were from mixed tribes—Gio, Bassa, Mano, Kroo (all from Liberia) and Sierra Leoneans. I was pierced in the chest by a bullet that entered and left a big wound. We were taken to Daru Military Hospital for treatment and I stayed there one month and three weeks.

When the government soldiers were in Bomaru, my father, who was a section chief, was arrested by the soldiers and interrogated. They alleged he knew something about the war and was collaborating with the rebels. He was tied up, beaten, and his mouth torn at both ends. He was loaded into a government military truck and taken to Pademba Road Prison in Freetown where he died after a week. My father's name was Lahai Kallon.

Narratives

The rebels started capturing our brothers and forcing them to join the RUF and when they went on an attack the Sierra Leonean boys acted as guides to show them the routes. Whenever they attacked a town and captured it they took all the civilians and ordered them to do what they wanted. You couldn't refuse. So we lived with them like that during the war.

The war disturbed everyone and almost everyone suffered. Everyone knows that war is bad. To avert all these negative things people should be good, especially in terms of business, and prices should be fair. During the war the rebels said there were no price controls in the country and people were making high profits. If the government sends things to villages and if the people use them honestly, nobody will grumble and there won't be another war.

2. Lucia
   It was Rogues and Crooks
   Civilian

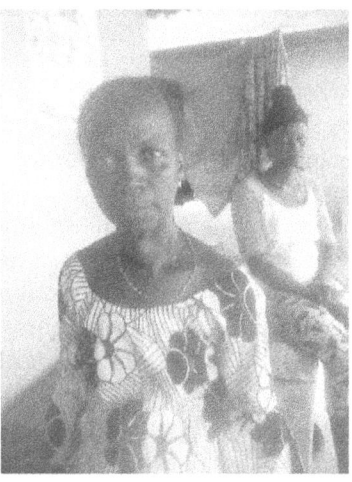

Lucia also lives in Bomaru. She describes the violence and looting that began after the initial invasion, and the politics of the conflict when the RUF arrested chiefs from the APC party.

I'm thirty-eight years old now. I was in Gumaru when the invasion took place on March 23, 1991. It's a few miles from Bomaru. We were processing palm oil in the morning when we heard gunshots and saw people running away into the bush, saying it was an attack and that people had been killed.

The East: Rebel Territory

The following day Chief Kallon called everyone hiding in the bush to come back to town but again we came under a very heavy attack. The rebels came into the town, gathered us together, and told us it was a real war. They didn't allow anyone to leave and guarded all the strategic locations. Some people who knew the village well managed to escape but one businessman from another place had some money and tried to leave at night. They caught him and shot him.

Foday Sankoh came to Bomaru. He said they came to take over the country because things were difficult and there was no truth, and that they were fighting for everyone so no one should be afraid. He told us the war would last two weeks. They called a big meeting in Pendembu where all the section chiefs and other people with positions were arrested and locked up. C.O. Kargbo said they were all APC chiefs.

During that time you had no property of your own—no child, no wife, no belongings. They hunted people hiding in the bush and brought them to town, then looked at the young boys and girls and took who they needed. From the girls they chose their wives. They took some of the boys to Baiwala and some to Pendembu where they had training bases at the school in Baiwala and at the vocational school in Pendembu.

I saw young armed men sleeping with old women. They raped mothers and their daughters together in the same room. If girls were small and their breasts were just coming out they called them "iron titty" and took them away toward Liberia as their wives. Most of them we never saw again. They took our young boys and gave them loads to carry. Most of the things people owned were taken to Vaahun (in Liberia). If a boy was fortunate he would come back, if not we wouldn't see him again.

If they came upon you cooking they would ask if you were cooking Momoh's soldier. Momoh (President of Sierra Leone) was the enemy they were fighting against. They would just take everything you were cooking. My husband was killed in the war. They also killed my younger sister and brother.

During the war if they asked you a question and you didn't answer they would tie you up and after more questioning they would kill you. When the government soldiers came to attack the rebels we would run into our houses. They came in big groups and surrounded the town. They didn't enter people's houses but if you tried to go out you could be shot. We couldn't go into the bush because we might meet someone who would kill us. Most of the time we hid in mud houses because bullets couldn't go through mud as easily as cement.

Bomaru and Baiwala were under rebel siege until the Kamajors came much later. The government soldiers would take over the village then the rebels would come back, so there were continual attacks. The rebels were strong because they had foreign fighters from Liberia. They would come and fight, then go back to Liberia.

Narratives

So many bad things happened. They were killing innocent people. By right, during a war it should only be between the combatants, but it was extended to the civilians. They split open pregnant women's stomachs and killed young children. They amputated children's hands. In front of me they took one man named Nyamoneh and dug out his eyes before killing him for collaborating with the government troops. They killed one alpha man (Muslim magic man) who was doing magic for them. They found out he was making fake magic, using cigarette papers in the charms, so the charms weren't working well though they hadn't given him any materials to work with. One day they went to him and mercilessly killed him. They boiled hot water in a big drum and dumped him in it.

What do I think brought the war? To me it was rogues and crooks. If someone is denied their rights, that person will go another way to find his or her rights which will bring confusion. Since the war a lot of truths have come. Some of them are human rights, children's rights, and rights for women concerning property so that she can have property if her husband dies. Now the property of a father goes to his children rather than to his brothers and sisters. All these things have improved. Everyone is praying it won't happen again. Everyone has seen the consequences. When war occurs, whether you have a hand in it or not you will suffer or your sister or parents will suffer. Even unborn children will suffer because if your mother is pregnant with you and she hasn't had food all day, even you will feel the pinch of war.

3. Jusu
Rebel Child
RUF Child Soldier

Jusu was just eleven or twelve years old when he was taken by the RUF at the start of the war and trained to be a fighter, and he remained with the rebels up to disarmament in 2002. Jusu refers to Foday Sankoh, the leader of the RUF, as "Papay" which is used in Liberia for "papa" or "father". He is a university student and asked not to be identified.

My present age is around thirty-three. I was in Sandiallu in Kailahun District when the war started. Sandiallu isn't far from Koindu and is located near the main road from Koindu to Kailahun town. I'll tell you everything I witnessed.

The East: Rebel Territory

At that time I was eleven or twelve years old and in primary class six, planning to complete class seven and go to secondary school.

We heard that war had entered Sierra Leone in Bomaru and that the rebel fighters were attacking towns and villages in the district. There was also an attack on Koindu which is a major business town bordering Liberia and Guinea. After the attack on Koindu people fled their towns and villages with bundles on their heads. As more and more displaced people moved into Sandiallu my father decided that we should go to Guinea.

We arranged bundles of loads and exited the town into the bush very early in the morning as the first cock crew. We communicated by whisper. It was the cool dry season and we travelled for two hours before we could recognize each other. We avoided the main roads. We were afraid of a rebel ambush.

We arrived at Mano-Sewaru Junction and tried to cross it quickly but were stopped by a group of rebels. "Halt! Halt! Halt!" a voice from nowhere repeated. The voice came from a mature bastard rebel, and a few seconds later we were engulfed by young armed men in their teens with their faces disguised. My father held my hand but he was shouted at to let me go alone. I was ordered under gun point and forced to move and I tangled my feet and fell down, injuring my knee. This caused me to get a kick from an armed boy. They started commanding us to pass, pass, pass to go to one side and gather with others at the junction.

They told us they were the rebels. They had commanders named C.O. Massaquoi and C.O. Momoh. These were strong commanders and whatever they ordered would happen immediately. C.O. Massaquoi spoke Mende and was from Pujehun. The rebels were all dressed differently. Some wore green and tied green cloths on their heads (the color of the SLPP party). Some wore women's wigs to disguise themselves and also to put on sticks when the enemy came so they would fire at the wigs. That was one of their techniques.

The commanders said the war would continue for three months to overthrow the APC because they were ruling the country in a bad way, and that the country should have facilities which the APC had denied the people. They told us that they killed any APC leader they found in a town. My own home, Sandiallu, had 2,000 or 3,000 people with three hundred to five hundred houses. I heard that after capturing it they gathered everyone at the barrie and asked for the chief. When the chief got up and said he was appointed by the APC government, they used a bayonet on his back to tear off his clothes, then put the weapon in his mouth and fired. This happened in front of everybody.

While they were still holding us, they sent some rebel soldiers to go on reconnaissance to Kailahun town. They had a special group to do spying missions

Narratives

called "rekkies". From Mano-Sewaru to Kailahun town is about seven miles, so we were held by another group while the reconnaissance was going on.

They captured an old man named Pa Sengu who had some money hidden in a coffee bag. They said "You, we're not going to kill you, but do you drink alcohol?" He said "No." Then they brought some alcohol and poured it on his head and took his money. The Pa was crying, telling them not to kill him. The rebels were glad because they had money and arranged for food to be cooked, then they started singing "See-o see-o, ah we day see you, mama mama mama we day see you, papa papa papa we day see you, auntie auntie auntie we day see you." ("We see you, mother, father, auntie", meaning they will find everyone.)

They were all glad because they had a lot of money and the fighting would only be for ninety days. They shot guns into the air so everyone panicked and before they could control the crowd some escaped, including my mother. I didn't see her again until later in the war. They said they were going to kill us but the commander said they should only bring back anyone who escaped. The men who had gone on reconnaissance returned and the food was ready but they weren't able to eat it because everyone was worried and disgruntled that some people had escaped.

They said they needed to go and attack Kailahun town before nightfall, before the escapees could warn the town. The spies estimated the military strength and decided that the RUF men could overpower the government soldiers there. A plan was made to attack immediately, and Daru would be the target after that because it was where the government barracks (Moa Barracks) was located. One commander, Rambo, whose real name was Charles Timber, had his own group heading to attack Daru while the group who captured us went to attack Kailahun town. I noticed that the rebels were speaking Liberian English and some other languages I didn't recognize. They said some were from Burkina Faso and were called Burkinabés.

With the RUF
They had already captured Koindu and Dia so they moved us back to those areas while they went to attack. They took me to be trained as a soldier. They took boys who were twelve, fifteen, twenty years old and warned us that anyone caught escaping would be killed. First they took us to Koindu. While traveling we had only bush yams to eat. We slept anywhere in the bush. We never slept in a village and we didn't change clothes. We were only concerned about saving our lives. There was one village we entered and only three hours later the government troops attacked it. Close to another town we heard gunfire and ran into the bush, but it was actually another rebel group sending a signal to let their brothers know they were there.

The East: Rebel Territory

They captured Kailahun town and sent another group to Baiima and Pendembu which are near Daru. So we were in a real war within the rebel zone. Anyone they captured they would train right away. My elder brother was also trained. We spent three months in training then went to the war front. Some guys were able to hide because they knew the bush in the area but some didn't hide, like Saffa, Benito, Abbaloto, and Chinese Pepe, who was a giant guy in the RUF.

Upper Kailahun District near the RUF headquarters at Buedu

The guns we used were Berettas, AK-47s, and RPGs (rocket-propelled grenade). During the war we mainly received arms from Liberia and from the front during attacks. As we advanced they supplied us with different types of weapons.

Our first mission was to attack Segbwema. I was dressed in a net shirt and had a wig cap on my head with a green piece of cloth tied around it. My Beretta was black and short and nearly the height of my hips. Before we ambushed the town, myself and two others were sent to spy. We planned to have a night attack if their military strength was big. Indeed, Moa Barracks was just seven miles from Segbwema and was strongly fortified. In the morning we hit, but had to retreat because we lacked adequate artillery.

Narratives

We returned to Sandiallu and from there moved to Dia and Kangama within the rebel zone. We were just staying within our own zone and weren't allowed to go into zones we didn't control. We started capturing villages within the district such as Ngeyehun and Manowa, where I was involved in a fierce battle and was injured. We proceeded to Bunumbu where I now just prayed for God's mercy. We just had to defend ourselves.

Before an attack we first made a base with our medical personnel. We didn't kill medical personnel who we captured unless they refused to go. We had our cooks and support groups 1 and 2. Normally sixty strong rebels were able to destabilize many armed government soldiers. The first twenty rebels launched the attack while the other twenty held strategic hidden positions. The first group fired at the soldiers who chased them, then the second group entered the place.

Foday Sankoh told us that he had brought the war and that we should support him. He loved little children and often called them around him. When they had meetings no big man could tell the children to leave. He opened primary schools in many towns in Kailahun District. One of my brothers has a results paper from an RUF Free Primary School. They used secondary school students as teachers.

He talked about the reasons for the war in the village square and some I can still remember were corruption, bad governance, no employment for the youths, and poor salaries for teachers and workers. He mentioned the go-slows that went on in schools, the teachers refusing to teach because they didn't receive their salaries. I recalled from my own school days one of my teachers standing and saying he was frustrated and disgusted with the whole system. Also the police weren't respected because their uniforms were old and their shoes had no soles.

The top men in the RUF would come and talk to us including C.O. Mohamed who was called Field Marshall, and Pa Gene. Pa Gene later tried to overthrow Foday Sankoh. He was a Liberian, a Gio. He was short, thick, stubborn and very wicked. He tried to overthrow Sankoh by saying he had not accomplished what he promised, to complete the war within three months. Pa Gene talked to everyone, both rebels and civilians, and started training small boys, age seven, eight or nine years. He called them the SBU—Small Boys Unit. Pa Gene wanted to kill Foday Sankoh but he didn't succeed.

Before that a lot of looting started taking place because the mission hadn't been accomplished. At first they said "looting not nice", "rape and killing not nice", but all of this started happening because there wasn't enough support to complete the war and everyone had to take care of themselves.

Foday Sankoh made Kailahun town his headquarters and brought a lot of good rebel soldiers there. He assigned various people as town commanders, even some small boys, and removed all the old chiefs. After that there were a lot of rebel campaigns—TOP 20, TOP 40, and TOP Final. During TOP 20 we were killing, looting, and raping. During this period anybody found in town was killed straight off, no question. Rebels left the field of fight and chased innocent people into the bush and killed them. Because of this, many young men joined the rebels to defend their cocoa farms. This carnage lasted about three months.

After that TOP 40 began. This was infighting between the Liberians and the Sierra Leonean junior commanders. Each rebel commander announced his own area of control and used young rebel boys to attack other rebels and kill each other for fame and position in the jungle. At that time only the strongest survived. It was a battle for supremacy. In the jungle, if you were bloodier than me you captured my boys and killed me.

The vangahun (the rebel term for foreign forces) were from many countries, not only Liberia. There were even some men from Mali and Gambia. Ranger, Mosquito, Issa and a few other Sierra Leonean commanders connived to drive these mercenaries out and shot and killed them when they were retreating from army attacks. Then Foday Sankoh became involved. He said the reason the war didn't succeed after the first invasions was because the foreigners had caused destruction, so we should now drive the foreigners out. He wanted to send the Liberian commanders back to Liberia and told the Sierra Leonean boys to take over leadership.

Finally there was TOP Final to kill all the foreign troops at the war front. Any place where they saw vangahun they would kill them, so the Sierra Leoneans drove them to Liberia and even crossed into Liberia and did looting before they came back. Now we knew that all the commanders were Sierra Leoneans and Foday Sankoh gave positions to many others. Most of them died in the war and only a few remain now.

After Foday Sankoh told them to get rid of the foreigners, Mosquito and Issa took over leadership. Before that Mosquito was just a boy while Issa was a junior commander with no say. Other top commanders were Rashid, Ray, Papay Zombia, C.O. Massaquoi, and Azis Tombolo. The last, Azis Tombolo, killed forty-five people in our town while they were trying to escape to Guinea, killing one after another and telling them to clap and laugh as they killed each one. That man was bad. I swear to God if I see him anywhere I will do bad to him. I don't mind abusing him. I think that was in 1992. They used to keep records of dates and killings but one of my brothers named Emmanuel was killed when they found a record on him. The rebels were cowards and didn't like educated people.

Narratives

Attacks from the Government

After the NPRC coup in 1992 we were attacked by government troops from all directions and were pushed back to Koindu. Foday Sankoh moved his base from Kailahun town to Sandiallu. During these attacks a lot of our rebel soldiers died, like Sunanimus who was my own brother. Kasia also died. A lot of people died.

I had a friend who was called Rebel Baby. He was one of my school mates. He was Papay's best bodyguard. Heh! The way he dressed! He looked like a dead man who they had dressed and brought back to life. They could shoot at him and nothing would happen but he was killed later in the Zogoda attack.

Once I was captured by government soldiers at Galema in Kailahun District. One of my brothers had given me a very nice haircut and before they captured me I dropped my weapon so they wouldn't know I was a rebel. The government soldiers first said we were Small Boys Unit but we denied it so they took us toward town. We met an old woman who was carrying firewood on her head. Her head tie included an old combat shirt wrapped with other clothes which I didn't see. I asked the old woman if I could use the clothes and she gave them to me. A government soldier named Sullay called to ask what was in the bundle and on opening it he saw the combat shirt and said "Ah, you're an S.B.U. soldier and I'm going to kill you."

He pushed me to the side to shoot me and told me to open my mouth. I was shouting that I wasn't a rebel and he asked for proof. I cried for help from an old man who was nearby but he said he didn't know me. He put the gun in my mouth but another soldier came and said I was a boy and he shouldn't shoot me. He still fired the gun but the shot didn't hit me. The second soldier kept saying "Don't kill him" and "God bless you." The soldier who was going to kill me said "Fuck you."

Foday Sankoh had one guy named Rashid (Mansaray). He was a fine, fair guy and very tall, and was second in command. Rashid was with Sankoh when he first organized the war from outside Sierra Leone, but he was a small boy then. However, he wanted to quit the movement and go back to Guinea so he betrayed us.

At the beginning of the war there was an agreement that anyone who betrayed the movement would be killed, even if you said you were going to see your father or your relatives, you were killed. They caught Rashid escaping and brought him in front of Foday Sankoh. Papay asked him "Weren't we both there when we started the war?" Rashid answered "Yes." Papay said "Why did you betray the cause?" Rashid couldn't speak Krio but he replied "I have never betrayed the cause, but if you people say so, let the cause work with me, with the procedure." So they told him to go to the war front, sending him where they knew there were government soldiers, and on his way he was killed.

The East: Rebel Territory

That very day we were attacked by government soldiers. They discovered that Foday Sankoh was in Sandiallu and wanted to capture him alive. Government soldiers entered Sandiallu led by Tom Nyuma and they used jets (helicopter gunships) against us. We had one rebel guy called Chinese who was with the ventral, which is a machine gun mounted on a big truck, hidden under a mango tree that he used to shoot down jets. The old truck is still in Sandiallu.

A jet passed by but they couldn't see the gun. Government soldiers were entering the town and the jet was passing around, firing at anybody they saw. There's a lady now in Sandiallu who tried to move from her verandah to get inside her house and the jet shot at her. She lost her legs and she was pregnant at the time.

The jet would go around and around concentrating on the place where Foday Sankoh was hiding, so Chinese opened fire and there was a heavy exchange between him and the jet. This made the jet move away and it gave Foday Sankoh a chance to escape into the bush before the government soldiers were able to surround the place. As Foday Sankoh moved we all moved with him, hundreds of rebels. Men didn't mind if they died before they would allow Papay to die. We all moved out before the government soldiers were able to capture him.

Opening the Jungle

Chinese was killed and we moved straight to the training base in Dia. Foday Sankoh had a vehicle and they put wounded men in the vehicle to take them to Dia. On the way we were attacked and everyone scattered into the jungle where we regrouped. That was when we opened the jungle, meaning that we started fighting from the bush and not from the main towns. (Referring to the start of guerrilla warfare at the end of 1993.)

Foday Sankoh opened Zogoda Camp when the government soldiers pushed us out of Kailahun town and captured most of our areas in the district. Mosquito said there was no hope that a proper war would start again. We decided to avoid Kailahun town and went through the bush to establish Zogoda Camp, Peyama Camp near Tongo Field, and Banana Island (all in Kenema District).

We used Zogoda as a base to attack highways. We looted vehicles and took things back to the camp. The few rebels who remained in Kailahun reattacked the government soldiers and pushed them down to Baiima. I went back to Kailahun while others went to the south and the north. The jungle was open. Things were nice. People could move from Zogoda to Kailahun and other places. We went on foot. We were all used to walking for days, from Kailahun District to Kenema District on foot.

They set up groups, for example, the Kono group was called Kono By Pa ("by Papay"). Those from Kenema were Kenema By Pa. These were their jungle names and when they would meet they would say the names. When we saw those of Kono By Pa we knew them from their new jeans and other clothes because they came from the diamond area. Those from Kenema had old clothing but were strong-hearted. We concentrated mostly on the Kono area because that was the target of the rebels.

We had land communication. Our Sierra Leonean commanders captured radios and walkie-talkies from the army. These Sierra Leonean commanders would just meet young men and give them guns without any training so they would become rebels straight off, and the number of rebels increased greatly.

Foday Sankoh ordered anyone who claimed to be a commander but who didn't have documents from him to be killed. Those who were harassing people were also killed such as Bassa Boy, Loma Boy, Sunday, Sunday to Sunday, Tuesday, Young Killer—a lot of them. One very bad guy in our area was named Prince. He would capture people, split their stomachs open and take out parts and give them to a brother saying "Go roast it and bring it to me to eat." He was killed by Mosquito and calmness returned.

Mosquito was one of the strongest commanders. He was Kono By Pa and they called him "Master". He was brave in killing. Everybody was afraid of him because he killed other commanders, the vangahun, and their boys. He pushed the government soldiers out of many areas in Kailahun, Kono, and Kenema districts. After capturing a town Mosquito would call the civilians from the soquihun (bush camp) and tell them everything was under control and to stay in town. He talked to people about the reasons for the war, why all the bad things started happening, and that he would put a stop to them. That made him famous and popular in the area.

Disarmament

In the end there was going to be disarmament and the war would end. Mosquito decided to go and fight in Liberia for Charles Taylor. I was at the last meeting they had in Kailahun when Foday Sankoh came from Lomé, Togo in 1999. He wore green-green (a green camouflage uniform) and he stood and they sang the RUF national anthem:

> RUF ("roof") is fighting to save Sierra Leone
> RUF is fighting to save where we are
> RUF is fighting to know where they are
> RUF is fighting to save Sierra Leone

The East: Rebel Territory

People are suffering without survival
All our minerals have gone to foreign lands
RUF is hungry to know where they are
RUF is fighting to save Sierra Leone

Where are our diamonds Mr President?
Where are our golds, APC?
RUF is hungry to know where they are
RUF is fighting to save Sierra Leone

Go and tell the president
That Sierra Leone is my home
Go and tell my parents they see me no more
We are fighting in the battlefield, we are fighting forever
Every Sierra Leonean is fighting for his land.

So Foday Sankoh came to Kailahun with some UN men after signing the Lomé Accord. They came in a helicopter that landed near the court barrie. The UN men came down first and we went to receive them, then Foday Sankoh and Morris Kallon and other RUF guys came down with Akim, Leatherboot, and other Sierra Leone Army men.

They told us to join the disarmament and that Kailahun would be the last place to disarm. They established Segbwema and Daru as disarmament points. So it went on and when they came to Kailahun the DDR (Disarmament, Demobilization, and Reintegration) people alleged that Foday Sankoh was greeting people saying *kpande na bafay* which means "Don't give that gun" in Mende, meaning that Foday Sankoh was telling people not to disarm.

I spent more than 90% of my life in Kailahun District. Everybody was tired of the war. To me the main reason for the war was to change the APC government. They talked about the corruption of the APC government all the time. As for the brutality, at the beginning everyone was working under Foday Sankoh's command to meet the three-month deadline for winning, but after that failed some fighters went back to Liberia to bring their brothers to loot. Anything they looted was theirs and they took it back to Liberia. It came to a time that Foday Sankoh lost control over them and they started killing mercilessly. I myself never had friends from Liberia but always talked to them in groups.

For Sierra Leoneans the war brought increased awareness. At first we weren't aware of many issues but now we are. Also, we now know many areas

Narratives

of Sierra Leone because we were walking all over the country. Now I feel free of the war because it has come and gone.

In order for it not to happen again we should like each other and not allow corruption. There should also be a change of attitude. In the university here we have a program called NESPA, meaning North-East-South Peace Association, to minimize corruption so that war won't happen again. If you are really aware that you are my brother you won't kill me, but at that time people were just killing mercilessly.

4. Jeneba
Saving the Lives of Others
Nurse with the Rebels

Jeneba was living in Kailahun District when the rebels attacked, and she was forced to work for them as a nurse. She explains how attacks and medical care were organized and the effects of the war on herself and her children.

When the war started I was thirty-five and now I'm fifty-something. I'm Sierra Leonean, married to a Liberian. I was living in Liberia but had to flee the war there, so I came to my home town of Balahun in Kailahun District. Three months later the war came to Sierra Leone. I didn't have money to leave the village so I decided to stay, and I had seven children to care for with the oldest being eight years old.

One day in 1991 we heard of war in Koindu so some people fled to the bush and others left the town. Initially I fled to the bush with the children but when we heard there was no danger we returned to town. Though I was a Sierra Leonean and a Mende my children only spoke Liberian, and when some villagers realized the attackers were Liberians they ran away from us saying we were Liberians.

Two days later the rebels entered Balahun. The first time they came there was no exchange of gunfire, only one gunshot that we heard at around 9 PM. They surrounded the village and moved in quietly. I wanted to go out and get water for the children but as soon as I opened the door I was halted by a rebel. He said "If you move, I fire" and then asked "Who stays in this home?" I told him "I and my children." He heard my Liberian accent and asked why I was here and I told him we ran from Liberia but now were encountering the same thing here. He asked for the house owner and I told him everyone was gone. I said I didn't know anything about the bush and didn't know where they were.

He asked me where I was staying in Liberia and I told him Gbarnga. So then the man told me to stay where I was and not to move or they would kill me. He went to call the commander and brought a colleague who asked me the same questions. I told them I was a teacher. Luckily for me one of the rebels I taught in Gbarnga came by and told them I was his teacher and they should do nothing to me. That calmed me down a little.

One day they told us the person who started the war was coming to visit and that we should all go to Kailahun town. On the way some people who knew the bush managed to escape but I went directly to the town. We all gathered at the roundabout in the center of Kailahun and they introduced Foday Sankoh. I saw him. He was wearing a ronko, a traditional type of shirt, with shorts.

Foday Sankoh addressed us, saying he hadn't come to remove chiefs or kill anyone but to change the system of government in Sierra Leone, the APC government, who cheated people and didn't pay government workers. He said that the doctors and nurses weren't satisfied, that those who made cocoa farms didn't get any money, and that soldiers weren't satisfied so the security of the country wasn't good. For these reasons they wanted to get rid of the government and make Sierra Leone straight. In the afternoon he gave us escorts back to our villages. Those who could crowd into vehicles went by road but I walked because I had my children with me.

A few months into the war some of the rebels came around and said they should have a new leader in the village. They made their own selection and chose one Chief Bundukarr. Any stranger who entered the town had to go to these chiefs first for identification. If you came as a stranger they would provide food for you because when the rebels initially captured Kailahun District they were providing food for the district. When they ran out of food they taxed the people to give them rice. The village was divided into six sections to provide cooking for the rebels, one section per day. The food was also for other rebels passing through town. They said the war wasn't only for them but for all of us, so let everyone contribute.

Narratives

Medical Work
One time as the war progressed they brought coffee to be husked in a mortar and said each woman had to beat one bag. I hadn't done this kind of work for over ten years and I told them I would die if I had to do it. I said I had been to school and done paperwork and not physical work. They asked what I could really do for them and I said I had some knowledge of medicine from a nursing course in Liberia and could do medical work. They said I could assist when a doctor came but if I ran away they would do harm to my relatives. They threatened me in that way. My relatives talked to me and asked me to stay.

Their doctor was a woman named Rebecca and they handed me over to her to work at the village clinic. Each time the rebels came they would check for me. They told me that if I was short of food I should tell the chief. Later they moved us to Kailahun town where they brought wounded rebel soldiers for treatment. They gave us medicine and we did the treatment. We worked at the Government Hospital treating people for free. None of the medical staff stole medicine to sell. Civilian patients were told that the nurses needed to eat so they brought vegetables and other food for us.

As the war progressed the rebels deployed us to different towns they took over. First they would take us to the town chief to introduce us and tell him we would take care of the people's medical needs including delivering babies. They also told the chief that when the farming season came they should help us make a farm and a rice swamp as payment, so the rice we harvested is what we ate.

Once you were a worker with the rebels they didn't allow you to go anywhere. The soldiers in the front, anything they captured they brought back some for us such as clothing, soap, salt, and other things they could share. This was one way they made sure we stayed at the hospital.

When the rebel soldiers went to attack they concealed medical people off from the fighting zone and gave us extra security. Before they attacked a place we took cover so we never saw firing but were on standby to receive emergencies, and they would move us to another position if the fighting

Pounding rice in a mortar

came nearby. Some of the problems we faced with treatment were: we didn't have drip stands and to make a tourniquet we had to use sticks and native rope from the bush. If a woman was in labor and there was an attack we weren't allowed to leave her. She had to be moved along with the medical team until she delivered. We couldn't leave our medical kits. If we did we would be embarrassed for losing them.

They only gave position or rank to those who went to the front and not to those who stayed in the rear. They gave us anything we needed, but because we didn't "turn the baton" (use a gun) we didn't get rank. We moved from Balahun to Kailahun town, to Giema, and then to Tongo Field. I always took my children with me because there was better security. They provided men to carry the younger ones on their backs.

We received food from the supply and had time to sit and cook. But it came to a time when the jets came in and we could never cook during the day so they couldn't see the smoke. We cooked very early in the morning at around 5 AM and wrapped it so we could eat it the rest of the day. They didn't allow anyone to make a fire again until seven in the evening.

Caused by Ourselves

Before the war started things were very difficult. Prices were high and if you criticized the government they might take you to Pademba Road Prison in Freetown. It came to a time when people prayed in mosques and churches that only war could change the direction that Sierra Leone was moving. So all these things, including difficulty with schooling for the poor, made the war start. The brutality during the war was caused by ourselves, the Sierra Leoneans.

When the first rebels came they only moved on the main roads and didn't go into people's houses. But our own brothers who were captured and trained as rebel commandos had grudges from before the war. So for example, if they had to pay somebody money but were unable to, they had someone go and destroy the person's property and harass them. Even if they hid their belongings, because they knew the person had things, they would force them to hand the belongings over. If you had a beautiful wife they would threaten you and rape the woman. If you resisted their demands they would kill you, but if the person agreed to give up his belongings he would be released to run into the bush.

I can remember one village called Bandajuma-Sinneh where a woman delivered two weeks before the place was attacked by the rebels. Her husband was a rich person so the rebels asked her to tell them where he was. She wouldn't tell them so one of the commandos raped her. She told him that she had recently delivered and he said "That's why I love you. You are my virgin today." The report of this incident came to Kailahun town and when the commando was brought there, he was told that the local people shouldn't be harassed, only high APC officials. The commando was tied to a light pole and shot in front of a crowd of people, so you can see they had discipline for cases they knew about, but if they didn't hear of an incident the person went free.

For attacks there was tight discipline. When they told us there was going to be an attack we had to wait for casualties and we just sat and prayed we wouldn't have too much work to do. After a battle, if there were a lot of casualties we worked until everybody was treated before we got any rest. The medical doctor, Rebecca, was also a soldier and went to fight at the front. She would send cases directly to us so those who brought the cases would say "Your boss woman said you should treat this case right away." Our work wasn't just to treat people. We had to provide food for the patients and we assigned women to do that.

Good and Bad
I was lucky they promised they wouldn't kill me if I didn't run away, and they didn't do anything bad to me or any of my children except for one child who was killed by God. I lost three children out of the seven. One of them died of malnutrition. That child was with me but as the rebels advanced we had to carry a lot of drugs and I had to leave the child in a place where he died. Another died of sickness but none of them were killed.

I felt bad about losing my own children while I was saving the lives of others. In general, the war brought destruction. Although earlier they said it was to change the APC leaders, even people who had no connection to the APC lost their lives, property, and families. On the positive side, before the war there was no freedom of speech and rights did not prevail. Getting a job was a problem. The war brought NGOs which weren't here before. They have come and given people the opportunity to work and speak freely. Now scholarships are available to everyone and not hidden as before (meaning only for children of officials). The war brought awareness and the government is now saying it should follow policies. Before, those in power made their own policies.

The most bitter experience I went through was the death of my children, and I couldn't even have ceremonies for them when they died because the war was too tense. No one came to sympathize with me. Sometimes we struggled just to survive. When they brought in cases we weren't allowed to attend to our family's needs but we just had to stay with the patient.

The East: Rebel Territory

5. Michael
Things Became Difficult
Civilian

Michael is from Dia in northeast Kailahun District, near the Guinean border and the town of Koindu, the second town the rebels attacked in the district. He remained a civilian throughout the war. Michael describes his experiences in the early years of the war.

I was born in 1974 in Dia, a town in Kailahun District, and was there from the time I was born up to the war. I remember when the war started in 1991. I was seventeen years old and in the second term of Form 3, studying at Methodist Secondary School in Kailahun town.

When the rebels attacked at the Koindu border they fought throughout the night. In the morning hours they took over the border from the Sierra Leone government soldiers and entered Koindu town. It was not really easy. The first people who came were Liberians and some of our Sierra Leonean brothers, but the majority were Liberians and Burkinabés. Some of them were even speaking French. I know one guy who they used to call Fullamanami and he spoke French.

I was in Dia at the time. The rebels were moving from Koindu down the road toward Kailahun town and attacked Dia on a Sunday morning when we were still indoors. Dia is eight miles from Koindu and it's around fifteen miles further to Kailahun town.

In Sierra Leone we used to have a tradition that when a prominent person died they fired native guns on the fortieth day ceremony, so we thought the initial attacks were that because nobody was thinking of a war. That is why some people stayed and the rebels found them. We heard about the attack on

Koindu but people were thinking it was like a war in the nineteenth century where people fought with cutlasses and native guns, not knowing it was a modernized war where they used machine guns and other things. It was a very challenging issue.

So they attacked Dia and rounded up everybody. We saw one incident: they were chasing a chicken belonging to one Fullah guy and he came outside and said "This is my chicken! This is my chicken!" and they shot him. He was the first person they killed. He was a Fullah by tribe. They killed him and everybody became timid. On that day they didn't kill any other people.

So we were there, they registered some people and were just patrolling, firing guns. After some time they left a few of their colleagues there and the others went ahead toward Kailahun town. Whenever they attacked, some of those that came would stay and those going to the war front would just continue. At the same time they were rounding up youths, getting people interested in joining them. That was how the thing came about.

At the initial stage in 1991, around April, some of us escaped to Guinea but after two months we were faced with serious hunger and had to return to Sierra Leone. I went with my mother, my sisters, and my brothers. We just ran away to a village in Guinea. We had to cross the Moa River which is the border between Sierra Leone and Guinea in that part of Kailahun District, but being that we speak the same language, the Kissi language, when we went at the initial stage they saw us as family members. People were in sympathy, but later they became angry and we had to return. At that point the war became tense and they closed the border.

Failure at Daru
To return to the initial story, the rebels in front captured Kailahun town and went as far as Daru but were stopped there. Guinean soldiers and Sierra Leone soldiers were based in Daru at Moa Barracks and the rebels found it very difficult to take over the barracks so they fought and fought. The soldiers killed one guy who was leading the rebels, the front commander. We called him Rambo but his real name was Charles Timber, a Liberian. They killed him right at the bridge as the rebels tried to fight their way to the barracks.

Also, according to some of the guys the Sierra Leone and Guinean soldiers put electricity in the water of the Moa River so when you got into the water you got shocked, so the rebels weren't able to take over the barracks because they had to swim across the river to get there. A lot of them were killed. Some of them were captured, but in fact those who were captured were killed. They couldn't hold them as hostages (prisoners).

The East: Rebel Territory

When they killed Rambo at the bridge in Daru, the war became difficult for the rebels. The Liberian and Burkinabé rebels started retreating. Some of them were saying that this was not their country and they didn't want to die here. They started killing our Sierra Leonean civilians. They were doing it in retaliation because at the initial stage they said they had come to free Sierra Leoneans, because Sierra Leone people had been suffering for some time from the one-party state and all the rest. They started killing people, looting people's property, and forcing people to carry loads. They took produce—cocoa and coffee—and forced people to carry it to Foya in Liberia so they could sell it in exchange for things they needed.

The bridge at Daru where Rambo was killed, Moa Barracks in the background

Around the end of 1991 the rebels recruited a lot of Sierra Leoneans. The Sierra Leoneans said that it was like the Liberians wanted to kill our people and that they should be asked out of the war, out of Kailahun District. So the Liberians became angry. They said they wouldn't go, but really it was because they had found a lot of things to take. They were looting Koindu and other places and had burned down all the markets.

I saw Foday Sankoh. He visited Dia near the end of 1991. He was stationed at Buedu and used to come to Pendembu and Kailahun town. At that time he was slim. He was not too tall but was a short, old man. At the initial stage he had control over the whole revolution. When he came they used to say "The Papay is coming! The Papay is coming!" He was really in charge and had control. What he said was final.

Those who went and trained before the war were trained in Burkina Faso and Liberia and some of them in Libya. We even had some of our brothers. I can still remember, we had a friend who hailed from the same village named Anthony who went with them. He went to Liberia around 1988 and came back in 1990 and explained to us that they had taken a course and needed young people to join them. He said everyone was going to enjoy it. They were just telling us that but we were looking at it as something different, and of course they were just coming with war.

They got rid of the Liberians, but some of them were still coming and forcing people to carry their loads. If you know Kailahun District they have a lot of plantations. When people buy the produce they have to store it for some time, so they were just breaking into the stores and taking it to Foya to sell. In fact I was very unfortunate at one point in 1992. We were captured and had to carry their loads to Foya and we spent about a week there. We were afraid to return because sometimes you might meet other people who would again force you to carry loads. So some people were killed in the process. If you refused they would just kill you and find another person to carry the load.

When the Liberians left Sierra Leone the rebels forced people to join them, telling them they were needed to fight for their country. At that time I was just going into the bush, sleeping from one place to another. We were moving, not staying anywhere because if you weren't lucky they would force you to join them. At that time they were taking underage children, training them for one or two days, and sending them to the war front to fight, so a lot of people were killed, not because of their own will but because they forced them to fight.

Before the war, chiefs had been using their power to put pressure on the young people. For just a small crime they would levy a fine on you, so some youths had to run away. When the war came and they had guns, they began maltreating and killing the chiefs in retaliation. When the rebels saw that you were a chief before the war they would just kill you and appoint their own town commander. This happened in Kailahun District when the rebels took over the towns.

Nobody Can Stop Reggae

After they tried to take Daru and failed they attempted another route. They had taken over Pendembu where there is a road that goes to Manowa. That was the road they used to reach the ferry over the Moa River that leads to Kono. They attacked Manowa, then came to Bunumbu and used the Gandorhun road to come

The East: Rebel Territory

to Kono. They were fighting in villages, moving up the road through Gandorhun. In that attack they came near Koidu (district headquarter town of Kono District) as far as Gandorhun, but were chased out and had to retreat. But they were still coming. That was what the rebels were doing—they were coming and going, on and off, on and off, until they finally entered Koidu town late in 1992.

They knew Kono was a diamond area and moved up there right away. They knew they could get diamonds to fuel the war and that was why they were consistently focusing on Kono, because as I said at the beginning, they were taking produce like cocoa to sell in Liberia in exchange for arms but diamonds were much more valuable.

At the same time some Ukrainians started coming. They were coming and going, and when the rebels finally captured Kono a lot of them went there. I saw them. They were white and told us they were Ukrainians. They used to come with planes and ammunition. They came through Liberia, flying to Kailahun and using vehicles that the rebels captured at the war front. All the arms and ammunition were passing through Liberia but I don't know who was really supporting them.

At that time those Liberian guys had small tape recorders we called "Ghana Bread" because they resembled a square loaf of bread that Ghanaians made in Sierra Leone at the time. They used to love the music of Lucky Dube and played his music almost twenty-four hours, especially the song "Nobody Can Stop Reggae" which always makes me think of the war when I hear it now. Everywhere they were based they used to play that music.

During this time I lost my elder brother and some other family members were killed. My brother fell sick in the bush and there was nobody to treat him. There was no medicine, so all of a sudden he died. That was how a lot of people died. There was one fellow who lost his wife because of that, because we were not staying in town. We had to keep moving. We couldn't even sleep in any of the villages because all of a sudden at night the rebels might come. A lot of people were killed. Some because of malice, some because of produce, or to steal belongings. It was serious looting. If you refused to hand over your items they would just kill you and forget about it.

Myself, I wasn't interested in joining the rebels. I wasn't interested in killing people. I don't like seeing blood and corpses. That was really the reason why I decided not to go with them. Some people got excited when they had arms. Some people were with the rebels because of hatred for other families. When a family had two of their children with the rebels they could protect them, and those who had nobody to protect them would be victimized. That is how the thing was going on. That caused a lot of people to go with the rebels because when you had arms you were superior. You could do anything you wanted.

Around the end of 1992 I escaped to Guinea again. We had to swim across the river and they took us to a refugee camp. Three of us ran away because they were just killing people all the time. I had spent almost one and a half years around the rebels.

We Can Easily Forget
Before the war it was only the rich people who were having a chance. If they had money it was like they could do anything, nobody could ask about it. The poor people were suffering. In fact, Foday Sankoh was a corporal in the army and they sacked him, then he became a photographer. He was really disgruntled so he went to Liberia and joined Charles Taylor. I don't know what arrangements he made with Charles Taylor, though they must have planned it in Liberia because a lot of our brothers went there.

One thing about Sierra Leoneans—we can easily forget because we are very friendly. We had people from the same place who did terrible things to our family members, but they are still there. Nobody has asked them to leave and nobody is chasing them out. When they first returned people didn't trust them. They thought they could just kill people all of a sudden, but now they are used to the system. People aren't having quarrels with them now.

The national reconciliation was good although some people are still afraid of going back to their original homes because of what they did. The reconciliation was really necessary, especially because everybody is just living together. They used to talk to everybody: let's forgive and forget, these are our brothers, it was not their way. Especially the project Fambul Tok (Family Talk) where those who have serious problems get in contact with the organization and they go to their homes and talk to the people. Those who have terrible stories and don't want to return to their homes, this NGO takes them to their people to say "I did such and such a thing, but I have come to plead that you forgive me."

When they were doing the disarmament they made a promise to provide job training and resettle people, which meant they would provide houses and things to start up life, but some of the trainings weren't proper. They trained people just six months for some skills. How can you train a tailor for just six months? Sometimes they trained carpenters for a short time and gave them tools and they just sold the tools and ate (spent) everything. A lot of training under the DDR program wasn't effective and many people are still without trades.

Socially the war has changed a lot of things. Before the war not everyone could speak Krio. This was one of the good aspects of the war. A good number of Sierra Leoneans were illiterate and could only speak their own languages, not Krio, but during the war people traveled. Some went to other areas, some to Guinea, some to Banjul and Liberia and they learned to associate with other people. They learned a lot about other tribes and cultures.

People can vote now, and that is one of the good changes. I remember when they brought Momoh to power (in 1985) they just handed power over to him. It wasn't democratic. They just said "Joseph Momoh, this is the power, you can just go ahead, you can be President." Now, to get a position you have to be elected, but people still aren't aware of who they should vote for. Sometimes they only see the politicians when it is close to election time. Politicians can just spend money before an election and don't do what they promised. That's the major problem we are facing now. Sierra Leoneans still aren't thinking wisely to elect people who can help them. In some places ward counselors are illiterate.

6. Jasper
Voluntarily Recruited
RUF

Jasper is from Tongo Field, a diamond mining town in northern Kenema District. He joined the RUF after attacks on Tongo Field and became a committed fighter. Jasper describes RUF tactics and his experiences in the war including an attack on Segbwema. After the Intervention in 1998 he was in the north, and he describes a food-finding expedition during Operation Pay Yourself and an attack on Kabala.

I was born on April 27, 1974 at Takbombu, Tongo Field and was there when the war started. At that time I was almost mature, around seventeen years old, and had some experience in life. We heard of war in Liberia and in 1991 we were hearing about the RUF rebels but didn't know what they were. We thought they had tails and asked people if they had tails.

As the rebels advanced through Kailahun District we heard heavy artillery echoing from Kailahun town and later heard that they had advanced beyond Kailahun and seized strategic locations close to Tongo. One night we saw flames from the direction of Peyama and some villagers who escaped told us the rebels were attacking. At that time government soldiers were based in Tongo and we saw them go to fight and return many times but they didn't succeed in pushing the rebels out. Many people left Tongo while others stayed.

Messages then came in that the rebels were planning an offensive on Tongo. One morning at around 5 to 6 AM we were woken by heavy gunfire and before daybreak the government soldiers retreated from the town. The rebels fired shots in the air so the civilians would leave. I ran to another town but again the rebels invaded that town and killed people. I got fed up with threats and oppression so I moved to Segbwema and was voluntarily recruited into the RUF. I and other new recruits were taken to Bokina Base (in Giema, Kailahun District), trained for just two weeks and given AK-47 rifles. Our mission was to attack the government soldiers' positions.

The first rebels who were killing people were not pure Sierra Leoneans. They returned to their homes because their mission did not succeed and they embarked on training Sierra Leoneans before they left. That's the idea I have of the beginning.

With the RUF

From the training camp we went straight to attack Bunumbu. It was an early morning attack and after an exchange of fire the government soldiers withdrew. We flushed them out of Bunumbu and chased them to Segbwema, then flushed them out of Segbwema. My squad was deployed at Tondola on the main Kenema-Kailahun road near Segbwema. The soldiers attempted several times to push us off the main road which resulted in a lot of casualties on both sides. An aircraft bombed our positions and killed civilians in their hiding places. We were trained to maneuver under any circumstances, but because of the frequent and serious hits we moved back to Segbwema.

The soldiers pursued us there. We allowed them to enter the town, then engaged them full time as was planned. For our tactics we had one team moving on a bypass and others using the main road. The bypass team went around to another side of Segbwema and entered the town while the government forces concentrated on the main road. In that way we took the town before they knew it.

The East: Rebel Territory

Tongo Field

We lost four men including Commander Freetown-Struggle who was shot in the abdomen and died on the spot, but an armored car was captured and burnt close to the Segbwema bridge. The government soldiers also suffered a lot of casualties. Later we attempted to attack Daru Barracks (Moa Barracks). I was shot on the right leg in Bombohun village near Daru. It wasn't easy to overthrow Daru Barracks and if we had succeeded in doing that we would have won the war.

In the bush we ate rice, cassava, bananas, and plantains. We didn't have supplies. I'll explain how we got our clothing. After an attack civilians would drop their clothing bundles and we would take them. Of course some people didn't take all their belongings when they ran away, so we went in their houses and took what we liked. Even if it didn't fit we took it and gave it to someone else. After an attack, if we succeeded we had a party to entertain ourselves. We played music and served ourselves to enjoy. In the jungle we organized dances but no one paid to enter. You entered by the barter system. People would give rice and other items to enter the dance.

I used to go out and buy goods and jamba (marijuana) for my colleagues. I went to Liberia to buy these things when we captured some money. I would also buy salt, Maggi, and soap. When I went to Liberia I would leave my gun at Bomaru checkpoint. When coming back they would return my weapon to me.

Narratives

When someone died we organized an overnight vigil for the body and had the burial ceremonies of seven days and forty days. We did this only for top men and big men. We had pastors and imams. We made our camp buildings of local wood with zinc roofs under big trees in the bush. This was to prevent planes and helicopters from seeing us. From there we left to go and cause problems. We were a guerrilla movement.

We had women with us and when we went to the front they stayed at the camp and cooked food. We had doctors who sometimes went to the front to take care of wounded fighters, for instance, when they shot me they just bandaged it quickly before they took me back to the camp.

I didn't worry when I went to the front because I had a mori man (Muslim magic man) who prayed for me before going to fight to give me extra power and protection. The mori men visited us in the front and we paid them for their services, so I was happy when I went to the front because I felt protected.

The guns we used were AA (anti-aircraft), RPG, GMG (general machine gun) with a long chain, Beretta, and AK-47. We had our own ways of shooting guns. If I shot in the rebel way others would know I was a rebel. When we went to attack a town we would put those with heavy weapons in one line, those with medium weapons in another line, and those with smaller weapons in another. We set the target and the smaller weapons would fire first altogether, then the medium weapons and then the heavy weapons. Then we would start shouting and enter the town. From the sound the people would think the whole town was surrounded. We normally shot in the air for civilians and to threaten soldiers who were there. After that the civilians and soldiers would all run into the bush because they knew we were stronger.

During the war we were attacked often, but it was difficult to drive us out of a place. Most times the attackers would withdraw. I was never in an attack where we withdrew. Sometimes we would withdraw a little, then come back to take the town again. I was a strong soldier. We were the only ones who had the patience to wait in the bush all day to ambush and even sleep there. Neither government soldiers nor Kamajors could do that. We had this zeal because we ate gunpowder and because they were supplying us with cocaine from Liberia. Our guns also came from Liberia.

We had passwords. If you became lost from your colleagues we had a way of talking to recognize each other. There was a question we would ask as a password. At times we had a particular whistle and a colleague would respond even if he couldn't see you. We also made signs with our hands from a distance if we saw each other. When we made an ambush we would lie down in twos or threes next to each other to talk so we wouldn't feel lonely.

The East: Rebel Territory

Segbwema in the early 70s

In the jungle we had different groups—rebels, former government soldiers (who had been captured and trained as rebels), and the Born Naked who I was. Some dressed in combat uniforms and others in civilian clothes. I had full military combat with boots. Our group was called Born Naked because of our hardness, and when we fought we took off our shirts and tied them around our waists or wore them inside out. We also did this to recognize each other because at that time both rebels and soldiers could be wearing combat uniforms.

I remember some of the tough guys I was fighting with. One man who died was a "harder" (a strong fighting man). He was a real man. Also Superman. Mosquito had a name but he wasn't really facing the front. There were many guys who were strong fighters like Gibril Massaquoi. The last time I saw some of them was when I went to Freetown, but I don't see them now.

Operation Pay Yourself

After the AFRC coup when the government soldiers joined the rebels, they divided up positions in the jungle, for example, if RUF was commander, SLA (AFRC) was deputy commander and vice versa.

During Operation Pay Yourself we had to find whatever we needed and we made special attacks just to find food. When we went on missions, if you were hard your hardness would help you find food. People used to hide their food in drums in the bush and we would capture the people and force them to lead us to the drums and take everything away. This was for us to survive.

Narratives

I was appointed commander for one mission when we attacked Malal, a river crossing point just after Makeni (in the north), and I was right in the front of the group. The people in the town were sleeping and I sent three men to cross the river and bring a canoe to our side. We left some guys there while others crossed the river quietly. We had men with us who knew how to paddle canoes. We went into the town but left some men at the river bank in case there was an attack from the rear.

We waited until 6:30 AM to attack. There air was foggy. A few soldiers were guarding the town but they ran away when we fired because it was dark and they weren't prepared. We stayed in the village for three days and got a lot of sheep, goats, rice, and other items and transported everything to the waterside and over the river.

I was involved in a mission to Kabala. We mobilized in Makeni in vehicles to attack (the AFRC/RUF were then in control of Makeni) then surrounded the town and attacked early in the morning. We entered and the soldiers guarding the town retreated and climbed up the hills then shot at us from the hills. We couldn't succeed and retreated. They captured some of our men and we had a lot of casualties.

We captured some soldiers too and brought them to the jungle as prisoners. We lectured them and talked to them so they wouldn't be discouraged and took them to work on the farm in Buedu (Kailahun) where they did weeding for us. We also captured some civilians. We didn't kill them but also took them to the farms. If we captured women, the men without women would take care of them. So we stopped killing and made the jungle civilized because we needed more recruits.

End of the War
Near the end of the war I was back in Kailahun District when some white people came from Liberia. They flew in by helicopter and landed at the vehicle park in Kailahun town then went to Buedu where the radio station was. The white people asked for Mosquito and had discussions with him. We waited and after they left we heard the meeting was for ceasefire and disarmament. After that I was in Segbwema when Foday Sankoh came and met us to talk about disarmament. The rebels told us we were fighting for justice and rights and that was the idea I had when we were fighting, but we knew the war was going to end and some of us were hoping to see our friends and brothers again.

Once during the ceasefire we caught some Kamajors in Kuiva-Mandu near Segbwema, picking cocoa pods to sell. We captured them but didn't kill them. We carried the cocoa and brought the Kamajors to the riverside. Other Kamajors across the river tried to shoot at us but the captive Kamajors stopped them. We negotiated peace and they allowed ten of us to cross while some Kamajors remained on our side of the river. I was one who crossed. We negotiated and had a dance that night to celebrate the ceasefire while civilians from the area came to watch.

What brought the brutality? When I was with the rebels we were not cutting off hands or raping women. If anyone did that they were killed or shot on the hand or foot. I saw them do this as an example to a guy who raped a girl. They shot him but didn't kill him. Any time we captured someone we had to take them to the commanders.

Segbwema in 2012

But there were RUF who were amputating hands. A woman named Adama Cut Hand started it. I saw her doing it. I knew her. She was a Sierra Leonean, very strong-hearted and a woman who feared nothing. The Sierra Leone women in the jungle were called "Wise". There were some women who were stronger-hearted than men and some of them went to the battlefront. When we went fighting with women none of them were wounded or died.

We won't have war again in Sierra Leone because everyone has tasted its bitterness. Even those who were fighting, you can't just say "Let's go to war." We all know the sweetness of the town. We rebels were like bush animals and have a bush scent. For war not to happen again they should find work for all those who were in the war and bring skills for us to learn. For me, I learned masonry so people know me as a builder and nobody will tell me to go to the bush for war again.

Narratives

Have I ever killed anyone? During attacks there was an exchange of fire and civilians ran. We would see civilians falling on the ground but couldn't see whose bullet it was. I can't say I never killed anyone. It's not easy to get all these incidents out of my mind. If I have some opportunity or encouragement I could forget them. They promised us a lot of things but didn't give them to us. On the disarmament card they only gave us A, you have disarmed; and B, 300,000 Leones (around $135); and C, teach us work skills, but not D. Nothing else was given and I don't know what D was.

I was disarmed in Tongo. I gave them everything—my gun, combat, and boots. Those who disarmed us were DDR officials, who were white soldiers.

7. Fatmata
I Became Involved
RUF

Fatmata was captured by the RUF early in the war and became a rebel soldier. She was involved in fighting in Kailahun and Kono Districts and in the north. Fatmata knew Foday Sankoh, Mosquito, and Adama Cut Hand.

I was born in 1964 in Gbunumbu, a village in Kailahun district near Koindu. I experienced the first attack there in 1991. That day I went to Koindu with some people to do business. The rebels attacked at around 2 PM when the weekly market was full of people. We scattered and I and others escaped via bush paths back to Gbunumbu. I left everything there and ran for my life. I can't recall the month because I'm illiterate. I didn't go to school. This was in the dry season, a few days after the Bomaru attack.

That day I escaped to a village three miles from Gbunumbu and from there we moved and stayed in the soquihun. A few days later the rebels raided the village and killed three civilians and made frequent raids on us in the bush. When government soldiers pushed them from the towns we attempted to enter Guinea but were captured. They took us to Kailahun town that day.

Rebel Training

From Kailahun we were taken to a rebel camp at Mende-Kelema (near Pendembu) where we began rebel training. At training there were both men's and women's parades, announcements, singing and ceremonies. Our song said "like Foday Sankoh kill them ooh, kill them, kill them ooh, kill them..."

The Small Boy Units were mostly trained to know how to fire and maneuver, then they are given guns to carry and operate. They didn't undergo proper training like the other RUF guys. Some of the boys behaved badly when they got guns. Initially we were sexually harassed by the Liberians, but when I finally became involved (as a fighter) nobody tampered with me because I was like them. Men were raping women in front of me. There were few women soldiers—three or four out of twenty.

When we were with the RUF they trained us. They taught us and we were their wives. For your own self-security and defense you needed to train, especially how to fire and dash forward when there is a target. I have even used my gun to defend my children which is why some of them survived.

If we were in a town and government soldiers attacked we ran, or sometimes we fought and killed soldiers and they killed rebels. As the war went on, soldiers continued attacking our positions and we always moved. We rebel women and girls were defended well in the attacks.

During that time we used a gun called a Beretta. It was a poisonous gun. If you were shot with it, before the next day you turned black and died. All those shot with a Beretta died. Foday Sankoh condemned it because they were killing too many people with it and they brought AK's and other guns. We got them all from Liberia. I saw it. Nobody told me.

They gave positions to women who went regularly to the warfront. At that time I had children so I didn't go far. I went on the second attack on Koidu (in Kono District). We were based at Ngaiya where we laid an ambush for three to four days. We had no food. We fed on plants and dirty water along the road side. I went on the Segbwema fight too.

Mosquito and Foday Sankoh

Initially I witnessed RUF meetings and stayed with Mosquito, cooking for him in Buedu. Mosquito was a citizen of Kailahun. His village is just few miles from Buedu town. He told me that Foday Sankoh called him to Liberia to join the Sierra Leone war, to help him accomplish his mission. Sankoh told Charles Taylor that Mosquito was his brother who he called to join him to pursue the war. According to Master (Mosquito), Charles Taylor agreed and more support was given to them to fight.

Some Sierra Leonean boys were trained and joined the Liberian and Burkina rebels. Mosquito became commander because he was a friend of Sankoh and he knew about the war plan. Mosquito was black, slim, and tall. He was simple but really strict and wicked. His commanders feared him a lot. He killed a lot. Really, he was a man who didn't say much.

I stayed with Foday Sankoh at Sandiallu and Giehun—just ask anybody who was there. Foday Sankoh was a simple man. He didn't normally go to the warfront. Sankoh used to tell us about the war. He said it was a contract that was given to him, but he didn't say who gave him the contract. He told me he was a poor man and an ordinary photographer working to complete his mission. Being together with him I saw rebels bringing guns and ammunition from Liberia. I never saw Charles Taylor in Sierra Leone. Foday Sankoh was always with us.

Amputations
What brought the amputations? My brother, let me tell you. I witnessed a lot of the things that happened. I had a friend called Adama. She was a rebel soldier. When Kabbah was in power he declared that all soldiers should go to the bush (referring to the AFRC/RUF being forced out of power in the Intervention) and people were pointing fingers at soldiers' relatives and burning them alive with tires. Adama's only child fell a victim to this in Freetown. At that time we were in Kabala. I know a lot of places in this country. We were sitting outside when Adama heard the news of the death of her child. Her eyes changed to red and she became Adama Cut Hand.

Adama started taking cocaine and brown-brown (brown heroin). When we were in the front she was always drugged. When we captured people Adama would just ask "short sleeve or long sleeve—which one do you want?" If you say short sleeve, she amputates your hand at the elbow level and if you say long sleeve she cuts the hand at the wrist. She really introduced amputation before others followed. This was a message to Kabbah for both the killings and the power he wanted. After the war Adama was driven in a vehicle in Freetown and was shown to the amputees. This is the lady I am talking about. She is still around and often comes to me.

I hid my AK-47 in plastic during the ceasefire and later used it to disarm. After I disarmed in Port Loko the NCDDR (National Commission for Disarmament, Demobilization and Resettlement) brought me to Kenema and I was taught gara

The East: Rebel Territory

tying and dying. Most of my family died in the rebel war. I had eleven children and only four survived. The rest died of hunger in the bush.

Now life is fine because some of my children survived, though I lost my husband who would have supported my children to attend school. I feel free now. Kenema is a neutral place and a big city. Everybody is busy finding daily living. Nobody cares who you were. There are a lot of top fighters moving freely around town.

Women who were involved in the war need help through training and money to do business and to help send our children to school. Most of us lost our husbands so we need help to support our families. I know how to do gara tying and dying but I have no money to do it now. Presently I stay at home the whole day looking after my grandchildren. The violence in the war was a result of indiscipline. Many men became commanders on their own and used their power to cause problems. Some RUF boys when in the front had all the power to wreak havoc.

8. Bolo
   Why Am I Fighting?
   SLA – AFRC

Bolo was a Sierra Leone Army soldier. He fought the RUF rebels in many battles in Kailahun and Kenema Districts in the first years of the war. After the 1996 elections he experienced the conflicts between the army and Kamajors. He was involved in the overthrow of the Kabbah government in 1997 and joined the AFRC junta which merged with the RUF. He describes ECOMOG attacks on the AFRC/RUF in Freetown and the retreat from Freetown during the Intervention when he traveled to Kailahun District with Johnny Paul Koroma.

Narratives

In Kailahun District Bolo joined with the RUF in attacks on towns in the east during the lead-up to their attack on Freetown in January 1999, though he escaped to Liberia and didn't take part in the attack on the capital.

I attended Christ the King College in Bo up to Form 3. From school I went to the diamond area, but didn't succeed in finding diamonds so I went to Bo to my father. I heard the rebels had attacked Bomaru. I stole a big tape recorder from my father, sold it, and used the money to go to Daru to join the military. They scraped all the hair from my head, I was trained and I started fighting from the grassroots. I was thirty-two years old at the beginning of the war and was a soldier in the Sierra Leone Army in the Sixth Battalion in Tongo.

My first deployment was at Kuiva in Kailahun District. I was given an AK-58. They trained us at the front. They mixed us with men who were already trained and when there was no fighting we had lessons. I learned military lessons one to nine. After some time in Kuiva they asked us to go for advanced training, so we were taken by battalions to Benguema (the army training base near Waterloo in the Western Area). We were trained and passed out, though it wasn't very good training because the war was tense at the time. We were immediately sent to the front line in trucks.

The first rebel attack I experienced was in Nyama-Jawei in Kailahun District. I was with the Tom Nyuma squad. He was a famous fighter and later became District Council Chairman in Kailahun District. The RUF attacked us with heavy gunfire very early in the morning when dew was falling.

Our main guards withdrew from their posts, so we moved from the headquarters and engaged them until we pushed them out of the town. We regained our position, but a little later they attacked again and captured the surrounding villages such as Kuiva, Jojoima, and Mobai. In this attack some of our men were killed or seriously wounded and we killed or wounded some of their men. Most of them were Liberians.

In 1993 during the NPRC period we advanced into Kailahun to clear out the rebels. We pushed them all the way back to Koindu and captured all the towns from Mobai, Pendembu, Kailahun town, and Buedu. We were well equipped. We used ground forces to attack with heavy artillery in our vehicles. We never took bypasses but always used the main roads because we were government soldiers. That's why the RUF were planting mines along the main roads, because they knew the government soldiers always used them.

Later we heard the rebels were re-infiltrating Kailahun District and had opened a new jungle (theater of operations) through a different area starting in Koindu, and we were sent there to fight. We fought hard, but they routed us and we scattered into the bush. Their forces were stronger than ours. I and other colleagues crossed to Guinea and the Sierra Leone Government brought us back to Freetown by ship.

From Freetown they sent us to OPS areas (deployment areas). That was the place where you got your pay, so no one wanted to stay in Freetown because we wouldn't be paid there. I was sent to Daru. In 1994 the rebels captured Tongo. The First Battalion went to Tongo and we fought hard but couldn't succeed, so they asked for a joint operation of the fourth and fifth battalions. We all gathered at Mano Junction and attacked Tongo during the day and captured it at around 2 PM. Heh! It wasn't easy. At that time Tongo was fertile. There was a lot of food, people, and diamonds so the rebels didn't want to give it up. We succeeded in pushing them out of the town but not too far, only half a mile. The government troops couldn't patrol too far.

We started forming groups to attack their positions to push them out of the smaller villages around us and we deployed soldiers at villages we took over. We started gaining positions. In Peyama, which was a strong rebel camp, Mosquito was the leader and there were a lot of other rebel commanders there. It was very difficult to move them out and a lot of soldiers lost their lives. This was a big diamond mining town in the Tongo area. The rebels and the government both wanted the place. It wasn't easy to take. We fought and fought and fought.

Later (after the 1996 elections) we heard of the Kamajor movement. At that time Hinga Norman was the Deputy Defense Minister and they asked the Kamajors to join us. This was because the rebels were guerrilla fighters and knew the bush and bush paths and the Kamajors knew the bush paths too, so for some time we fought together.

However there was infighting. It happened that the Kamajors attacked our position at Petema in Kenema District and killed one lieutenant, and it became very serious. Also in Tongo they opened heavy fire on our troops and we fought against them for two days. In the end we drove the Kamajors out of Tongo.

Later Hinga Norman sent a message that the government soldiers had a bad intention and wanted to overthrow the government. The Kamajors attacked Tongo again and pushed us out. We escaped through Kono and when we arrived at Bumpeh we met some Military Police trucks and joined them. We were taken to the RDF Camp Charlie (near Mile 91). We were there with Akim, a famous fighter for the government, and were ordered to advance to Brackford Camp, a rebel camp in Rotifunk (Moyamba District) where we launched an attack.

Joining the AFRC Junta

Before the AFRC coup Johnny Paul was deployed at Rutile as a government soldier. The Kamajors attacked the government troops there and killed some of them. When no action was taken from Freetown, Johnny Paul ordered his

Narratives

Manowa Ferry

troops to retaliate and they killed a lot of Kamajors. Hinga Norman came to Rutile, but Johnny Paul and his troops didn't allow him to land his helicopter. Hinga Norman went back to Freetown and told the Kabbah government that Johnny Paul had plans to overthrow them, so Johnny Paul was arrested and put in prison.

We were fighting in Moyamba when the AFRC overthrew the government. We had a two-barrel artillery gun and were engaged in fighting the rebel called Superman. We weren't informed about the coup, but when the AFRC was fighting ECOMOG for the State House they sent a message to us to withdraw from fighting the rebels and ordered us to take our artillery gun back to Freetown so they could use it there.

We went to Freetown with the gun and there was heavy fighting around the State House. The Nigerians shelled the area around the Treasury Building with mortars when we used that area to attack them. The first floor of the Treasury Building was burned out. We used our gun to drive the Nigerians out. We flushed them out of the State House.

Tamba Gborie, a corporal, led the coup against the SLPP (the elected Kabbah government) and announced it on the radio. He was an ordinary soldier and didn't have any knowledge of government affairs, so they looked for someone to lead their government. Johnny Paul was chosen as the most appropriate. I was in the Akim group that went to break down Pademba Road Prison to free Johnny Paul. We freed all the prisoners though our aim was only to free Johnny Paul. He was wise, educated, and had good ideas.

The East: Rebel Territory

After that the AFRC called the rebels to join us in town because anywhere you went there were Kamajors fighting us. There was no respect for soldiers. We had two forces fighting against us—the Kamajors and ECOMOG—so the AFRC bosses decided to call the rebels to town to consolidate forces.

They interviewed Foday Sankoh on the radio (from Nigeria) and asked him what his aims and objectives were now that the AFRC had overthrown the government and called his forces to town. Foday Sankoh told his fighters to join the government soldiers and after that I started seeing live rebels in town. I was in Murray Town Barracks.

After the overthrow, civilians came into the streets demonstrating against us and asking for military intervention. The civilians didn't want us in power, so we told them that if elephants and leopards fight, it is only the grass that will suffer, and the grass will be you, the civilians. At that time there were sanctions and embargos against us. No ships or planes arrived in Freetown.

It wasn't easy because ECOMOG was fighting us and there was no concrete organization. This was the time when Maxwell Khobe or "Lionheart" came from Nigeria to head ECOMOG. Khobe came with Operation Mopping Up and Operation Stand-Stop. ECOMOG fought us heavily. At first they were firing from ships into the city and they killed a lot of civilians that way. The AFRC took the bodies to the National Stadium and Johnny Paul said that this is what we were trying to avoid. "Among the corpses are there soldiers?" he asked. "No, they were all civilians."

Intervention—Freetown to Kailahun

The pressure from ECOMOG continued. Johnny Paul called us in a meeting and said, since the pressure was too much and since we were citizens of Sierra Leone and since ECOMOG were foreigners and were destroying the city, let us give up the city to them. We wanted to take the route through the eastern part of the city, through Waterloo, but ECOMOG was camped at Jui on the highway before Waterloo. They had blocked all the ways to leave. We fought to get out but couldn't beat them, so we had to go around the peninsula through Tombo. There a lot of soldiers drowned in the sea.

We went around the peninsula. ECOMOG didn't know this route, and we came out on the highway to Makeni. Johnny Paul was with us. At this time we were on Operation Pay Yourself because there was no salary, so whatever we could get was our pay. We passed through Makeni, Kono, Kwellu-Ngieya, to Bunumbu, we crossed at Manowa Ferry to Pendembu then to Kailahun, Buedu, and finally to Kangama. There we camped with Johnny Paul.

It was in Kangama that we formed a strong connection with the RUF. In Kangama I met top rebel commanders—Mosquito, Issa, Mike Lamin, Morris Kallon, and other big men. They fought alongside us. They told us we were fighting for good achievements in the country because a lot of things were going wrong. They had brought the war because things weren't going straight. There was no good freedom of movement, if you didn't have money you couldn't get educated, and other things. If you looked into some of the things they said, you could see they were true.

We stayed there for nine months. Initially we didn't understand jungle movements because we were trained as government soldiers and only understood military tactics. They told us to take zinc from houses to make camps in the bush, but we said no, because we were soldiers we wanted to live in town rather than in the bush, so we stayed in towns.

In the jungle, when there was no food we went on food finding. When we heard that ECOMOG had a supply of food, arms, and ammunition we were glad. We drove them off and took it. We weren't attacking the Kamajors for food because they were just farmers and we wouldn't get anything from them, but if they attacked us we would defend ourselves or we would attack them when their farms were ready to harvest. Really, in the jungle we were getting our food and arms from ECOMOG. We called it a self-reliance struggle.

Return of the AFRC/RUF
At this time Guinean soldiers were fighting us along the Guinea border while ECOMOG fought along the front. We were trapped between them. They called a forum in the jungle and discussed where to go, but there was nowhere to go so we decided to fight to gain territory. (Referring to attacks by ECOMOG on Kailahun District after the Intervention and attacks made by the AFRC/RUF on major towns during the advance on Freetown.)

We started attacking the Nigerian positions and captured a lot of things which we used for fighting. We divided into groups so we could gain a large area. There were around 1,500 armed men in our group. We bypassed ECOMOG at Daru and attacked and captured Segbwema. We captured other areas like Manowa, Bunumbu, and came back up to Kono. These were the combined forces of RUF and the AFRC junta.

When the rebels were on their own they would just hit towns and withdraw, but when we came together the war became more intense because we had more ideas than the RUF. We started capturing big towns and occupying them. Before, the rebels never stayed in Kono long, but it was during this time that we stayed in Kono a long time. We captured Kono and Makeni and Lunsar, so

The East: Rebel Territory

it was very advantageous that we joined together. We had ECOMOG pinned down in Daru Military Barracks and the only way they could move was by helicopter. They couldn't use the main road to Kenema until disarmament.

Once when we and the RUF were fighting the Kamajors, the RUF captured one beautiful girl whose father and mother were killed. They wanted to rape the girl, so she held onto my uniform and I said "Let this girl go" and we even cocked our guns against the RUF. At that time I was too bloody and could have killed those RUF. I threatened them and they left the girl alone. This happened in Hangha when we were flushing the Kamajors out. We slept in Hangha and first thing in the morning we attacked Kenema by way of the airfield. One of our men was shot dead at the bridge. At that time the Kamajors were across the bridge defending Kenema. The Kamajors opened heavy fire on us, but we succeeded in pushing them back and we entered Kenema. The girl was still with me. She was a Fullah. I left her in Kenema. I lost her around Hangha Road.

The Kamajors hid in houses in Kenema and the civilians identified them to us out of fear. Once after capturing one of them, with plenty of medicine (magic charms) on him, we undressed him and pushed him away from us to shoot him. He started crying. They started making fun of him and in the end they killed him.

Three Hundred Dollars
One time I took my men to go on patrol when we heard there was an attack on ECOMOG by other rebels at Mende-Kelema. The ECOMOG forces were all scattered and they didn't know any bush in this country, so some were missing in the bush. We captured one. We heard the sound of someone breaking palm nuts. He was lost and hungry. I commanded my men to deploy on the ground. We moved closer to the sound and I saw someone sitting on a palm tree. He had removed his boots and leaned his gun on the palm tree. He was standing on thatch because his feet were wounded from walking. He had a compass on his chest with a radio and $300 in his pocket. We captured him and I took the $300 from him. I had a pair of sports shoes and I hid the $300 in them and sewed it in tightly.

I took the Nigerian to our commanders with the radio and the compass. On questioning him, he told the commanders he had $300 that was taken from him. They called on me to present the money. I denied having it and as soon as I denied it they ordered me to drop. I was tied up with my elbows joined in the back. They had five men with canes flog me until I passed out. They flogged me mercilessly but I didn't give them the money. They beat me!

As they were flogging me, another commander came and rescued me and asked the beaters that if the enemy had killed me, what would they have done, and maybe the Nigerian was lying. Now you're beating him for the enemy. If he had the money he would give it to you with this heavy beating. What made RUF law very strong was the beating. If they flogged someone they would flog you until you were unconscious or until you died.

At the end I was released and they gave me a pass so I ran away to Monrovia with the money. In Liberia I joined the Taylor forces and we captured Voinjama and Zorzor. I saw Charles Taylor in Monrovia at the time we were going to capture Voinjama. I also saw his son Chuckie. They came in a helicopter gunship. We were supplied with desert combat uniforms (blue camouflage). I fought against the LURD rebels in Liberia. I returned to Sierra Leone and moved between Kailahun, Kono, Makeni, and Lunsar. These were places of AFRC and RUF activity. I rejoined the forces there.

Later they called for peace. We went to Kenema for peace talks and enjoyed ourselves for a time, then returned to Segbwema. I left the military after the disarmament. I disarmed, went to Service Continue but no benefits were given to me. They didn't give me anything except some training, so after the training I went to Liberia to stay with my sister. I was in Liberia when they gave benefits to other soldiers. My parents asked me not to join any other force and to just forget about everything, so I didn't ask for any more benefits.

I have all my documents intact. In the military they called me "Identity". There is no big man in the military who doesn't know me. The former army chief of staff knows me. We were all in Sixth Battalion at Tongo and Kono. There was compulsory retirement and my name was on the list.

There's nothing I'm afraid of now. Nobody will ask me to take up arms again. If you tell me to do that I will prosecute you. To fight a guerrilla war isn't easy, especially in the rains. You don't have any way to start a fire to cook something. We could only start a fire by opening a bullet and moving a metal or trap wire back and forth through it until it ignited. I know everything about war. There's nothing anyone can tell me.

The struggle in the military is too much, especially when you're not a big man. You're just a sufferer. You're being used as a tool. There's nothing in the military I don't know. I'm able to train men from lesson one to lesson nine. Eh! I suffered a lot. It was war. When war comes, at the end of the day if you don't take up arms, your fellow man will kill you for nothing.

Men under arms didn't enjoy during the war but I couldn't leave because they would kill me. During that time, before disarmament, if you decided to leave the army, people would look at you badly and they would kill you at night. So you just had to stay in the army. I didn't mind if I died there. If you quit, you're a public enemy. When we fought and I got fed up, I would ask God "Papa God, why am I fighting?"

The East: Rebel Territory

Hangha Road, main street of Kenema

Some people were raping and killing to make the war more fearful. To me personally, I can't deny that I didn't kill anyone during crossfire but I never captured a civilian and killed him. Let God be my witness. As soldiers our motto was to save life and property, so I wasn't there to rebel against civilians. If I ever killed civilians willfully let their blood fight me.

I fought to retrieve the land and that's why I have nothing wrong with me presently. I have some bullet marks but you can't play with arms or knives without getting yourself injured. I was shot three times. The vein on my right foot was cut. They also shot me in the back of my head where there is a mark, and again on the arm. All this happened in the front lines.

Why the War Didn't Succeed

When they brought the war initially, if they hadn't started killing people and burning houses and committing atrocities they would have succeeded. When the Liberians came they were the Special Forces (foreign fighters) who Foday Sankoh chartered. After they fought for some time there was a lack of support from Foday Sankoh, so they decided to lay an ambush for him. Sankoh made a report to Charles Taylor that these men had rebelled against him, so Taylor advised Sankoh to arm the Sierra Leoneans and take out the Special Forces.

Narratives

Sankoh came and explained to the Sierra Leonean rebels that they should get rid of the Special Forces because they were killing and eating people. These were the Gio tribe in Liberia. They called the place *Fewahun-Nemi*, where they were eating people. It means "a big pot is boiling" in Mende. So Sankoh set his men against the Special Forces to flush them out. This was the time when they brought in the TOP 20 and TOP 40 and TOP Final to get the Liberians out of the country.

Really it was the Sierra Leonean rebels who did bad in the country. Some did it out of grudges, for example, you have killed my brother so I'll kill yours. You have burned my house or my village so I will burn yours. This is called a "turn debt". The good thing the war brought was a revolution, a drastic fundamental change. Initially we didn't know our rights. We didn't know anything. The revolution brought a lot of changes. It brought awareness in the country. If there had been no revolution the country would still be in darkness.

For me I don't believe a war will happen again because when they say "armed struggle" it means the person carrying the arms himself is struggling. Eh-h-h. An armed struggle isn't easy. Even the least important man knows the suffering from the war.

I agree that people were raping, killing, amputating, and destroying property, so you can see today some of them aren't doing anything. "The evil that men do lives after them." Some people were acting outside orders. People were doing this because they didn't think the war would come to an end.

KONO DISTRICT: DIAMONDS AND BLOOD

Kono District, also part of the Eastern Province, is located to the north of Kailahun and Kenema Districts. The district headquarter town is Koidu, formerly called Sefadu. Kono was a major target of the rebels because of its large deposits of diamonds. There were many attacks on Koidu, and the rebels often stayed in rural areas to mine diamonds when they weren't in control of the town. For the final three years of the war the rebels occupied the district, mining intensively and building up their forces to continue their attempts to take power and to help Charles Taylor fight against LURD in Liberia and Guinea.

The main headquarters of the RUF was in Kailahun District to the south, and the route they used to attack Kono District first crossed the Moa River, then traversed a number of small towns including Bunumbu, Bandajuma-Yawei, Malema, Kwellu-Ngieya, and Gandorhun. Heavy fighting took place along this road to keep the rebels out of Kono District, and the Kamajors and ECOMOG stationed troops to guard it until December 1998, when they were forced out by the rebels and AFRC on their push through Kono to attack Freetown.

Kono District is the home of the ethnic Kono people, though many ethnic groups live there. Before the war Koidu was a prosperous mining center, but the AFRC/RUF burned most of the town when ECOMOG expelled them in 1998 after the Intervention, and it is one of the places in the country where the effects of the war can still be seen. The district has received few benefits from the millions of dollars in diamonds that have been mined there, and workers in the main foreign-owned diamond mine work under exploitative conditions.

1. Allan
   Everyone Wanted Diamonds
   Civilian

Allan is from Kono District. He talks about events that took place up to the Intervention in 1998 when the AFRC/RUF attacked Koidu and he fled to a refugee camp in Guinea. After the war he worked as a counselor with civilians, former fighters, and communities. This part of his narrative is at the end of the book.

I was born in 1965. In 1991, I was in Kono teaching Physical Health Education at Koidu Secondary School, then I went to college in Makeni. In 1991 the rebels attacked Gandorhun, south of Koidu, but were fought off by government soldiers and vigilantes. However the next year in October they came through Gandorhun again and invaded Koidu causing people to run away from the town. I think they were here for over two weeks before they were forced out. After that they went back to Kailahun District and reinforced.

They started making hits on Koidu again early in 1993. I was a student in Makeni, and I came to Kono to look for my people. At that time the Kono students in Makeni made convoys to come to Koidu. We wouldn't take the main highway because it was too dangerous. There is a road passing through the forest at Waidala where they are mining now, so we would go that way and take the road to Tombodu and then to Koidu. I came with some friends and went in search of my mother who had escaped from the town and was in one of the villages. I found her and my sister but my brother-in-law had died. He became sick and there was nobody to treat him.

I stayed with the family for a week, then college reopened so I had to travel back to Makeni. We traveled on foot because we heard that the highway was dangerous with ambushes and they were just killing people, so I was afraid to go back by vehicle. In 1993 the road was terrible.

First we walked two days to a village near Kabala. We slept there and the next day moved towards Kabala but were stopped and accused of being rebels. They said some of the Konos were turning into rebels. They only let us go when we produced our student ID cards. Fortunately after that we met the Tamaboros and they had a vehicle the government had given them and were going to Kabala. We gave them some small money and they took us on board. We slept in Kabala and in the morning joined a group for Makeni. I think it took almost five days.

They would Sit Here and Mine

Kono was a rich area. Everyone wanted to mine diamonds. The rebels were trying to overrun the town but they weren't strong enough. They would come and loot the shops and commandeer vehicles. When the government soldiers came back they would also sit here and mine. They would be mining again and the rebels would come, drive the soldiers back, then the rebels would mine for some time. That was how the thing was happening.

It was the same with the Nigerians (ECOMOG). They were here doing mining and sometimes were taken by surprise by the rebels and the rebels were able to push them here and there. Their main attention was not on the war. They were mining in Koidu town and around the town in Tombodu, Bumpeh, Small Sefadu, and Number 11 which was one of the most productive areas. Those areas are mined out now. There is only sand because they were mined intensively during the war.

In 1994 the rebels took over Koidu completely. That was when the NPRC was in power and the next year the NPRC made an agreement with Executive Outcomes who were South African-based mercenaries. They did the fighting and were very good. The rebels were forced out of town. Of course the rebels stayed around the environs but they weren't able to come into town. Again in 1995 the rebels advanced on the city from Gandorhun and Executive Outcomes mounted a defense that was a massacre. They killed hundreds of rebels at Wordu. The EO soldiers told the civilians "Go and see your brothers, the rebels" (meaning go and see the bodies).

Narratives

Downtown Koidu, district headquarters of Kono District

I came back to Kono in 1995 after EO pushed the rebels out and started teaching at the same school. The NPRC was in charge and they had their office in a big house in town. At that time the rebels were still trying to get a grip on Kono for the diamonds. They would come, the government soldiers and EO would drive them out, and they would come again. The rebels would come and people would run away. Like, the rebels would be in Gandorhun and you would get the news from people running from Gandorhun so we would pack and go far back into the villages where there was no mining, like in Sandor. I remember one village I was in about forty miles from here. The rebels never attempted to go there.

But at the time we were also suffering at the hands of the government soldiers and vigilantes. They were just hanging around taking food from people. Some didn't want to fight. They went to the villages with their guns, groups of them forcing the villagers to do things.

There was a change of government in 1996 after the election when the SLPP came into power with Tejan Kabbah as President and the situation became more normal. People were going to school but the rebels were still around in the bush and attacking roads. At that time they were spread out over the entire country with Kailahun as their rear camp.

At the Yamoussoukro Peace Talks (in 1996) Foday Sankoh said that if they wanted him to cease fire the government should stop using EO mercenaries, so they made that agreement and the South Africans transformed themselves to this diamond mining company that is working here now (referring to Branch Energy, Executive Outcome's sister company). After that no one was to have mercenaries to fight with you. It was politics. Foday Sankoh said that if the mercenaries were out he would lay down his arms, little knowing he had a plan. That was his tactical way of getting rid of them.

I was in Kono and just teaching. I never took the risk of traveling. I was afraid, seriously. I had to stop going to Freetown or anywhere. The rebels would attack and stay a day or two then be driven away by the government soldiers and ECOMOG.

It was a shock when the AFRC took over in 1997 and invited the rebels from the bush to join them. Koidu town was just full of them. There were no soldiers fighting for the people. They were just doing things. People's lives were at risk. They would go out at night and attack. If they knew you had money, if you were lucky they would leave you alive, if you were unlucky they would kill you. Life here was just like survival of the fittest. It was terrible.

The ECOMOG soldiers had retreated to their own camps at Koakoyima (on the western edge of Koidu town) and some other deployment areas in town with some loyal government soldiers who hadn't joined the AFRC junta. At that time Executive Outcomes were no longer fighting. They were miners. If Executive Outcomes had still been fighting the situation wouldn't have been like it was.

After the Intervention
The AFRC said they would rule for a short time then hand over the government to civilians through elections. There was a meeting in Guinea but they wouldn't agree to step down and that started the fighting in Freetown. ECOMOG forced the AFRC and the rebels out of Freetown and they left through the peninsula. A large group of them came to Kono.

I was in Koidu, but when I heard that they were on their way I fled to my village which is three miles from town. We had problems there. They would come and chase us into the bush and take food and things from us. They captured one person and beat him to death because he had joined the youths to fight against them. I think the youths succeeded for just one day fighting against them in town. I headed to Sandor and from there traveled on foot for two weeks to Guinea.

When they came to Koidu they started burning houses. They would command those who were with them "You burn ten houses on this street" and that was how they put fire to houses. It was because they considered the youth of this place to be their enemies. That was one of the reasons they burned down the town. The other reasons were that they wanted people to completely fear this place, and they wanted to have a clear place to fight so they could stay and do their mining. They just kept some houses to live in. Even the villages, like my village, didn't have a single house left. Everything was burned when I came back in 2003.

The Civil Defense Forces and ECOMOG were fighting together against the rebels and AFRC soldiers. They asked chiefdoms to send people to join. Even the Konos had a Civil Defense Force called Donsos. They were just hunters like the Kamajors but not as strong as the Kamajors because it wasn't easy for them to get arms, so they were easily overrun. The fighting against the rebels here wasn't organized. There were a lot of rebels and everyone was just heading for this place to get diamonds.

I was in Guinea at Nyaedou Camp near Gueckedou from 1998 and we were getting news over the BBC and from people who escaped. At the start it wasn't easy. We had to work on the Guineans' farms. For me, I wasn't used to doing stumping and we would work all day for just 500 Guinean Francs (around 50 cents). I did that for one year.

There wasn't enough food and no money and I had ten people with me—my late brother-in-law's children, my own children, and my mother. The UNHCR was giving us food but it was just sorghum which we weren't used to eating. They gave us sorghum, bulgur wheat, oil, and beans but not the things you needed for condiments. We had to go out into the villages to get odd jobs to buy fish and other things. I wanted to do teaching but at the time the Liberian refugees were doing all the teaching. When we went to apply they thought we wanted to take their jobs so they found ways to block us.

I was there when the rebels attacked the camp in 2000. The rebels attacked Guinea because the Guinean government was helping the Sierra Leone government fight against them. Also, Liberians fighting against Charles Taylor were based in that area so the rebels wanted to drive them out.

I did odd jobs for nearly a year and then secured a job with Enfants Réfugiés du Monde who needed people with teaching backgrounds and experience working with children. I was responsible for the recreational areas, constructing gyms and goalposts. I didn't come back to Sierra Leone until 2003, almost two years after the war ended. I had a job and was also bitterly afraid to come. At one point I was about to come back and got as far as Conakry but my employer asked me to stay and work in the camp where they were transferring refugees. They were bringing refugees back by convoy and it took over a year.

Kono District: Diamonds and Blood

2. Jammie
I'm Going To Die
Civilian

Jammie describes a brutal incident that took place during the 1992 attack on Koidu. In 1998 she traveled with Johnny Paul Koroma's group when they were retreating to Kailahun District after the Intervention, then she went to Kenema where she experienced an attack on the town.

I'm forty years old. I was in Motema near Koidu when the first attack on Koidu happened in 1992. I was at the hospital doing night duty as a volunteer. The attack started at the NP petrol station on the highway so I ran to a village and we took cover under a big rock where nobody could see us. We stayed there for over three days. We had people who went and spied and came back to tell us what was happening. The rebels succeeded in taking Koidu and before they left on the third day they were firing sporadically throughout the town. We went to town and saw some houses burned but the NDMC (National Diamond Mining Corporation) camp where we stayed wasn't destroyed.

We saw government soldiers from Freetown coming to secure the town. They said they would give us escorts if we wanted to go anywhere in town but we decided to move to Makeni. We walked on foot to Masingbi in a big group and camped there for a day, then we moved on to Matotoka and met Paramount Chief Bai Kafarie who is now dead. He had a ring in his nose. He took us to his village called Luporo and let us camp in big NDMC containers, then he went to Makeni and secured rice for us from the Red Cross and told us they would take care of us. At that time I was pregnant, almost at term, and later had my first boy.

My husband was a policeman and he was still staying in Koidu and asked me to come back. A police truck took me back and I stayed with him in the Police Barracks. Two weeks later there was another rebel attack. There were a lot of people in the town. One rebel group from the south was called Yamotoh ("soft to chew" in Mende, a cannibal group).

During the attack I ran to the police station but my husband told me not to hide there because it was one of the first places the rebels would come. He asked me where we should go and I said "I don't know. I left once and you called me back here to die." All the police wives decided to move toward Tombodu because the main highway to Makeni was under heavy attack. There were six of us, all with our husbands, and all of us breast feeding our babies.

There were some boys in the rebel movement and also some civilians who really hated my husband. Some of them were his high school mates. On the way we were captured by some of these rebels. At that time I had his police uniform and some pictures in my suitcase and one of my friends told me to throw them into the bush, so I did it quickly.

Four of the rebel boys came and told us to open our luggage but they didn't find anything. They called my husband and tied him up. He shouted to me "Eh Jammie, I'm going to die." When I looked at him I started crying and one of the boys told me not to cry or they would kill me too. I knew one of the rebel commanders. He was from Kailahun and is still alive now and we have met since the war. He commanded the boys to kill my husband because people had told him he was a bad man.

They undressed him, removing all his clothes, then tied him up and put him under the sun. They gave me a bottle of soft drink and told me to enjoy myself while they were killing him but I didn't drink it. One of them asked me "Won't you drink it?" I said "No, I'm too disheartened" ("me heart spoiled" in Krio). He replied "We'll kill him anyway whether you drink it or not." At that time I was crying in my heart because my husband was looking at me while he was lying under the sun.

They brought a very long knife and sharpened it in front of us and told me to move further away. They told me to forgive them because my husband was a bad policeman and they cut off his penis. He shouted and they stabbed him again. I cried and they told me again they would kill me if I didn't stop. They finally cut his throat and I saw him defecate and die. They told me to go and lick his blood as a sign that he was my husband.

All the men who did this are still in Kono and I still see them. One is presently a motorbike rider (motorcycle taxi driver) and I have ridden with him back to my village after shopping in town. They all attended Kono Model Academy and were in Form 2 together before the war. When I see them now they pretend nothing happened between us and if I have the chance now I would even do good to them. I feel that way because after the war they told us to forgive everybody, and also because if I hate them and there is another problem, I will be one of their targets.

After they killed my husband they gave me Le 10,000 Leones (around $5) to buy food for my child. When people ask me about the war I tell them nothing. People heard the news that they had killed my husband but I just say I lost him.

To Kenema

In 1998 I decided to move from Kono to Malema, my original village where I stay now (located on the road between Koidu and Kailahun). I joined a walking convoy to travel there from Koidu town. At that time I had another child, a girl, with a junta man. In the convoy was Johnny Paul Koroma who was sick and in a hammock. They left Johnny Paul in a village called Madina while his boys went ahead to clear the way. This was in the evening and they decided to wait until night to travel with him, but there was a battle and they decided to bypass Kwellu-Ngieya where the Kamajors were in control and were ambushing the juntas and rebels as they moved back to Kailahun.

I left the group and went straight to Kwellu-Ngieya where we met some Kamajors and they stopped us and asked me where we were going. I was answering in Krio and someone told me to speak Mende because the Kamajors were Mendes and they might think I was a rebel. Luckily for me one of the Kamajors was a brother from my village and they escorted me to Ngiehun-Konjo, the Kamajor headquarters. From there I decided to go to Kenema and I travelled in a Kamajor vehicle along with Kamoh Lahai, their initiator. He sprinkled something on me before we left so I wouldn't spoil their magic spell.

I left my first child behind in Tentihun near Bandajuma-Yawei when I went to Kenema but later I heard she was ill so I went back to get her. She was all swollen and I took her back to Kenema. We were in a truck and a Fullah was the driver. As we were driving we heard gunshots and met some ECOMOG soldiers in Bunumbu who asked us to take their wives with us to Kenema. We reached Kenema in the morning and I took my child to the hospital where she stayed for three months.

When we were in Kenema the rebels attacked the town. Father Charles, a Catholic priest, gave us a vehicle to take us to Blama to camp at St. Joseph's Secondary School. There were more than 14,000 refugees there and I was part of the Center for Victims of Torture counseling group, the only woman who did that work. They had a place for us but I stayed with a friend who was a cook for the priest. I still have her picture with me. They gave me a room and registered me at the camp where I went for supplies. There I had my third child with a pastor in 2002, but we are separated now. He didn't leave me. I left him because he wasn't responsible.

Narratives

3. Kumba
A Command To Cut Off Our Hands
Civilian

Kumba was living in eastern Kono District after the 1996 elections when the rebels went on a rampage of brutality including the amputation of limbs.

I'm fifty-seven years old. When the war began I was in Koidu. One day during the rainy season in 1992 we were sleeping and we heard gunshots so we went along Koidu Yard, around Gbesse-Kandor. When the attack was over we came back to town but later, when the rebels were controlling Koidu, we decided to go to Sukudu in Soa Chiefdom. There we made farms. Before I left Koidu I saw Foday Sankoh at his headquarters in Konomanyi Park.

A few years later in 1996 at around 4 AM the rebels attacked Sukudu and we were all captured. They knocked on the door and when I opened it there were armed men surrounding the house. I saw that some people had been killed and others were tied up so they couldn't escape. Our boys and girls were lined up to be taken away, but then they passed a command to cut off our hands. Some feet were also chopped off and it happened to a lot of people. They killed more than twenty people. My son was one of those killed that morning and my husband was also killed. They took twenty-five boys and girls away. Only three out of the twenty-five came back.

The rebels had been looking for soldiers, but when they didn't see any they amputated us. When they amputated us they said "Go tell your father, Tejan Kabbah, to give you another hand." One man named Momoh had both legs amputated and they broke the bones in one of his arms. Recently they put an iron rod in his arm so he can lift things. He spends all his money on medicine. There's a clinic here in Koidu, the Amputee Clinic, that treats us when we are sick.

Kono District: Diamonds and Blood

After they chopped off our hands my uncle's son took me to Guinea, to Gueckedou, and the UN took me to the hospital there. I stayed in Guinea until they brought us back to Sukudu in 2002. One woman came to register and move us to the Amputee Camp in Koidu and build houses for us. She has built each amputee a house with two rooms and a parlor and she's also going to build more. The UN used to supply us with food but now everything has stopped. Presently we survive on the little garden work we do. From this we pay school fees for our children.

I don't really know what they fought for in this country. We, the poor ones in our villages, our only occupation is farming and we suffered the consequences. Amputations happened in a lot of chiefdoms in this area. I pray that war will never happen again. The war that happened here spoiled human beings. There was no reason for it to happen. War is happening in other countries but they just kill people. They don't torture you like they did in Sierra Leone.

I don't know why the rebels caused this havoc and were so bloody and wicked. They weren't staying with us, they just attacked us. Before the attack we were always afraid it might happen so we used to sleep together and check vacant houses before sleeping.

The war made Sierra Leone go backwards. In Kono, where the war was fought, there are no good roads and this causes accidents. Since the war they have built stores and NGOs have built schools, hospitals. barries, and hand pumps.

For all that has happened in Sierra Leone we should unite to avoid war. If the authorities come together we won't have war again. If they're not at peace we, the poor ones, will suffer at their hands and a war will come again. When the war came the authorities just got into planes and flew away.

Kwellu-Ngieya, on the Kono-Kailahun Road

Narratives

4. Momodu
The Kamajors were Fighting for Peace
Kamajor

The Kamajor Civil Defense Force was one of the civil militias formed early in the war to protect civilians from the rebels. They worked with the army until the AFRC coup, when the army joined with the RUF rebels, leaving the Civil Defense Forces and ECOMOG the only forces fighting on the side of the government.

Momodu was a Kamajor stationed along the Kailahun-Koidu road at the small towns of Bandajuma-Yawei and Kwellu-Ngieya. He took part in fighting the RUF when they were moving from Kailahun to Kono to join forces with the AFRC after the 1997 coup, then engaged in continual fighting during the junta period. In late 1998 there were heavy attacks along the road as the AFRC/RUF moved from Kailahun to Kono on their way to attack Freetown, and the Kamajors and ECOMOG were forced out and retreated to Kenema. Momodu explains how the Kamajors used magic in their fighting.

I was born in 1970 and was in Kenema District when the war began, living in a village doing mining. I fled to Guinea around the border area near Kono but in 1995 I decided to come back to Sierra Leone and went to Kono. The government had formed a Civil Defense Force and I decided to join it because we were being harassed by young men in the bush, both rebels and Kamajors who would threaten anyone who didn't belong to them. We were trained in Kenema. At that time there was war all over the country and people were being chased and killed anywhere.

We were in Kenema up to the time the AFRC overthrew Kabbah in 1997 when we moved to Bandajuma-Yawei. The AFRC had invited the rebels to join them in Freetown and the rebels were passing through Bandajuma from

Kailahun District on their way to the capital. We were moved to Bandajuma so they couldn't move and molest us. We all met at the main junction at Kwellu-Ngieya to stop them.

We fought for nine days and nights. We just lived on coco yams. There was no rice. We didn't sleep or wash the whole nine days. We only smeared *nessi* (oil the Kamajors used for protection) on our bodies. If it was on your body and you were hit by a bullet it just felt like something bit you, but the bullet couldn't penetrate your skin.

The rebels brought twelve vehicles from Kailahun and we captured all of them along with one of the bodyguards of Akim and a medical person. Both sides suffered a lot of casualties. We killed the bodyguard when he tried to kill one of our commanders. ECOMOG came and took twenty-five of us to Bandajuma to protect the road. We stayed there with the ECOMOG soldiers for nine months during the junta regime.

The juntas were attacking us every day and night in Bandajuma. They had a base at Gandorhun where we and ECOMOG also attacked them during the daytime. The ECOMOG soldiers gave us additional training and arms because they were relying on us to fight.

When the fight intensified ECOMOG told the civilians in Bandajuma to leave the area. We were receiving frequent messages from the juntas that they were coming to take over the town. When our commanders went to Kenema to receive more arms they were attacked and many of our forces were killed. In 1998 they drove us out of Bandajuma. We were chased to Kenema where we regrouped, but then we were attacked again in Kenema.

Controllers and Laws

When I was fighting I didn't feel anything. I was just trying to survive the war. We used magic means from our karamoko (Kamajor initiator) to protect us. The initiator in our area was Kamoh Brima. They gave us a controller that worked like a human being. If there was going to be an attack it would tell us. It was made of a cow tail and decorated with cowries. If an attack was coming the hairs of the tail would come together and stand straight up then fall down and stand up again, repeating, with it happening more frequently as the enemy came closer. The controller could direct bullets to go anywhere you pointed.

There were differences between the groups of Kamajors. Those in the south used leaves for their magic. We didn't use leaves. Those in the south ate human beings but we didn't. In the south they had "born naked" who fought naked but we didn't do it. I still have my magic because I'm still following the laws they gave us. No bullet can penetrate my skin. The laws are: a Kamajor can't take away anyone's property, you can't rape a woman, and you don't shoot unless an enemy shoots first. There are certain things you don't eat such as snakes, snails, and palm kernel oil. They didn't give us reasons why we couldn't eat these things. It was a law. We couldn't look at naked women. The rebels used the tactic of sending women they captured to the town naked, thinking it would destroy our magic. Any Kamajor who killed a civilian would be killed if it was reported to the commander.

About the amputations, there was a war in Angola but they weren't amputating hands. It was something unique in this war. They put people in houses and burned them. They raped women. There was AIDS in Sierra Leone but this caused it to be spread more. I think hardship brought the war and it was also caused by the politicians. The human rights and democracy we have now came because of the war.

The Kamajors were fighting for peace. We weren't fighting for political power but to have peace within our own chiefdoms so people could return and make farms and harvest their cocoa. At present there are a lot of former rebels living here peacefully and sometimes we sit together and talk about the war. Sometimes when we talk we tell them, as a joke, that they were the bad boys we were chasing. Some of them even show us their wounds and say they received them from us. When we were in the CDF they promised they would build houses for us after the war, but when we disarmed nobody mentioned it again, and the money we received at disarmament was very small.

The road through Bandajuma-Yawei

5. Massah
Remembering The War
Civilian

Massah lived in Kwellu-Ngieya when ECCOMOG and the Kamajors were fighting the AFRC/RUF along the Kailahun-Koidu road. She stayed there until late 1998 when ECOMOG and the Kamajors were forced out during heavy fighting.

I don't know my age but I'm around seventy years old. When the war started I was living in Kwellu-Ngieya. My youngest son, Komba, was sick and I didn't know the rebels had passed through the town and that the other people had gone to hide in the bush. Later I heard shots from the fighting in Gandorhun and I took my sick son to the bush where he died.

All the young men and women left Kwellu-Ngieya during the Kamajor era and I was the only one in the town. I used to cook for the Kamajors but when things became difficult they would just come and take our food from us. There were many killings in the town. A lot of Kamajors, rebels, and government soldiers were killed so we moved to another village. ECOMOG soldiers were in Bandajuma, but one day someone came and told us that the ECOMOG soldiers were packing their things because if the rebels came and attacked them they couldn't fight them off. When this happened I finally left the area and went to Kenema District.

I was in Kenema when my elder brother died in Freetown and I went there. Later when I came back I saw that my son had joined the Kamajors and I decided to go and stay with him, but unfortunately he was killed the day I arrived. They had gone to Bandajuma to engage the rebels and he was killed there. I didn't see his corpse, only his bones which they packed and brought to town.

Narratives

I never talked to a rebel because I was afraid of them. I never saw a woman being raped. When I heard of rebels coming I hid. During that time we got food from selling kola nuts to traders. There was a Fullah man who used to bring us rice to exchange for kola nuts. If there was no rice we ate bush yams and bananas. Once I went for a month without eating cooked food. In the bush we used to sleep on sticks and if it was raining we didn't lie down, we just sat and covered our heads with leaves.

There were a lot of difficulties so we decided to go to Fangamandu in Guinea to a camp called Mange. When I was traveling to Guinea I was only wearing short trousers so someone gave me a lappa to enter the camp. We were given a bag of bulgur and a tin of oil for four or five people per month. We wore our old clothes. After we were there six months one of my children asked me to come to Freetown and sent someone to collect me.

Whether war will happen again we have to talk to God, because God has everything in his hand. If you say something won't happen but God says it will happen, it has to happen. The government said they would provide zinc to rebuild our burnt houses but after the war nobody helped us. It was only because one of my children built a new house for me that I have this house. To stop war from coming again we should know what to do, because we say we are independent and not under the white people.

6. Finda
Massacre in Tombodu
Civilian

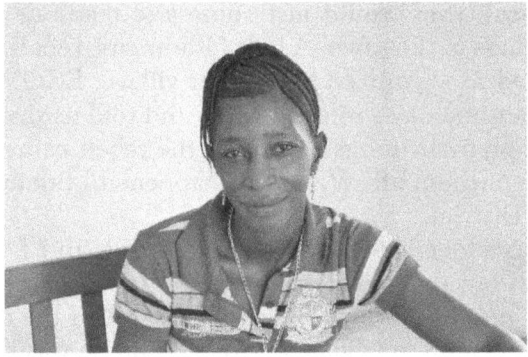

After the Intervention in 1998 the AFRC/RUF retreated to the north and east and took over Kono District, initiating Operation No Living Thing with extensive rape,

amputations, and murder of civilians. Finda was present at Tombodu, a town a few miles from Koidu, when a massacre took place.

I'm over thirty years old now. I was living in Kamadu, a village near Koidu town, and was there when the first attack happened in 1992. I had gone to a nightclub in Koidu with my sister the evening before. The club was packed and we came home at around 5:30 AM and the attack started at 6:30. We ran to Sandor Chiefdom and stayed there until we heard that government soldiers were in control of the town, then we returned. The rebels didn't burn any houses but just looted, and the government soldiers also looted the town when they took over.

SAJ Musa was in charge of the government troops. They gave an order that anyone who wasn't a resident should move seventeen miles away so they wouldn't be mistaken as a rebel. Later I heard that SAJ Musa left the country but came back to fight after the AFRC coup. For me, I wouldn't leave the country then come back again to fight.

After that I got married and the second attack happened. By then I had a child who was two weeks old and when we escaped I put the child in a plastic baby bathtub and carried it on my head. We went into the bush but the attack didn't last long so we came back.

Tombodu

In 1998 the rebels (and AFRC) took over Koidu and the whole area. We tried to escape through Tombodu but they captured my husband and I. The day we were captured they killed twenty-two people in front of me.

My husband was taken and beheaded right in front of me. I shouted when they beheaded him, and because I did that they took me and dropped burning plastic from plastic bags on my leg. After they killed my husband they beheaded another man who they alleged was a soldier but I knew he was a civilian. It was just because of his strong body that they thought he was a soldier. They used a native mortar placed upside down to behead him and they killed the others in the same way.

They threw my husband's body in Savage Pit where many bodies were thrown. Savage was the name of a rebel who cut off people's heads and threw their bodies into the pit. After that they put a lot of people in a house and killed them all by burning the house. They did this because they were tired of beheading people. The house is a memorial in Tombodu now where the bones are kept. They also killed people by making them lie on the road and running a vehicle over them from up on the hill, then they threw their bodies in the pit.

I was also in line waiting my turn and I urinated on myself from fear. It was coming to be my turn when other rebels who spoke Kono came, and when I spoke with them they said I was their Kono sister and they shouldn't kill me. That is how I was saved.

One woman, they put a stick through her body from her anus to her head and set her up her like a cross at the checkpoint called Janama ("hell") Checkpoint. I don't like going to Tombodu now because I see that checkpoint and Savage Pit and remember what happened. I almost went crazy that day.

Memorial in Tombodu for people burned in a house

I don't forgive those who slaughtered my husband. They made us suffer and any time I see my child I remember my husband. If those men are dead now let them judge them there, but if they are alive in any village one day they must come out, and if I see any of them all of you will know about it. It's easy to forget if you do bad.

I was lucky and one rebel felt sorry for me because they had killed my husband and because I had a child, so he told me to follow him. I was afraid and thought he was going to kill me but it was the only thing I could do. He helped me escape and I tried to go to Guinea, but at Koakor I was captured by rebels again. One of the commanders took me as his wife and I had to stop breast feeding my child because he was raping me (from a traditional belief that the child will get sick from the breast milk if the mother is having sex). The day he captured me he raped me.

One day the rebels killed a man and cut him open and cooked his body parts and gave some to everyone to eat. I didn't eat any. I went away to the toilet while they were eating and they gave me all the pots to wash as punishment.

They did this every day for two weeks. I was never forced to use a gun but some of the women took guns willingly. One woman boss was named Monica. They didn't respect those who didn't take guns and there were days when they flogged us twenty-four or more times.

One day they sent two civilian men to go and catch fish for them. They were escorted by a rebel and when they returned one had caught some fish but the other one hadn't, so they cut off both his hands and told him to go and tell the soldiers what they had done. The man who cut off his hands was later killed at Koakoyima when the Kamajors and ECOMOG controlled Koidu. He had gone to buy palm wine and met the man whose hands he cut off. The man told the Kamajors and they took him away. No one has seen him since.

I saw some of the rebel big men—Staff Alhaji and also Issa at Koakor in a vehicle, and also a Koranko rebel named Demba Marrah who was later killed in Koidu. Issa had people pushing the vehicle (because there was no fuel) and they pushed it from Koakor back to Koidu. Every morning they talked to their boys and told them not to take the war too easy. It was Operation No Living Thing and they shouldn't spare even a fly.

Some of the young boys didn't want to fight but were given guns by force. When they went to the front some of them didn't return—either they escaped or were killed. The rebels were so brutal because of the drugs they were taking. Some of them cut their bodies and put drugs in the cut then put a plaster over it. Some put the drug on a piece of paper and sniffed it. After taking these drugs they would kill human beings like they were animals.

They took us everywhere they went. When they took over a village they let the people stay there while they built camps in the forest around the town to sleep in. When ECOMOG jets came they wouldn't see the camps but would drop bombs on the village and kill civilians. Most of the people who died were civilians. When there was an attack they would show the women hiding places where we could meet them after the attack. You had to struggle and try to reach the place to save your life. During these attacks a lot of people escaped.

My Escape
I was with them for weeks and finally escaped to Guinea one day when they went out to fight. The way I escaped was this: one morning they told me to fetch water. I carried my child on my back and when I went to the stream a civilian called me from the bush and helped me run away. He carried the child for me.

While in the forest I fed my child water from young banana stems. I entered Guinea the same year, in 1998. It was difficult to cross the border because the Guinean soldiers called us rebels. If you weren't able to speak

Narratives

Kissi, Mandingo, or Fullah (languages used in Guinea) you couldn't enter. It was fortunate that the man I escaped with spoke Kissi and told the soldiers I was his wife and that I was a Kono. I hadn't eaten rice or good food for a week. When I had rice at the border it caused me to have severe abdominal pain and I was admitted to the Gueckedou hospital.

In Guinea we got food by pounding rice for people. If we pounded three or four bags they would give us seven cups and I would sell two cups for soap, salt and other things and eat the rest. In Guinea I found my mother but she died and we buried her there. Life wasn't easy. Only God owns life. We would have died in Guinea.

At the present time things are still difficult. I make money by going out early in the morning and buying fruit and vegetables to sell in the market, and from that I raise my two children who are thirteen and fifteen years old. I won't marry again because I have to take care of my children, and if I get married he won't be interested in them.

7. Tamba
   Helping The Men
   RUF Child Soldier

Tamba was abducted by the AFRC/RUF when they attacked Koidu in 1998, after they were expelled from Freetown in the Intervention. He was with them when they burned houses in Koidu town and carried out Operation No Living Thing, and he describes some of the terrifying experiences he had as a child soldier.

In 1998 I was in my village, Yardu village, living with my grandmother. On the morning the rebels (and AFRC) launched their attack on Koidu she asked

Kono District: Diamonds and Blood

me to go to the farm with her to pick beans. As we were walking we heard the sounds of bombardment coming from the town. I counted the number of explosions until it became very serious and intense and I also heard small arms fire. Grandmother decided that we should return to the village and as we approached we saw a lot of people running away saying the rebels had attacked.

I saw someone who was shot by a stray bullet so we just took a few things and ran into the bush. I didn't encounter the rebel forces. It was only my elder brother. He was captured because he insisted on going back to get some belongings. We stayed in the bush for one month and ten days, in the forest behind the Bafi River in Sandor Chiefdom. We've never seen or heard from our brother again.

My grandmother was afraid of the rebels so we had to leave and go further. In our second hideout we were chased and caught and they gave us loads to carry to some villages. After that we were released in a town in Sandor Chiefdom but while going back through the bush we were caught by another group of rebels who gave us more loads to carry. This time we brought the loads right into Koidu town.

They told us boys that if we didn't become rebels they would kill us so some of us took guns. I was using an AK-47. All our guns had just a single magazine or no magazine so we could carry them. Among our group we had a very young boy whose gun was longer than him.

After that we were sent on a mission to get food and goats. The rebels put us in front for the attack so we couldn't escape while they were in the rear. It was at Yardu and many of my comrades were killed. You can see this cataract in my eye. It's from a fragment that hit me. The attack failed and we attempted to escape from the rebels but were caught and they killed one of our guys which filled us with fear. I decided not to try to escape again. My responsibility was to attack places to get food but I can't remember if I killed anybody. God is the witness.

You would be very afraid if you saw a group of rebels. They tied red cloths around their heads and arms and rubbed blue ink on their faces and hair to look fearful. Some wore different colored socks—red and black. Some wore combat clothes and others wore T-shirts.

I was with them to help carry things. We were boys helping the men. They gave us guns to protect ourselves because there was no one to protect us. I followed them as they did things. There were many boys in town like me shared by battalion. Sometimes I had to hold people who tried to escape.

We the young boys were sleeping on the house verandas while the rebels were sleeping inside, or some of them outside. There were no covers and the cold killed some of our friends. There was no food, just unripe bananas. We would scrape the inside of the banana out with our fingers and put it on a fire to get something to eat. They didn't give us any food. They had guns, they watched us while they were eating, and they kept the leftovers.

Narratives

We used to eat good food when we attacked villages. We killed goats and chickens and captured civilians to cook for us. The rebels gave us cocaine so we were no longer afraid. The only problem we had was that medical care was very poor. Some of our colleagues died from illness or injuries. They amputated arms or legs of those who were shot but if you weren't careful you would just die. We didn't have extra clothes. What you were wearing, you laundered it then sat while it was drying then put it on again. We called it "wash and wear". Some slept in the towns while others slept in the bush. At daybreak we couldn't see some of the fighters because they'd run away.

I was living in Koidu town with the rebels. If you were living there at that time you were a rebel. You had to join them. They were digging diamonds in the town. You know Konomanyi Street and Post Office Road? That whole area was dug for diamonds. You couldn't move around town because there were pits everywhere. They would break down houses and dig for diamonds or dig inside houses. We saw a lot of diamonds being produced. At that area in Koidu, if you processed just one bucket of gravel you would get a lot of diamonds. We saw diamonds with our bosses, so many we thought they just picked them up.

Mosque and shops, downtown Koidu

I didn't see many Lebanese here then. There was only one but he is gone now. He was captured by the rebels for his money. No shops were open. They even dug under the shops thinking the people who ran away left diamonds and money. There were no vehicles in Koidu town. Everyone went by foot. In the center of town there were almost no people going by.

Kono District: Diamonds and Blood

Most people left Koidu when the rebels came but some stayed behind to loot. Sometimes the rebels killed them when they found them looting. A lot of people left things in their houses when they ran away so others wanted to loot them. People were looking for watches, clothes, money, good shoes, TV sets and tape players. They would take the zinc from the roofs to sell and when they burned the house they would take the metal window frames.

Outside Koidu there is a place where they cut off hands. I saw them doing it. They asked people if this was the hand they used to vote. The people would beg them not to cut off their hands so they would ask them if they wanted to die. The people would say no and so they told them to put their hands on the board. They had a big board and later it was eaten by ants who came for the blood.

They used a cutlass and only hit one time to cut it off. The person was surrounded by rebels slapping the person. One rebel held the person's fingers while the hand was cut off. I heard a story that they made a mistake once and cut off the rebel's fingers. Sometimes they told other civilians to hold the person's hand. They didn't cut off people's hands to make them afraid. People were already afraid of them. They did it from wickedness, to make people strain.

After they cut off someone's hand they would tell him to sing and be happy so they would laugh when they were feeling pain. When they had a lot of people they captured they would put them in a line. They would kill or cut off the hand of one, then skip the next, then kill or cut off the hand of another one. After that they would tell the people left that they were lucky and take them to be workers—digging diamonds, carrying things, or doing other work. If they saw someone physically fit they wouldn't kill him. They didn't kill young women but took them as wives.

The rebels made the civilians work for them. Even a Caterpillar machine, if it wouldn't move they would tell people to push it. Can you imagine pushing a Caterpillar? They would tell them to move it or they would be killed. They would hit you and say "push". They used their gun butts to hit people. You had to pull it. It was just wickedness.

When I was in Koidu the Kamajors would attack the town to try to drive out the rebels. It happened continuously. They exchanged fire but the rebels usually drove them away because they had more ammunition and a stronger position. The Kamajors wore a special fighting outfit made of country cloth with a big pocket in front. It was based on the old paramount chief clothing with a country cloth cap and cowries and other magic things attached to it. The cap was long with the top laying over to one side. The Kamajors colored the country cloth brown by pounding kola nuts and dipping the cloth into it. All this was done to make them look fearful.

Narratives

The main part of town was controlled by rebels and Koakoyima was controlled by the Kamajors and ECOMOG. The boundary was Congo Bridge. Nobody crossed the bridge. If the rebels captured a Kamajor or Oga (the nickname for Nigerian ECOMOG soldiers) they would cut off his head, and if the Kamajors captured rebels they would cut off their heads. The Ogas just killed rebels. They didn't cut off their heads.

They would cut your head off, put it on a stick, and leave it at a road junction. At Congo Bridge I saw many heads lying in the road. Both sides were putting heads there. I even saw heads of girls who the rebels had raped and killed. I saw them cutting off heads. There were no cameras here at that time or I would have snapped it.

Mission to Bombali
This is about the Makeni area where the rebel leader sent me and some others. It was a Temne area and we went to find food because there was a shortage in Kono District, but we had trouble in one village. The Temne people had a native way that they could send white powder on you and it would make sores and a rash on your body that you had to scratch. If you scratched it water would come out and there was no medical care. I have scars on my face and body from the powder.

Farm hut

Because of that we left the area and on our way we were attacked by Kamajors. I was lying inside a house under the bed during the attack and a Kamajor came into the house and shot around the ceiling, putting holes in the zinc. They captured one of my colleagues named Abu and he told the Kamajors I was in the house. He wanted them to capture me because he didn't want to die alone. I heard it and went out and hid at the back. I didn't feel bright and couldn't run so I just sat and I heard Abu crying "Don't kill me." They took him away and I never saw him again.

After that I came out and looked for my colleagues but didn't see anyone. I dropped my gun and took off my shirt because it was a combat shirt and just wore my jeans. I walked to a farm and saw an old woman and she asked me "Where are you going?" I told her I was running away and she said "Don't run, my son, come here." I told her we were attacked by the rebels. I didn't want to tell her I was with the rebels. She took me to a farm hut where they gave me water and cooked cassava and washed me with native medicine until I felt better. My feet were very swollen. I slept and stayed there a long time.

After a while people started going back to the town because the rebels were gone. My hair was very bushy. There was no barber there, so I was afraid to go into town because people would say I was a rebel. I told the man I wanted to barb my hair but he said there was no blade so he gave me a cap to wear. I put it on and looked at myself in a mirror and decided I couldn't go to town because my face was so ugly from the cuts and scars. I knew they would kill me if they thought I was a rebel.

The man said "No, let's go to town. I'll be by your side." He liked me a lot because I was very hardworking on his farm. In the town the man and I went back to the house and I found my gun. I told him the gun was left by a rebel and that I was attacked there by rebels. He was afraid when I took the gun and told me to put it down, that it wasn't good. He thought I would shoot him but I showed him that it didn't have a magazine. I put it in a rice bag and we dug a hole and buried it. Later I went back and dug it up and took it and started walking back to Kono.

I was on the main highway near Masingbi and I saw a group of people and decided to forget about the gun. It was in the bag and I just left it by the side of the road. Someone said "Hey, you dropped your bag" and I told him to forget about it. He went and looked inside, thinking there was something valuable, and shouted "Hey, it's a gun." People panicked and ran asking "Who brought it?" They started looking for me so I ran into the bush.

In the evening I went back to Masingbi town and was lying against a wall behind a house. A very old man came and asked me why I was lying there. I told him I was tired and he asked me to come inside because it was dangerous outside. I went inside and slept. He called his family and told them there was a stranger. They asked me where I was from and I told them I was from Kono District and that I wanted to go back but it was too far. They told me not to go because I was alone and someone would kill me, and the road was so lonely and sad—you couldn't see anybody on the road. They said I could stay with them and they would take me back when the war came to an end.

The next day I saw a symbol the rebels wrote by the side of the road. It was three crossed lines. I saw it and told them that we should leave, but they didn't understand why I was saying that so I told the old man to believe me and that the two of us should leave. The next day the rebels attacked and killed and captured some people. I told the old man that what I said was true and he asked how I knew it. Then he knew I was with the rebels and told me to leave. Anyone who saw me would know I was a rebel because my hair was so bushy.

I was around Masingbi almost five months. I saw rebels but didn't want to join back with them. People I met gave me food and I slept in houses or in the bush. I decided to return to Kono because I was afraid people in Masingbi would kill me.

There were no vehicles and I had to walk back. When I was going back I saw a fearful thing by the road, a little baby sitting near her mother, crying. They had cut off the mother's head and put the child next to the body. There was no head near the body. The baby was crying loudly and I went to look at it but stepped back. I wanted to take the baby but didn't want people to see it with me because they would think I killed the mother.

I called a woman and said "Hey, there's a baby there." The woman took the baby and started crying when she saw what they had done to the mother. I stood and watched her cry, then told her to leave because people might come. The woman took the baby and we went into the bush.

The baby was crying for breast. There was no water or food and it died. I cried when the baby died. Tears came from my eyes. The woman cried too. We tried to arrange a grave for it. While I was doing that we saw some men coming from far away. I told the woman and we hid. The people came and passed by. They weren't rebels and I called them "Uncle, this child has died." They helped us bury the baby. After that I was so sad. I couldn't eat and was feeling bad.

I told the woman I was going to Kono and she said it was too dangerous and hoped I would stay there, but I left and went to Njaiama Sewafe with some other people. We stayed there for a month but then the rebels attacked the town. They harassed people but didn't kill them. They just took things and took girls to sleep with even if the mother cried for her daughter.

After that I told one man I wanted to go to Koidu to look for some people I had been doing gold mining with before, who had money and gold they owed me. I walked all the way until my heels split. There were no vehicles on the road, just people walking who you could join if you wanted. Some of them you were afraid of because they might be rebels. The road was so lonely, you couldn't hear anything.

Disarmament
I was in Koidu when disarmament started and I disarmed as a rebel. When you disarmed they gave you 50,000 Leones (around $20) so I took a gun from someone who had two and disarmed to get the money. Some people disarmed more than once.

After disarmament I just walked around town helping the Pakistanis (UNAMSIL peacekeepers) build and fence their barracks and put sand in bags to make guard posts. My mother was staying in Kenema at that time. I learned tailoring and completed primary school. I'm a tailor on my own, though there's not much work, and I go to secondary school.

I try to forget about the war because it affected my education. I'm 23 years old and still in JSS 3 (ninth grade). I thank God for life because I have no injuries except my eye. I see little future at this time but if I can be educated to the college level my dream will come true. Because of the war many people were able to travel and go to other countries. Some people have even gone to America. I think these are the only good things the war brought. Life is not easy here.

If you asked people what we were fighting for they wouldn't tell you anything. They were fighting for vanity. We didn't fight for wealth. The only benefit was when you destroyed something. After the war I didn't see any of the commanders because those who destroyed Kono went to live in Kailahun and those who destroyed Kailahun came to live in Kono so people wouldn't recognize them.

I remember only General Issa and Mosquito when they came to Kono. We admired them so much, seeing the real commanders who issued the orders. Top men used to visit us in the bush and they talked badly. They told us that if we burned so many houses they would give us a higher position like sergeant or corporal. At that time we didn't think about anything because we were small. We had women commanders too. One of our commanders' wives, who loved little children like us, sometimes wouldn't allow us to do anything. She would say that we were small and that they should leave us alone.

I can't explain all they told us that brought the war. As soon as they captured us they gave us a gun, whether we were trained or untrained, it wasn't their business. They only taught us how to shoot. In the morning there was no order. They just dispatched us to a place. They were compensating elder rebels who did great destruction. They praised them for doing a lot of destruction. A single guy would go and destroy a whole village.

When war comes to a country the youths are more involved. The old people and women weren't that involved. It was more the youth-men who killed each other. All this happened because there were no jobs for youths. When you are idle the next thing that comes to your mind is to do bad. If you are engaged and earning a salary, having money in your pocket, you won't think to do bad.

When they captured you there were only two alternatives—either you joined them or they killed you. They didn't want you to be able to identify them later. If you knew somebody before the war and you saw him later with a gun, he would kill you or ask somebody to kill you because he wouldn't want you to tell people he was a rebel. One thing I believe: if your own time hasn't reached you won't die. Most of the things we were doing were under command, but it's up to God if you will die.

THE SOUTH: SELF-DEFENSE

The Southern Province is an area of forests and farms, traditional villages and small towns. The largest city is Bo, which is considered a center of education in the country. The Mendes are the principal ethnic group in the south. Traditionally members of the SLPP party, they were strongly opposed to the one-party state of Presidents Stevens and Momoh, but the brutality of the RUF led most southerners to reject them as an alternative.

Initial RUF attacks on the south took place simultaneously with the first attacks on Kailahun District. In 1994 the rebels established Zogoda Camp in southern Kenema District and spread quickly through the south, looting villages and killing and abducting civilians. They attacked Bo and a large army convoy traveling on the main highway through the south in December 1994, then two major mining companies the following year.

In response to the rebel attacks, the Kamajor Civil Defense Force was organized to protect local villages and towns, with its principal initiation center in Bonthe District. After the AFRC coup in May 1997 the Kamajors expanded and, with ECOMOG, fought the AFRC and RUF in late 1997 and early 1998 to restore the Kabbah government to power. During these operations (the "Intervention") the AFRC/RUF were forced out of the south. The area was protected by the Kamajors and mostly free from attacks after the Intervention,

Narratives

though the war continued in other parts of the country for three more years. During this period it was dangerous to travel between the south and Freetown as any of the factions could attack and loot vehicles and kill passengers.

1. Bobby
   Liberian Connection
   RUF – SLA – Kamajor

Bobby fought for three groups—the RUF, the army, and the Kamajors. Before the war started he was abducted and trained by Charles Taylor's troops at Gbarnga, Taylor's headquarters in Liberia, and he took part in the first attacks on the south in 1991. He quit the RUF and joined the Sierra Leone Army in 1996, then joined the Kamajors in 1998 and returned to the south to fight against the RUF and the AFRC.

I am around forty years old. In 1990 I was living in Senija (in Pujehun District near the Liberian border) before the war started and I went to Monrovia, Liberia on a business trip. At that time the Liberian war was on. During this trip I was told that diamonds had been discovered at Gbarnga along the border with the Ivory Coast and that there were people looking for men to go to mine, so I decided to go. We went in a truck that was transporting diamond miners to the site.

On arriving close to the point we were held by Liberian rebels who told us that they were the diamonds we had come to mine. There was no way to leave because we were surrounded by gunmen and we knew nothing about guns.

There were 368 rebel soldiers at that place with Charles Taylor, General Vannie, Prince Johnson, Oral Vannie, Kortorko, and Pepe. They said they had brought us to train to remove Samuel Doe, the current President of Liberia, and started encouraging us by giving us $150 U.S. each.

We were camped in a village near Gbarnga. We trained for three weeks and a day and were now strong and powerful men. We were divided into four groups with commanders from Liberia, Ivory Coast, Libya and Kuwait positioned on the borders of the three countries of Guinea, Sierra Leone and Ivory Coast. Other training bases were opened to increase our number and I attained the rank of colonel and was commander of my group.

Mission to Sierra Leone
We were informed that there would be a mission to Sierra Leone and the commander would be Foday Sankoh. We went to Monrovia for a meeting to discuss the mission, and Charles Taylor and Foday Sankoh said they would give $300 U.S. to colonels and $500 U.S. to generals. The meeting was concluded and we returned to our bases to inform and organize our boys.

Charles Taylor called some of us to go for guerrilla training. Our new trainers were from Burkina Faso and Libya and we went to Gbarnga where we met them and where 162 men were trained as Special Forces in a big forest between Liberia and Ivory Coast. As part of the training we were flown in a helicopter and dropped at various distances to find our way out and back to the camp. We were dressed in full military combat and carried gari, jamba, rum, and some had cocaine.

In the forest, as I moved to find the base I smelled a bad odor that seemed to be a dead and decaying animal. I moved slowly to find out what it was and saw one of my jungle men dead with his belly cut open. Looking around I saw a very big animal like I had never seen before up in a big tree. I aimed my gun at the animal and shot eight rapid bullets which brought it to the ground. Others responded to my shots and I knew I was near the base.

After two weeks in the jungle eight men were killed by wild animals. We received our final training, passed out, had identity cards issued to us, and returned to Monrovia ready for the Sierra Leone war. It was 1991.

Within a few days we crossed to Sierra Leone. I led my group to Zimmi, then Gorahun and established a training base in Gissiwolu in Pujehun District. There were only a few trained Sierra Leonean boys in our group. I was in the first squad as deputy commander on the Guinea Road (the highway near the border from Sulima to Kailahun). A guy called Gadafie was my commander.

We advanced to Gegbema then to Joru which we failed to overrun. We attacked and fought there twenty-nine times against Sierra Leone soldiers backed by ULIMO who were a group fighting Charles Taylor's troops in Liberia. Others from our group were engaged in Kailahun and advanced through Kailahun District, though we were eventually pushed back into Liberia from both Pujehun and Kailahun Districts.

Street in Zimmi, Pujehun District

According to what we were told in Liberia, the war was to restore the SLPP back to power because the APC had killed and oppressed the people. That was why we initially used palm fronds on our heads, used green bags, and wore green material and even tied green cloths on our weapons when the war started, signifying we were rebels of the SLPP.

We were strongly advised to avoid hostilities and brutalities especially against civilians, but as the war progressed some young Sierra Leonean rebel recruits went out of command and harassed, looted, raped, amputated, and killed innocent people which diverted the course of the war. Anyone found guilty of these crimes was punished by the commanders. We respected the validity of life, especially we, the Special Forces who entered from Liberia.

In the front we carried nothing with us except food and our weapons with money we took from dead people's pockets. If you go to areas now where I was based no one will ever say Colonel Bobby committed crimes and everyone welcomes me whenever I visit those places. Captured soldiers were never killed and some were reformed to join the rebel movement, though some of them were engaged along the highways attacking vehicles and caused havoc that brought a bad reputation to the RUF. That was why some of us quit.

The South: Self-Defense

Foday Sankoh and his men promised us high positions upon completion of the war such as recruitment into the military, police work, company work, learning new jobs, and helping us travel to overseas countries, but all failed because the revolution failed. Foday Sankoh fought alongside us in the first two attacks on Joru. I didn't see Charles Taylor fight in Sierra Leone, only in Liberia. Many of the RUF Generals were executed by Taylor for allowing ULIMO soldiers to invade their areas of control. They were alleged to have connived with ULIMO.

In the Bush
In the jungle we had many kinds of plants we used for food like *nge kowi*, or we chewed raw cassava or *katatay* which gives water to drink. After the Joru attack failed I was in the bush for three days and my food was a big cobra I shot and killed in the forest where I slept. I cut open the belly and roasted and chopped (ate) some and took the balance to the base.

We wore both civilian and combat clothing. The combat was from killed soldiers but I used civilian dress most of the time. We were supplied with combats from Liberia by Foday Sankoh, especially we the top commanders, but we supplied our boys too.

If an attack was tense we used a captured civilian as a spy to find out the passwords and dress code of the enemy. Some enemy groups would decide to fold a sleeve of their shirt or wear something in the wrong way. This was mostly done at night for easy recognition by group members. Night fights we named "shaw shaw mission" (be "sure" who you are shooting). No one was allowed to shoot a gun until the town was surrounded and major points were deployed.

One could only sleep if you were at the headquarters. At the war front no one slept. Commanders at the front slept during the day while being guarded. At times you just relaxed and were woken up by gunshots from undisciplined boys. Before we launched an attack we prayed in both Muslim and Christian ways, sang songs, and said the national anthem and the RUF pledge. Commanders would advise their boys and hope we all returned in good health. In the war, those who died were said by God that they would lose their lives.

As a rebel I went into battle against Tom Nyuma in Joru, Mende-Kelema, and Tongo Field. He and his boys used to defeat us but sometimes we defeated him, like at Bendu Junction. Mosquito, who became an icon in the rebel movement, joined us at the Gissiwo Base, the first rebel base in Pujehun District. He didn't cross with us from Liberia.

Leaving the RUF

I decided to return to Monrovia. At that time refugees were being taken in ships from Monrovia to the deep water quay in Freetown so I thought it fit to escape from the armed struggle and go back to my country. I was in the refugee camp in Monrovia for days, then joined a ship to Freetown. At the dock a few guys and I were arrested and taken to Pademba Road Prison for three months. I was later freed and transported to Mano-Taiama refugee camp in 1992.

After months in the camp I moved to Kenema, then to Gbandogeneh in Kenema District to mine diamonds. There a daughter of one kamor (a Muslim magic man) from Bayama accused me of being a rebel. I was apprehended and brought to Kenema Military Brigade for interrogation. I admitted being a rebel in Liberia but told them I had dropped arms and come back to Sierra Leone as a refugee. My refugee documents were requested and I told them that my wife had taken them with her to Zimmi. I was taken to a prison and held until 1996.

With the help of Captain Strasser (head of the NPRC government) I was freed and recruited into the Sierra Leone Army. I was trained at the Show Field in Kenema. As a government soldier I fought in many towns along the Daru road. We fell into rebel ambushes many times, especially at Bendu Junction. After three months of brave battle against the rebels with no promotion I decided to quit, which I did.

In 1998 I joined the Kamajor society and was initiated by Chief Kondowai. In the Kamajors there was no training. We only trusted in the mystic power of the society though some were fake and only a few were real. That's why many died in attacks except a few who had some military background. I went to Zimmi as a Kamajor and there we were attacked frequently by AFRC and RUF but were unable to defeat them. We crossed over to Liberia, regrouped and retook Zimmi where we stayed until UN troops disarmed us.

My Armed Struggle

I felt nothing bad in my entire armed struggle. The game was to attack and defend when the need arose. The most important thing was that my own life continue, and indeed God guided me. I didn't sustain any bullet wounds because my body was protected and no bullet could penetrate it. I had washed my body first in this country then again in Nimba County in Liberia by a Fullah man.

The war brought some positive things. It enlightened us about happenings around the world, made us free, made us know our rights, human rights, and democracy. I don't believe that war will happen again in this nation, but one

The South: Self-Defense

can't underrate anything because in this world anything can happen. As for me nobody will convince me to go to war again. If I had lost my life my wife and children would suffer for nothing. Even the promises made, none were fulfilled. Let there be stringent laws that avert people from planning wars.

2. Ansumana
Southern Villager
Civilian

Ansumana describes brutal attacks on his village in Moyamba District when RUF fighters were moving through the south from 1994 to 1996.

I'm around forty-five years old and I was twenty-five years old and residing in Takpanga village when it was first attacked. That day my elder brother Morie and I took our mother Nyanda to Njama town, seven miles from the village, because we were receiving frequent threats from the rebels that they would visit us as they were based close to the village.

On our arrival home from Njama that evening hundreds of people were there from nearby villages and every house was full. At 11 PM we all went indoors to sleep. The village was perfectly quiet but then I heard the sound of boots and woke up Jebeh, my wife. She panicked and I calmed her down, then I went slowly out of the bedroom into the parlor. My brother was with us and he was awake too.

A lot of people came into the parlor. We listened keenly and heard a loud shout at the house of a wealthy man named Uncle Joe Meyei. The rebels had knocked at his door and captured him. Another uncle named Gbagema was also captured. We heard shouting and shots from every part of the village and we were sure it was a rebel attack.

We all escaped through a window—my wife, my handicapped brother and others, and went into the bush to hide. In less than an hour we saw fires in the town. They burned four houses and three kitchen buildings that night. Gbagema, Foday Karbondeh, Princess and many others were captured while trying to escape. After looting homes of items and food they beat some villagers but no one was killed. Those who were caught carried the looted items for them.

After that we were planning to plow the fields so we decided to go to the bush and make camps, being afraid to sleep in the village. We didn't see or hear the rebels for two months so we thought they wouldn't return. We finished planting our farms and were weeding them. The rebels were then advancing toward Mokanji and Rutile in Moyamba district where bauxite and rutile are mined. The attack on our village was forgotten, and because we were not used to staying in the bush some people started sleeping in the village again.

Attack on the Village

It was close to harvest time. Again the rebels attacked towns and villages near us, moving through the bush to find people. They had been defeated and suffered heavy casualties by the South African mercenaries at Rutile and while retreating they killed, amputated, raped, and burned towns and villages. People were hunted, beaten, and killed for no reason. One morning I was chased on my farm and they captured some women and took them away. Later some of them returned after being sexually misused but some never made it back. Men were beaten to death, farm huts burned, and rice cut down.

This harassment became worse and I decided to flee to Bo. This was in 1996. My family and I stayed with my aunt at first. Things were extremely hard and for two months we ate only bulgur which was supplied by the UN. One evening I got a message that my three-tin rice farm was due for harvesting (a four-gallon tin denotes the size of a rice farm). Strong-hearted men like Foday Ndaima and Borbor had never given up staying in the bush. The rebels had again stopped raiding after being flushed out and pushed back from Bo district by the army and ULIMO soldiers.

We left Bo town and went back to the village to harvest the farms. The situation was peaceful. Soldiers were deployed in towns and villages and calmness and sanity returned again. Since life was completely difficult in Bo many of us settled back in the villages. We harvested the farms peacefully, then brushed the harvested areas and planted tabe beans.

The South: Self-Defense

Takpanga village, Moyamba District

One evening a fighter jet flew over from the direction of Freetown. On the third day after that, on a Wednesday night, the village was attacked again at around 6 PM. We had left the farm and were cleaning around the house and it was getting dark so we decided to take our baths before we ate.

We went down to the river to the men's washing place and met around ten other men taking baths. Other people were coming from the bush. The only person I didn't see was Pa Joe and he later told us that when he was coming from the bush he met the rebels on a bridge close to the village. He asked who they were and they tried to stop him but he ran into the bush.

The rebels rushed into town before Pa Joe could warn us. John Ndaima was the first one they captured. They told him to sit on the ground while they surrounded the village. There were around two hundred of them. They left John Ndaima with a guard who had only a matchet so he took advantage of that and ran into bush.

The guard reported it and the rebels became angry and bloody, wounding and killing anyone they caught. They cut people with their matchets who fell and died from their wounds. They gathered a lot of people and brought them to the center of the village and started killing them with knives. I saw all this from a hideout close to the village. Uncle Ningeh was held and hit with a matchet on the neck. He fell and put a hand on the bleeding cut and they cut off the hand. He fell again and didn't shout and the rebels thought he was dead so they didn't do anything more to him. They killed everyone around him.

Narratives

Matchet or cutlass

A woman named Princess fell down, covered with blood. A young girl named Madie was raped and killed by men dressed in full military combat. Her corpse was given to an old woman named Kadie, and they told her to tell everyone they had done this and would be back the next morning. They said they were heading for Njala where a university is located.

On Thursday they came again and stayed for three days. The corpses were decomposing and many were dumped in the well in the center of the village. We were afraid to enter the village and stayed in the bush. Foday, Borbor and I spied on the village every morning and late at night to see if there were rebels, and after we saw they were gone we entered. There was blood all over the stones in the center of the village. From where I stood I counted over fifty corpses and the stones on the ground glistened with human oil.

I saw family members among the dead who included Madie, Yea Batu, and others. We didn't proceed further into the village but returned to the bush. Auntie Mary's son Umaro was found in the bush screaming in pain with RUF carved on his back. We went back to Bo and stayed there until the war ended. Umaro died a few years later which I believe was a consequence of the humiliation inflicted on him.

In Bo I stayed with my aunt on Sewa Road and later registered at the Splendid Camp at Shelmingo as a displaced person. We received bulgur, butter oil, blankets, cooking utensils, land to build a small house, and a tarpaulin for the roof. Life became hard. Some brothers decided to initiate into the Kamajor Society to revenge. Community leaders and chiefs met and contributed money for their initiation and transport to Tihun, the place of the chief initiator. I didn't join any of the warring factions—the government soldiers, rebels, or Kamajors.

We couldn't recognize any of the rebels because they were wearing disguises, dressed in combat, and had marks on their faces. They did many bad things to us. We weren't involved in government matters but they just came in and destroyed our village and killed our relatives. They took all our zinc roofing to make their camps from where they attacked highways, and now we have to cut thatch to make roofs.

Since the war there hasn't been any progress despite promises to rebuild our houses. They've built one mechanized hand pump well. I don't think war will come again because the bad things that caused the war are being changed, and you can't repay evil by evil, bad by bad.

3. Foday
Protecting the Village
Kamajor

Foday is from the same village as Ansumana. He joined the Kamajors and fought the rebels in Bo and Moyamba Districts. He was in Bo when there was fighting between the Kamajors and the AFRC/RUF, and a prominent paramount chief was killed.

I am also from Takpanga and the girl named Madie who the rebels killed was my daughter. We went to Bo but things were hard. I didn't go into the displaced persons camp because I had many children and they said I was bringing other people's children so they wouldn't register me. I didn't receive any supplies despite trying to register many times, so we returned to the village to get food. That was when Madie was killed. I went back to Bo and joined the Kamajors.

What I know is, the rebels had no chance to return to the village again because the Kamajors protected it. I was initiated into the Kamajors and after that we aimed to remove the RUF from our area. We came together in Bo where we planned the fight. We attacked places where they waged havoc and they counter-attacked us too, but we gained support from the populace and retook Bumpeh, Balahun, Nyagoihun (in Bo District), Njama-Kowa, Mano Dasse (in Moyamba District) and many other villages.

Camp Vendahun was the main target after we retook the small villages. This was a rebel camp located between Njama and Bumpeh Chiefdoms near the Foya River which flows between two hills. The camp was in a large valley. It was built in longitudinal rows, partitioned with bush between each row that they never brushed. They looted all the nearby villages to build the camp. There was a church, a mosque, and a cemetery. They cooked only at night so nobody would know where they were.

It was a fierce and tough battle to remove the rebel soldiers from this camp. We went on the offensive and fought heavily for days. We suffered many casualties but succeeded in removing them. ECOMOG soldiers weren't needed to do this. The Kamajors accomplished it alone. Some rebels escaped and based themselves along the Freetown highway where they attacked vehicles.

One day (during the AFRC period) we heard that eight Kamajors had been killed at Njala so we decided to go and bury them. While waiting for a vehicle at the Distinct Office in Bo we were attacked right in the town by soldiers and rebels (AFRC/RUF). This happened because there was fighting in the town between the Kamajors and those who supported the AFRC. During this attack Paramount Chief Lagbeyoh was killed. He was taken by the soldiers to be escorted home but they killed him because he supported the Kamajors.

There was heavy shooting in Bo that day. I escaped with Paramount Chief Quee of Njama-Kowa and gave him some medicine to drink and pour on his head which would protect him from bullets. This was near the High Court in Bo. I went directly to the Police Station with him. After that Paramount Chief Quee always recognized me because I saved his life.

After the war we went back to the village and decided to change the well where many people were thrown into a mass grave.

4. Baby Seiya
He Proposed Love
Civilian

Baby Seiya was abducted by rebels during an attack on her village.

I was in Mattru Koi-lin-ima (Mattru on the Rail Line, a village west of Bo) when the war came to our area. They attacked our village and I ran into the bush. There was no food so we returned to town and were caught and taken far back to the Tikonko area. They gave us food but I refused to eat it because I wasn't used to that type of food. We slept outside in the cold and I had only a single sleeveless dress to wear.

One of the commanders proposed love to me but I refused him. Then one of the rebel women came to me and convinced me not to be afraid of him, so one night I was called upon to sleep with him. I was still afraid but I did it. He did nothing to me that night, to be honest. We were then taken to a forest and I developed a severe abdominal pain that is still continuing at this time.

When we were with the rebels we saw them capture and kill a lot of people. We also saw women raped in front of us. I saw everything. I don't know the real names of any of the rebels, only their nicknames. One was The Killer and another one was Cobra. They never talked to us about why they were fighting except that they were fighting for a political party. They didn't give us any reason why they were killing and raping people, they just went on doing it.

I became very unhappy, especially because I had left my children behind. My husband and one of my children disappeared and I've never seen them again. My sister was killed on the day of the attack. When we returned from captivity they showed me where my sister was killed.

Narratives

I was with the rebels for a year. One morning when we were sent out to find food, government soldiers ambushed us and we were freed. We were brought to Bo and interviewed and were there for two weeks, then released.

During the election in 1996 we couldn't vote. If you voted and they saw the ink on your hand they would cut off your hand. A lot of our brothers from this town joined the rebels and I know them. I see rebels I knew during that time on the street begging. Some never returned. Some are insane but others whose families are well-to-do were sent back to school and are doing well, living a good life.

The bad things about the war were that it killed a lot of people, destroyed homes, and cut off sources of food. Presently we are living in other people's homes. Whenever we have elections we are afraid the same thing will happen again. In order that war doesn't happen again we need to unite.

5. Borbor
Initiation
Kamajor

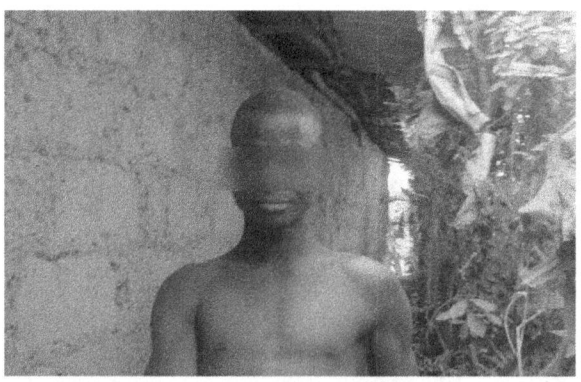

Borbor was initiated into the Kamajors in 1996 when the faction was expanding. He was involved in attacks on the army base at Koribundu in 1997 after the AFRC coup. He also took part in the first Kamajor attack on Bo during the Intervention when the Kamajors took over the town, though the AFRC/RUF returned and forced them out on their retreat from Freetown. We obscured his identity at his request.

I was born in 1977 in Bonthe District and I'm thirty-five years old. At present I'm doing masonry work. I was in my village when the war started. The rebels entered the village at two different times, first in uniforms dressed as soldiers and the second during the AFRC period.

The first time they gathered everyone in the barrie and chose some of the young men to go with them. I was with this group. They didn't kill anybody but took things they wanted and used us to carry their loads from one village to another. Their base was in Mattru Jong in Bonthe District. They took me up to a village called Gola near Mattru Jong and left me there so I returned to my village.

In 1996 we heard of the Kamajor initiation and the town chiefs were asked for people to be initiated. I was one of those chosen. The first Kamajors came from a small village called Kaiwanjama in Bonthe District, then they moved to Talia-Yorbeko and made a big initiation base there.

I was initiated in a village called Makosie, the main base of the Kamajors in Bonthe, called Base Zero. I was taken into a small, dark room and my body was cut all over with razor blades. It was very painful but I couldn't leave because there were stronger men there than me. After that they put something in my eyes that burned and I couldn't see anything, then they gave me something to drink from a calabash and put something in some food which I ate. They made a shirt for me called a ronko that had magic writings all over it hung from strings. The writings were in Arabic on folded paper that were for protection.

There were different types of Kamajors. The first group were called *Baoteh* which means "don't change" meaning that if you are a Kamajor you can't change to a rebel as the government soldiers were doing. It also meant that if you face fire you can't turn and retreat or you will lose your protection and die.

Another group were called *Jombobla* and they could disappear and track down enemies. I joined this group and I have the ability to disappear. We acquired that power in a graveyard. After someone is buried, on the seventh day you go to the graveyard at night and the initiators tell you everything that is going to happen. If you are strong-hearted you take the initiation yourself, or you can pay the initiators to take it for you.

Before leaving your house to go to the graveyard you open every door and window. In the graveyard at midnight you see something coming out of the grave and you have to take it and run to your house. If you have the doors and windows open the ghost that is following you won't harm you, but if they're closed the ghost will enter and harm you.

Another group of Kamajors are the *Ba-nyamolie* meaning "don't ask me." The meaning is not to ask someone why they are initiating people, or, because some Kamajors were doing bad things around, when people talked about it they said "Don't ask me." The last group was called the *Gbamuleleh* and they were very powerful Kamajors.

After my initiation I wore the ronko and they shot at it and nothing happened. To keep this protection you have to follow laws. First you can't touch women when you're wearing a ronko. You can talk to them but you can't touch them. When you go to bed with a woman you have to wash before putting on the ronko, if not, when you go to battle you will be killed. Also, you can't take anything that doesn't belong to you.

This was the period when there were a lot of Kamajor initiators and it became a business and people paid money to be initiated. The main initiator of the Kamajors was a man named Kondowai. He had been a herbalist treating fractured bones in the traditional way. All the Kamajor initiations involved human beings. When a child died they removed it from the grave and pounded it in a mortar and used it to make the magic. They divided the child into parts. They pounded the head, then the hands and other parts. Some people worshipped the head and some people worshipped other parts.

Growth of the Kamajors
Before the Kamajors came the rebels were harassing people everywhere, taking food and possessions. Kondowai initiated some hunters in the Bonthe area who were still using traditional single-barrel rifles. They would go to rebel positions and attack and kill some of them to drive them from the villages. In this way they started becoming well known. Some people came together, Pa Koroma, Joe Timindi, and Moinina Fofana, the top men of the Kamajors. They called Kondowai from the bush and asked him to start initiating.

They expanded the initiations and drove rebels from more villages. As the Kamajors took over villages they initiated the young men who were there, and every chiefdom was asked to send young men to be initiated to protect their areas and the number of Kamajors expanded greatly. They began deploying Kamajors at main junctions. I was deployed at Sumbuya Junction where there was a Kamajor base led by Commander Banja, one of the great fighters of the war. I had an SMG (small machine gun).

There was one Kamajor group called the Death Squad made up of a few men who were strong and hard-hearted who formed the group themselves. They would attack soldiers and take their weapons and do things that were surprising even to the commanders to revenge things that had been done. This caused the soldiers to stay out of towns.

Before the AFRC coup we fought alongside the government soldiers but fell out with them, and after the coup most of them joined the rebels. The way we fell out with the soldiers was this: some government soldiers were deployed at Sumbuya with us, headed by Lt. K.K. The Kamajors always got food from the bush but the government soldiers took food from villages during attacks. Because of this the Kamajors became angry with the government soldiers and went to Lt. K.K. to complain. After that the government soldiers opened fire on the Kamajors and these attacks spread around the area. They killed two Kamajors that day in Sumbuya and we all retreated to Base Zero.

Fighting the AFRC/RUF

The first attack I participated in was at Koribundu after the AFRC coup. At Sumbuya we started receiving threats from the soldiers in Koribundu that they would go to Base Zero to see Kondowai. We left our base at night and some of us surrounded the town while others entered. We engaged them at 6 AM and fought for hours but weren't able to beat them and withdrew. We were scattered and some of our brothers were shot. I escaped into the bush with some others and we went back to the base. We continued these attacks many times and the soldiers also attacked us at Sumbuya.

In 1997 most of the south was controlled by Kamajors except the main towns on the highways which were controlled by the AFRC/RUF. At Base Zero we had supplies coming by helicopter and Hinga Norman used to come on these flights. We received arms to continue attacking.

The number of Kamajors at the base increased to over 1,000 and we decided to attack Bo and push the AFRC and RUF out of the town (referring to the first Kamajor attack on Bo during the Intervention). They called on Kamajors from other areas to converge to attack Bo and we gathered at Bumpeh, 16 miles away. We moved to Bo at night and launched the attack early in the morning. We fought for some time and thought the soldiers (AFRC and RUF) had left the town so we entered, but they were hidden in houses, culverts and other places.

We were in Bo for two days. We entered on a Friday. Some Kamajors began looting televisions, telephones, and other things and hid them in the bush outside town. The soldiers converged on Sunday wearing civilian and Kamajor clothing but wearing the ronko inside out so we didn't know they were soldiers. We thought they were Kamajors from other villages.

That morning they started shooting at two main roads in Bo—from the airfield area and from Mattru Road where they hid guns and set an ambush. They chased us in town and killed a lot of our colleagues. Some were captured and beheaded. As we were retreating they killed many of us. They burned houses of relatives of Kamajors and killed some of them. I was lucky and escaped. Later ECOMOG came and took over Bo with some other Kamajors, though I didn't go.

I didn't know the causes of the war. We were only fighting for peace. I used to hear people say there would be fighting in the country before things could go straight. Now we know each other and won't be afraid of anyone who tries to bring war again. If someone shoots a gun we won't run, but will want to know

Narratives

where the shot came from. If anybody tries to enter this area again I will just get my gun and kill him.

The war brought bad things. People had to sleep in the bush and they didn't eat good food. They burned people's houses and raped women. The Kamajors were doing these things too—beating up people and abusing the elders, killing people if they said anything. The good thing about the war is that the towns opened up and became bigger. People have more understanding and it has become more civilized. We shouldn't repeat the mistake of setting groups up to fight each other. During the war if you were in any faction you suffered.

6. Makambo
A Soldier of This Country
SLA – AFRC

Makambo joined the Sierra Leone Army and fought the RUF in the south and east, but after the Lomé Accord the army was downsized and he was demobilized. He returned to the south, joined the AFRC and fought the Kamajors in Zimmi, believing that he was still a member of the Sierra Leone Army and angry that the army had to fight the Kamajors and foreign ECOMOG troops to regain its position. Co-author Bernard spent a few days with Makambo at a ghetto (a place where drinks and jamba are sold) to record this account.

I'm thirty-nine years old now. I was in Magbele Chiefdom, Pujehun District when the war started. The first attacks I witnessed were in 1992 to 1993. At that time I didn't join the military yet. I didn't run away but defended myself as a soldier would. There was a lot of destruction. Those who were caught were killed, those who escaped went into the bush and lived. That was God's own issue. We were very angry with the rebels for attacking.

The South: Self-Defense

During these attacks I was a vigilante soldier, then I joined the army and went many places to fight including Rutile. We had training at Benguema and from there I was deployed to Kono in the 9th Infantry Battalion. When I was there we just stayed in the barracks. We weren't attacked and we didn't go on any attacks. Later I was deployed at Kuiva in Kailahun District where we were attacked by rebels. When they attacked us we pushed them to Bombohun (a village near Daru). We fucked them up!

After Kabbah became President in 1996 they disbanded us so we were nothing. They removed us from the army. I went back to Zimmi and joined the AFRC junta. I am a soldier of this country. I became a junta rebel because I was forced out of the army. In Zimmi the Kamajors attacked the town and we fought them off. I still felt that I was part of the national army so that gave me cause to fight them.

I am a soldier of this country. I felt nothing during attacks though I didn't feel fine because I wasn't with my parents, but that was the only reason I didn't feel OK. My concern was always to defend myself no matter which side I was on. I was always a soldier of the national army.

I was called Major because of what I did, but I wasn't a real major. It's because of the mission I was on, to give me high morale. I used a gun called "Multiparty 58". I felt proud when I attacked and cleared a place. I came back and I felt proud, especially when I pushed them out of my own base. When we cleared a place we would take all the food and properties and bring them back. I was the boss and everything I did was final because I wasn't responsible for bringing the war. I did this because there was no food or other support.

After becoming a junta soldier I met Manowa, one of the greatest rebel fighters. I heard of Foday Sankoh but they said he was in Nigeria. I never saw him. I saw Momoh Rogers, another tough RUF fighter who stayed in one of the up-garrets in Zimmi.

The war came because the government ignored the people. For example, if you come and give me something, I'll do anything you ask me to do because I don't have anything else. I'll fuck up anybody. I'm doing nothing now. Presently I just feel that anything I'm doing is war.

Another thing is—what is for me, give it to me. If not there will be a war. This is called gbosh-gbosh-gbash-gbash ("corruption and conflict" in Krio). If I don't get what I should because of corruption it leads to conflict.

About the brutality, rape, cutting off hands: my own heart is my own heart and we were living in the jungle. If we were given an order we had to execute it completely. The orders were coming from above. That is all. I don't want to say more.

This zone was Mosquito's zone. At that time the RUF and junta soldiers came together to fight against the Kamajors and ECOMOG. We didn't want to see them. The Kamajors were illiterates and that's why we were fighting against them. We were fighting them because they didn't want to know better.

I can't give any reasons why I was fighting. They brought the war here. I don't know why they organized the war. They met me here and I fought here. We were under them and they asked us to join them to fight the war. I just had to fight because war is war, and we fought bitterly. The war was fought seriously. Where I stay, where I eat, if you want to come and destroy it...that's why I fought strongly.

I have documents that prove I fought for this country but I received no benefits. I was in the infantry. I was a confusionist. The infantry is just people who go and destroy. I fought because I wanted to save my life, so I could see myself at the end of the war as a warrior.

Those I was taking my commands from were Mosquito, Manawa, Colonel Ego, and Papay Bomy—"Bomber"—and they are all still here intact except Mosquito. Some of them are farmers. They are nothing to me now. I'm a hero in this community.

After the AFRC coup the army and rebels joined together tightly and we were getting our commands together. I enjoyed when we were clearing the road from Kenema to Daru and to Baiwala. I enjoyed myself in the movement because I was moving tactically. You don't stand before me. If you stand before me I will become very angry and get rid of you. This is what is called a massacre. If you bring me any mission I swear I will accomplish it. If I don't, let God destroy my future.

We used to sing:

"Kill it, kill it, it's born in reggae.
We kill, kill, kill.
I will kill you if you try me."

I didn't bring the war. It wasn't my business. I just had to fight. Once I joined the movement, whoever tried to stop me, it would be very bloody. I felt fine when I was fighting. I was in places where I could defend myself. It was God's own business to save my life.

During the war I had a lot of women and children. Out of all those women I have only one now. I got no benefits from the war. They promised us a lot of things but didn't give us anything. The men in Freetown are stupid.

I'm not educated and I never held a pen or pencil. It was due to my hardness and hard work that the British took care of me. When Kabbah came to power they tried to remove me from the army. They said I was a sickly somebody. They promised to give me benefits which they never did. They only gave me my transportation and empty papers promising things. I'm an angry man but one person can't fight a dozen.

Early in the war the rebels looted my father. This is still affecting me. The other thing the war did was prevent me from going to school. The war brought a modern cleaning system to the country (community cleaning under the NPRC) so the environment is cleaner now. This is because we used to flog people to clean their environment.

There was no commander who told people to go and rape. It just happened in the front because there was no control. The same thing happens now. Recently a miner dropped a plastic bag with three pieces of diamonds. A police officer took it and is now being held for taking it. Was he sent by his bosses to take the diamonds?

Who brought the war? The people who brought the war were bullshit! Nobody can contest that. Will war come again? There is a song that says "We have seen today but we haven't seen tomorrow." I can't answer that question because it's above me. Some people are driving luxurious vehicles and living well while some of us are suffering with no benefits. From the army I became a dregman (someone who lives hand to mouth). If you have money you are somebody in this country. If someone calls me to do something for money I'll do it.

I joined the rebels on the military junta issue. During this movement I would search people and take everything then go and enjoy myself. In the national army there was no payment. In the jungle no one had a right to be richer than others. We would search them and take it. That was the order of the jungle. We had only the clothes we were wearing.

When we joined the rebels we lived with them in the bush. In the jungle I didn't sleep well because the Kamajors and ECOMOG from Ghana and Nigeria were hunting us. We were attacked at Bombohun but we pushed them back. We responded bitterly. I used a machine gun called "Jungle Movement".

We used to pray in the morning in the Muslim and Christian way. We prayed that the Tejan Kabbah people would have peace of mind for us and stop attacking us because some of us wanted to see our parents. We, the junta soldiers, were all over Daru in 1997. From there we moved back to Kailahun because ECOMOG was still chasing us. I don't know who called the ECOMOG soldiers to come. They met us fighting brother to brother and they took one side so we decided to fight them heavily. We fought heavily in Kailahun until the war was over.

During the war a lot of big men visited us. Even Foday Sankoh came and talked to us. He is now dead. One-Man-One, Lavelie, and C.O. Gbane came. They used to talk to us, telling us to fight. It was just our business to fight, and in fact, if you don't go to the front they will catch you and flog you as a mature person. These guys were rough. If they tell you to shoot someone and you don't shoot, you're a dead somebody. That's what the orders said.

Presently I'm not doing anything. If there's any mission I'll do it. My hands aren't amputated. My eyes are good. Presently I'm vigilant and can run any mission to get anything I need until I die.

Good things I will follow. I'm a human being. God made me to live and so I should live. Presently there's no mission in Sierra Leone because of the situation. This makes me feel disgruntled. I'm a man who had three or four women during the war with plenty of children. They're all gone because I'm disgruntled. This came from the APC movement (the party currently in power), not during the war—now. I'm a hard-working man. I wasn't a bad guy in the army or in any community where I lived. I have documents to prove this. But I swear that if you bring any mission to me I will accomplish it because I'm a dregman. In fact I will accomplish a mission even beyond your satisfaction. If anyone stands in the way of how I'm making my living I'll fuck you up. Because you are nothing.

7. Bernard Sifoi
Bo School
Civilian

Bernard Sifoi was a student in Bo during the second half of the war. He relates events he witnessed there and during travels to Moyamba and Freetown. He was in Bo in May 1997 during the AFRC coup, and during the Intervention in February 1998 when the Kamajors took over the town.

The South: Self-Defense

I was born in 1982 and was nine years old, in Primary Class 3, when the war began in 1991. I lived in Mano Dasse in Moyamba District in the south. I remember one day when I was in primary school I saw my father with the Green Book from Libya which talked about grassroots revolution. There was Green Book 1, 2, and 3 and he had bought all three. He didn't allow me to read them but just explained to me that it was about planning war and at my age it might influence me. His teacher colleagues were coming to borrow and read the books, though the books didn't lead him to join the rebels. Later he was in the CDF as an eye to give intelligence to security forces. They were using teachers to send messages as educated men.

I fully understood the gravity of the war in 1994 when I completed my primary education and entered the Bo Government Secondary School, a boys boarding school. The government soldiers were controlling Bo and the rebels attacked the town on Boxing Day that year. I was on holiday in Mano Dasse so I didn't see it, but the rebels were driven out of town the same day by a coalition of government soldiers and people of Bo, mostly youths, using matchets, sticks, and stones.

During that school year we would sometimes break bounds and go to town. At that time the rebels controlled most of the area around Bo and many of the towns in the south. We went to watch soldiers returning to town after battling them, bringing causalities and rebel captives from the war front.

One day I witnessed the execution of seven alleged rebels who were captured in Mattru Jong, all in their teens. They were beheaded at seven different roundabouts, one killed at each roundabout while a crowd followed. They were killed by ULIMO forces based at the Liberian border who were aiding the government to fight the rebels while they also fought Charles Taylor. I stayed to watch it all because I wanted to see what was going on.

It was horrible and cruel. They cut off the head while holding the man standing up and the headless body would try to run in any direction. They would then kick it down and enjoy watching it die, kicking it and shouting to rejoice in its death. After that they cut open the abdomen and ate the liver raw, then burned the body with old tires. This operation was headed by a female called Kadiatu Cut Hand. She was there doing the beheading and eating the liver with the ULIMO soldiers. People said she was a Liberian.

The Coup and After

In May 1997 the AFRC overthrew the Kabbah government and invited the rebels to join them and this move was opposed by the government and its allies, the Kamajors and ECOMOG. In Bo the coup caused vandalism and looting of shops before daybreak. I was staying in the school dormitory and was awakened by gunshots.

At daybreak there were only a few armed men in vehicles going around town so we decided to go out and see what had happened, and my friends Gassimu and James and I all left the campus to go to the town center. I was amazed at the destruction. Famous Lebanese businessmen's stores and shops were broken into and looted with only torn plastic, cartons, broken glass, and paper littering the streets. People were moving around and among them were thieves toting any item they could get.

The AFRC started beating and killing relatives of Kamajors and burning their houses. Our school closed and we all went home and didn't return for a year. The coup happened on the day before we were to take our Junior Secondary School Exams so we weren't able to take it until the following year. I stayed at my aunt's house in Bo as it wasn't safe to travel back to my home town because of attacks on vehicles by the Kamajors, AFRC, and rebels.

Carpentry workshop at Bo Government Secondary School

In February 1998 the Kamajors attacked Bo (during the Intervention), capturing it from the AFRC troops who they threw out of town. The Kamajors beat and killed relatives and friends of the AFRC in revenge. I was working at my cousin's shop and we heard about the Kamajors shooting in the town and people being killed. Anyone thought to be a rebel was killed. During that time if someone was caught stealing, people just shouted "Rebel! Rebel!" and if the thief ran they would kill him straight off. Because of this, when thieves were caught they would stand still and say "I'm a thief, not a rebel" so people would only give him a beating.

Because of the fighting I decided to go back to my father's at Mano Dasse which was forty-four miles away. I took plastic items from my cousin's shop to sell and left Bo. After six miles we were blocked by armed AFRC soldiers and they held us the whole day but didn't do anything to us, though they took items such as salt, cigarettes, and bullets away from people who they suspected were supplying the Kamajors in the bush.

We reached Taiama Junction that evening and met another checkpoint with soldiers and queued for them to check our baggage. I was wearing brown boots and one of the soldiers asked me to give them to him. I was afraid but told him they were the only boots I had and he didn't take them. Later someone told me to take off the boots and hide them in my luggage so after that I was walking barefoot. They searched the whole vehicle but didn't allow us to go. Then a big vehicle came from Freetown and they were busy searching it so a group of us just walked away. We walked down the road to Njala to a curve where the Kamajors often ambushed AFRC troops, so when we reached that point we knew that the soldiers would be afraid to follow us.

We walked seven miles to Njala and slept there. In the morning we were walking to Mano Dasse, another seven miles. Unfortunately one woman who was with us was carrying a picture of her husband who was a soldier and we were stopped at a Kamajor checkpoint. They found the picture and took everything away from her. They even took off her wig and scraped off her hair, manhandling her. They took her to their headquarters at Mano Dasse with all of us. They put her in an open drum at the chief's compound and covered it. They brought charges against her as a collaborator and beat her. I left and went to our house. My father went to the chief's compound and negotiated her release, though they kept all her money and things. I still see this woman now.

A few days later, while I was in Mano Dasse the AFRC/RUF attacked Bo (referring to the AFRC/RUF reattacking Bo during the Intervention), retaking it from the Kamajors and killing a lot of them including one of my cousins named Samuel. Then the Kamajors and ECOMOG retook the city. In August I decided to return to Bo because school was reopening after a year and we had to take exams. I walked to Bo using the old railway line because I was afraid of roadblocks on the highway. Different areas were controlled either by Kamajors or AFRC troops, and to cross a zone you needed a pass which cost 500 Leones (around 25 cents).

In December, when school was closed for holidays, I was staying with my aunt and we were afraid to go out but we managed to get bulgur, gari, and cooked cassava. The Kamajors killed a lot of young guys they alleged were

AFRC/RUF or a relative of them. People were happy that ECOMOG was there but a lot of people were killed for revenge and others went into hiding because of their connection with the junta.

Holiday in Freetown
Bo was controlled by ECOMOG and the Kamajors but the highways were still dangerous. The AFRC and RUF were in the bush and some settled along the highways attacking vehicles. They had camps in the bush from where they would attack vehicles such as Okra Hill Camp to attack the Freetown highway.

I took my exams and was promoted to Senior Secondary 1 and decided to go on holiday at my uncle's house in Freetown. I left Bo at around 5 PM in the back of a trailer truck. I couldn't go by bus because I didn't have enough money. We were stopped in a village after Mile 91 by a group of Gbinti militias and had to sleep there and stay the whole next day because there had been an attack on the Freetown highway just ahead of us. Later, by evening time, some vehicles came from the Freetown direction and said the attack was over so we moved on. After just four or five miles we saw a burning vehicle and some bodies with other people wounded. They said the AFRC/RUF had attacked the vehicle and there were also some loyal government troops around who we thought might have been involved in the attack. The driver gave the soldiers some money and we left.

After my holiday in Freetown my uncle recommended that I take the government bus back to Bo because it was faster and safer. We left in the morning and just after Masiaka we were stopped by armed men. I saw dead bodies whose heads had been cut off and put on sticks, one facing Freetown and the other facing upcountry.

They shouted at us to come down. They told us about the heads, that they were bastards who had attacked them that morning. I saw the driver go to their roadblock booth and give them money, jamba in a plastic bag, and a lot of bread. They shouted "Bravo!" to the driver and didn't take anything from the bus. They were in half uniform—half government and half civilian—and said they were government soldiers. At that time the situation with the government soldiers and rebels was confusing. They had joined together officially through the AFRC coup but some groups had separated and were fighting each other. Any of the factions, including the Kamajors, stopped vehicles on the highway to get money and loot.

We continued to Bo safely with the driver giving money at each checkpoint. All of us were afraid but nothing happened. I returned safely to Bo, started Senior Secondary School, and graduated in 2002.

The South: Self-Defense

There wasn't any further fighting in my area and I was in Bo for the disarmament. There was a radio announcement that all the combatants should disarm and they went to the Coronation Field, the main football field in Bo, for disarmament, then they were taken to Gondama where there was a disarmament camp.

In general I can say that the atrocities in Bo were caused by the Kamajors and AFRC soldiers. The rebels weren't involved much in Bo town. The people of Bo are still proud they prevented the city from being overrun by RUF rebels in 1994. The city was badly affected by the war with people killed, loss of businesses, schools closed, people displaced from their homes, outbreaks of disease in the displaced person camps, overpopulation of the town by refugees from the rural areas, lack of food, and other things. Presently the city has returned to its former position as a center of education in the country and is expanding and developing quickly.

8. Mr Tucker
Around as a Young Man
Civilian

Mr Tucker is a resident of Bo. He took part in fighting the rebels when they attacked the city on December 26, 1994 (Boxing Day in Sierra Leone), and he witnessed the killing of Kamajors by AFRC junta soldiers in 1997. During the Intervention the Kamajors took over Bo, but AFRC/RUF troops re-entered the town disguised in Kamajor clothing and held it until ECOMOG arrived a few days later. During this period he moved around the city, socializing with friends and getting into situations where he could have been killed.

Narratives

I'm forty-five years old now. I was living in the Moriba section of Bo and I personally encountered the incident on Boxing Day, 1994. That morning I was at home and I started hearing sounds like gun shots. I went outside and heard that some of the sounds were coming from the new Police Barracks and others from the direction of Mattru on the old rail line. Everyone was familiar with the sound of rebel guns. The small artillery shots were followed by heavy artillery. That was how the rebels coordinated their shooting. People in the township knew it was the rebels and were expecting them because they had sent messages warning us.

We had young men in every area of town organized into vigilante groups. At night, check points were mounted and the vigilantes probed into luggage and personal effects to justify people's status. As God will have it, any family man has to organize his family. I was married and had three children—a boy age eight, the second was five years old, also a boy, and the last was three. My wife asked me what to do but I didn't have anything to say. I just said to spread mats on the floor under the bed and have the children go there and I asked her to stay with the children.

A very close friend of mine came to enquire about us. We were supporters and advisors of the vigilantes and I saw him dressed like a soldier ready to fight so I also went in and dressed in jeans. I had one long weapon which I called "Papa". I called it that because it was the eldest person of the house. It was a

Police Barracks, Bo

stick with four-inch nails in it. There was also a rope on it to carry like a gun. This was my own weapon. I put it on my neck and went out with my friend.

Masses of people were evacuating the fighting zone to safer areas in the center of town. We headed toward the shots and all the young men came out as if the shots were music, wanting to know where it was coming from. Government soldiers were in the town staying at the army barracks, getting ready as a brigade to fight. There were other people moving luggage from one place to another, some not even knowing where they were going. People were coming from all parts of the town, rushing away from the shooting.

My friend and I followed the other youths toward the fighting area to see what was going on. My squad set out to New London and on our way we learned that six people had died from stray bullets. There were a lot of civilians gathered at New London because the people of the township had made a decision to repel any invasion. Civilians shouted "Rebel!" as they encroached on the town. We started chasing them as their ammunition got finished, and we caught and killed some.

The soldiers had gone first along the Mattru old rail line to engage the rebels and we saw a group of them in a vehicle coming from the battlefront singing, and we joined them. We didn't hear any more gunshots as the soldiers had gone in and combed the area. Some youths were shot down with many wounded in saving Bo. Bo was prevented from rebel infiltration that 26th day of December.

Calm returned to the township. The attack only lasted around three hours and there was jubilation now that it was finished. The police, soldiers, and civilians had pushed them out, particularly the young men who had chased them with sticks like my own "Papa", cutlasses, slingshots, and any other weapon they could get, even swords. There were also women among them.

Soldiers Against Kamajors

In the south the war was being fought in the countryside and livelihood became a big problem. Displaced camps were overpopulated and though NGO food aid was coming there wasn't enough. Since some families were large, men decided to return to the bush to organize a unit consisting of hunters to force rebels out of their villages so farmers could return and plant rice and other food crops. These local hunters were later renamed the Kamajors.

When you say "Kamajor" it originally meant those who went into the bush to hunt. It's a Mende word—the name of the traditional society of hunters. They were also called the CDF—Civil Defense Force. The Kamajors had secret rituals that bestowed mystic powers on them to withstand bullets. They could disappear and had the power to redirect bullets back to the shooter.

The Kamajors were supported by the government with arms and ammunition to fight alongside the government soldiers against the rebels. They were well motivated and repelled rebels from the countryside, concentrating them in bases at certain places.

At the initial stage they were fighting alongside the government troops. They would go with the government soldiers to fight rebels, but as time went on their relationship began to sour. The way we noticed it, the Kamajors and soldiers were all our brothers but when they went to the warfront the soldiers would do things the Kamajors didn't like such as conniving with the rebels in looting.

In 1997 the AFRC overthrew the legitimate civilian government of President Kabbah in a coup from which Johnny Paul Koroma became the junta leader and head of state. He called the RUF to cease fire and invited them to the towns to join them. We then lived with three armed factions—the Kamajors, the AFRC soldiers, and the rebels. This altered the Kamajor–soldier relationship. They had formerly been allies but now were enemies and the soldiers were the allies of the rebels.

The rebels didn't stay long in the town and went back to the bush. I still gave my support to the Kamajors whose office in Bo was on Mahei-Boima Road. When they were fighting at the front now they had more casualties than before because they were fighting former government soldiers along with the rebels.

The war had taken a U-turn. Shots from soldiers we trusted were turned against us. I survived because of my greater powers. A Kamajor named Kill-Man-No-Blood told me that he would spear any soldier as they were now rebels too. One of the Kamajor initiators built Base Vaahun (near Bo) to initiate as many devoted men into the society as possible to match the strength of the AFRC soldiers and RUF.

At one point in Bo the AFRC soldiers said they wanted to make peace with the Kamajors, though it was a trick. They called a meeting where there were important people from the military, Kamajors, chiefs, paramount chiefs, and civilians—all respected people. They met at the Methodist High School. I was there myself. It was a colorful event, seeing the Kamajors and the soldiers who had formerly been fighting alongside each other. The peace between them was put in place and it was assumed that all was over and solved.

The Kamajors decided to invite the soldiers to Messima where Base Vaahun was located to show they had reconciled. There was a woman there named Mama Munda, a Kamajor initiator, who no one knew where she got her mystical power. So the soldiers were running, jogging, and singing to Messima. After that in return the Kamajors decided to go to the soldiers' barracks where the brigade stayed on the Bo-Freetown Highway.

The South: Self-Defense

We joined the group going to the barracks but something happened when we passed through the center of Bo town. We were going through Kortigbuma on the road to the barracks and the soldiers suddenly started firing, shooting people. I saw two or three people fall down and die in front of me. We all ran back to town. At that time the AFRC had their Secretariat Office in the middle of the town by Fenton Road and I didn't have any alternative but to run there for safety. I wasn't alone but I was mostly aware of myself.

What happened that day wasn't good to see. I don't like to talk about it because it was the first time I saw anything like that. The heavy fighting going on all over town was terrible. With my own eyes I saw three people dressed as Kamajors coming toward the AFRC Secretariat. The first Kamajor succeeded in passing by and went down Old Gerihun Road. I don't know what happened to him. The second one climbed up on the roundabout in front of the Secretariat. There was an anti-aircraft gun at the Secretariat and they fired at him. He had something in his hand. It was wrapped with red poplin with cowries on it and had a tail like a cow. As they fired the gun he passed it over his head. I believe it was to control the bullets. It was some form of protection. They pumped the gun toward that fellow and we saw him turn around and around and finally disappear. He disappeared from that place. I don't know how I could ever feel when I saw that. I was overwhelmed with different feelings. They weren't able to kill him.

Roundabout and former AFRC Secretariat (at left) in Bo

Another thing happened in front of me as I came out of the Secretariat. I was finding my way and people were running down Old Gerihun Road. We hid in a market area and saw the third person who was dressed as a Kamajor. We didn't know it, but soldiers were hiding in the culverts around town. Suddenly we saw the soldiers come out of the culverts with RPGs. They shot at the Kamajor and he was blown to pieces. I never want to see anything like that again. It was a terrible thing to see.

My only plan was to reach my home because I had left my wife and family there. After some time the firing stopped and I ran straight home taking shortcuts and avoiding streets. At the junction by Prince William Street there is a school called UBC where many people were hiding, and we heard the sound of vehicles and took cover. In the vehicles we saw soldiers. There were three vehicles that passed by, and in the fourth which was open in back was the renowned Paramount Chief Lebbie Lagbeyoh. He was in the vehicle with the soldiers. So the convoy passed by. The firing stopped so I went straight to my house which wasn't far away. I knocked on the door and my wife understood it was me and opened it.

My wife asked me what had happened and I wasn't able to talk. She calmed me down and I saw my children and touched them all. They gave me some food and I sat down to eat. I heard a friend call me and I opened the door. He said the AFRC had killed the paramount chief. The vehicle was heading toward the soldiers' barracks and my friend was following it. The vehicle stopped before reaching the barracks and there they killed the paramount chief by slitting his throat and cutting open his belly and packing it with stones. They also killed all the Kamajors around there, some by beating them to death.

So I ate some food with my friend and changed my clothes. I told my wife that I wanted her and the children to go to the village within the next two days. My friend also decided to send his wife and child to the village. He had one child, four years old.

The next few days things calmed down and I managed to buy some food as soon as we were able to go around the town. I sent my family to the village with some food and was left in Bo alone. What I went through wasn't fine. What was going on in town wasn't fine. After a few days the Kamajors took revenge on the killing of their colleagues and the paramount chief and launched an attack on the barracks. The battle was fierce and a lot of Kamajors were wounded.

During the battle some soldiers went to the Kamajor base at Messima to destroy it. They set fire to it and it burned down because it was made of thatch. The Mommy Initiator was there with some other initiators. They set fire to the place where she was and she disappeared. They weren't able to kill her. After they burned the place they saw a big cat running from the fire so they believed the Mommy had turned into a cat and run away. That kind of thing really happened.

That whole night there was continuous shooting in Bo. Before daybreak the Kamajors withdrew from town. Bo was now completely occupied by AFRC soldiers and there was looting and breaking down shops. They killed people who were supporters of the Kamajors. The town became quiet but people were worried. We were just there, like myself. I was alone at home. I closed up everything and left. We had to sneak around because if you stayed at home and they went there they would loot your house.

Intervention and Return of the AFRC
The Kamajors regrouped and added to their powers and launched another attack (the Intervention in February 1998). In town the AFRC soldiers' attention was on looting and enjoyment. A very large number of Kamajors came and drove the soldiers out of town. We didn't see any more soldiers around. If there were any soldiers they would have to be loyal ones who weren't involved in the fighting. But in any case, the Kamajors took over the town for that time, but you know, in any society you get initiated into there are rules and regulations. And we human beings are easy to forget them.

The Kamajors were very happy and we hailed them as brothers, but what did they do? They started stealing people's televisions and tape recorders and looting the same way as the soldiers. They weren't supposed to steal and kill. Doing these bad things would affect them because of their mystical powers. They were especially supposed to stay away from women but some of them were womanizing and it destroyed their power. After all these violations they forgot they were at war.

The AFRC planned their tactics to take back Bo (referring to the AFRC/RUF taking back Bo after the Kamajors forced them out early in the Intervention). One morning we saw four Land Rovers. I was at Mobile Sewa Road and a convoy came and passed by. They were all dressed as Kamajors with red ties on their heads and cowries on their shirts. They were shouting "safe, safe" which was the code word of the Kamajors. So they passed all over the town, but they were soldiers dressed as Kamajors being dropped at various points, distributed around the town.

Just then we heard firing in town. I left the area and everyone ran back to their compounds. The AFRC soldiers came and took over the town. There was heavy shooting and no discrimination about who was killed. They killed drivers and took their vehicles and burned some of them, even with people inside. They started burning houses, some of them big houses. They went from house to house, knocking at doors. If you didn't open they shot at the door and went inside, killing people and raping women. The girls were at their mercy. They would take the husband out of the house, rape the wife and girls, and if they were unlucky they would be killed. This made many people run to the bush.

There were a lot of corpses in the streets. There were no market places where people sold food but we knew where the market people lived in our communities so we could buy food, though it was expensive. As long as you had some money. I had money. I was wearing two pairs of jeans and my crepes (tennis shoes). I had my first aid with me and I was just praying they wouldn't capture me.

We moved from house to house to get information. If we heard they were coming to this side we would move to the other side, and we continued like that. On Sewa Road I entered a walled compound of one old Pa who worked for the Ministry of Works. One of his children was a footballer who was popular on Sewa Road so I stopped to see him.

There were a lot of people in the compound and they brought cold rice for us to eat. They heard that the soldiers had set a house on fire at Njagboima where there were people inside and that made a lot of them leave the compound. But for myself, because my wife and children were in the village, and because I had money I could buy cookery (prepared rice). People would say "There is food over there" and you would go and buy it quickly for 500 or 1000 Leones (25 to 50 cents). You drink water, you get cigarettes. Sometimes I bought one packet of cigarettes and a lighter.

One guy from Njagboima came to the compound and confirmed that they had burned the house with people inside so we put all the luggage and televisions up in the ceiling to hide them. The compound was walled so it seemed a little safe but the soldiers needed vehicles, money, chickens, goats, and other food items and there was a Mercedes Benz parked inside the compound. Two visitors saw the car and said "These are the things the soldiers are looking for." So the guys in the compound and the visitors all went up and hid in the ceiling.

I was alone, lying on the verandah quietly, and I saw a soldier boy pass by. He was a young boy but he had a gun and a big tape recorder. He climbed over the gate into the compound and came straight up to me. He held me and shook me but I knew he was a boy and I was bigger than him. He asked me for the key to the vehicle and I told him I had come to visit people but didn't find anybody there and I didn't know anything about the place.

The boy said he had seen me in the town. He was filthy and was wearing a mask so I could only see his eyes, nose, and mouth. I had a small waist bag that had my documents. He asked me what it was and I opened it to let him look. The boy put his hand in and pulled out the documents and started tearing them up. His gun was still on his back. He wanted to take the bag so I moved

The South: Self-Defense

Sewa Road, Bo

a few steps back and he took his gun. I noticed he was getting angry and he pushed me toward the vehicle.

Near the Benz was a water well. The people hiding in the ceiling heard us argue and the boy told me I was stubborn and that I had to give him the key to the vehicle. He pointed his gun at the ground and we stood chest to chest. I stayed near him so he couldn't shoot me.

I wanted to shout to get the others to come and help me but I was afraid there were other soldiers around, and those who were hiding might be afraid to come and help. We were still arguing about the vehicle key. He said he would kill me if I didn't give him the key. The boy shot the gun between my legs to threaten me. Ah! When he fired the gun it made my heart strong. The gun was between my legs. I smelled the gunpowder and there was a big hole where he shot.

Somebody from the ceiling shouted loudly and it caught his attention. He said I had told him there was nobody there, and I told him I didn't know and hadn't seen anybody when I came in. At that moment his soldier friends were trying to find out where the gunshot came from. Suddenly I saw another soldier dressed in a soldier's uniform with two guns. The boy shouted to him "Soldier! Come inside and let's finish this bastard pikin." In my heart I said to myself "I'm not a bastard pikin. You're a bastard pikin!"

The other soldier tried to climb over but he had two guns and had to call the boy to hold them. The boy told me to move with him toward the gate but the Benz was parked near the wall and the place was tight, so I went by the tight place and the boy passed around by the water well. To get the guns he had to walk some distance from the vehicle. I knew the compound because I used to go there, and when he turned his back I ran toward the kitchen and to the toilet. I climbed on top of the septic tank and jumped over the fence. I fell into an old trash hole and laid there in perfect quietness.

I saw four soldiers, well armed, coming toward the place where I was lying. They met with some other soldiers and stood there for a time. There was an old Pa who used to sell firewood there, also hiding near me and who saw me when I fell from the wall. When I saw the soldiers I took an old dry leaf, a big leaf, and held it to block the view so they couldn't see me. The four soldiers headed toward the same compound I had just escaped from where the boy was with the Benz.

Myself, I didn't see anybody else pass by so I stood up quietly and took a short cut, passing through Pa Zorokon's place. As I went around a corner I saw two soldiers standing there. As soon as I saw them I sat on the ground and started begging them not to kill me. They told me to get out of their sight. I walked fast to cross the street and saw two soldiers with guns, smoking jamba. There was a woman with them but she wasn't dressed as a soldier. They asked me where I was coming from and I said I was looking for food for my children. They asked me where I worked and I knew that there was premium to kill teachers because they wrote letters for the Kamajors so I told them I worked at the Ministry of Works as a security guard at the gate. I pretended to be very sorrowful. The woman shouted at me "Go!" I didn't turn from them. I walked backwards because I was afraid they would shoot me in the back.

I ran over the B Line to Maria Street and saw some guys cooking bulgur in their house. I saw my footballer friend running for his life with a big wound on his knee and blood running from a wound on his forehead, looking for a place to hide. He came in the parlor and fainted. We put water on the wounds from a big pot that was boiling in the room where they were cooking. They put salt on his wound and tied it. We ate the bulgur and I left.

I came out at Vacoma street, heading back to my house. I saw four guys appear before me, all with guns and smoking jamba. They told me to sit down on the ground, so I sat there and they threatened me that I was a Kamajor. They asked to look over my body for the initiation marks of the Kamajors but I was wearing a long sleeve shirt, so they said they were going to shoot me but instead they released me and I went into one old building. I told myself I wouldn't die.

I sat down inside the old building on Vacoma Street and smoked cigarettes. There were people hiding and doing business in spots. They didn't want anyone to know they were around but people went there to get food, even some soldiers who were decent and who ate, paid, and left. But some could misuse you and not pay or break up the place, so people had to be very careful to do that business and they made a lot of money.

I was buying groundnuts from a boy and I saw two other guys coming and invited them to eat the groundnuts, but they told me just to leave so I shoved the groundnuts in my pocket and went right to the middle of town. I found myself at Kissitown.

When you were around as a young man you could see other young men moving around. At that time the soldiers didn't want to see crowds of people but there were some moving around and the soldiers also had civilian friends. You could be enjoying yourself with friends, but suddenly it could change and they could shoot you. They could easily shoot people. It was during the "revo" (Intervention) before ECOMOG got to Bo that these things were happening.

After a few days they burned down the Southern Motel on Sewa Road and had civilians joining them as AFRC sympathizers and supporters. There was one guy named Agba Robinson who was very powerful. Ah! That guy had a mind. He led the group to burn it down. I was there and saw everything. We were drinking palm wine and we saw a vehicle with AA going toward the motel. They shot around first to scare people away then climbed down from the vehicle.

The Big Gun (Agba Robinson) came down dressed in a very big gown. He stood outside while some soldiers went inside. One man went with them to loot but he was shot as he came out carrying a sewing machine. The soldiers shot him because he was a thief. They wanted to burn everything and didn't want him to take anything out. They just shot him down with one shot. They burned the hotel completely to ashes.

You know what happened inside the compound I escaped from? The soldiers went inside the compound and raped one of the women. To get the Benz they killed a guy who was a secondary school teacher. The soldiers pulled everyone down from the ceiling and an argument started about the Benz. The teacher was shot in the mouth and fell by the water well. That was how he met his death. It took two days before they took his body out. The soldiers took the Benz away before the body was taken.

One fine day ECOMOG came to take over. They entered the town walking alongside the Kamajors. The Kamajors knew the area so they were able to fight off the AFRC and rebels, and ECOMOG and the Kamajors took over, so the sympathizers and supporters of the AFRC and rebels began to suffer in return. There were many casualties. They would set fire to places of the sympathizers and supporters. They would kill people and do other bad things for revenge. "Do me, I do you. Your own regime has passed and my own time has come."

ECOMOG was mostly made up of Nigerians and they spoke pidgin English. The Kamajors were our local brothers from villages and some didn't even know how to speak Krio. Some Kamajors looked fit militarily and strong and the Nigerians admired them and fought alongside them. Sanity finally came.

9. Margaret
It Pays to be Kind
Civilian

Margaret also lived in Bo during the war, and she describes some of the problems she and her family faced.

Foday Sankoh was a cousin of my stepfather. I knew him in Bo in the late 70's and 1980's and called him uncle. At that time he was a gentleman and a quiet man, to be honest, so I was surprised when I was by the radio and heard his name announced as one of the rebel fighters. I told my mother and she said it couldn't be the same man, but later we realized it was. He was a photographer and had his studio by the Rex Cinema on Mahei-Boima Road in Bo. That was in 1984 when I was about to get married, and I met him and told him about my wedding and he promised to take snapshots and make an album of black and white pictures. Only one of the pictures survived. The rebels destroyed the rest. A friend of mine found it on the street and gave it back to me.

The South: Self-Defense

Margaret on her wedding day (Photo by Foday Sankoh)

There were several attacks on Bo. The first was by the rebels on the 26th of December, 1994, then later there was very serious fighting between the soldiers and the Kamajors. It happened every now and again. Another one where we were really, really disturbed was in 1998. That was the last attack, then after that ECOMOG came.

When the rebels attacked in 1994 they got up to Tikonko Road where our marital house is. We were at home at the time and they were shooting all over. I went out to climb up on the roof. They tried to stop me but I told them I wanted to see what was happening so I could tell the story later, and also so we could decide if we should stay or not.

So I climbed on the roof and saw a woman with a gun wearing a military uniform and hiding in the banana trees. After some time she would come out and shoot and shoot and shoot and shoot. There would be another shot different from hers, and when she heard that she would go back into hiding. After I saw that I told my husband the place was not safe and that we should move into town to find another place, but he said we should stay there.

That woman, when the youth mobilized themselves to drive the rebels out, was caught and they killed her by the Clock Tower. They cut off her leg and stripped her naked—there were no knickers on her. Oh, my God. I was ashamed. We went to watch. They displayed her body at the Tikonko Road Roundabout. She was fair in complexion. It wasn't easy.

After the AFRC Coup

There wasn't much trouble in Bo before the AFRC coup but when that happened the groups were fighting for power and there was serious fighting going on. Even those who came to rescue us were fighting for leadership.

In 1996, before the coup, Kabbah was in power and the city was controlled by the Sierra Leone Army and Kamajors, and they were going out to attack the rebels in the countryside. After the coup in 1997 the AFRC and RUF took over Bo and there was a lot of violence because some of the civilians supported the Kamajors and had killed rebel sympathizers and burned their houses.

Narratives

After the AFRC took over we the teachers were not teaching because they were not paying us. We were doing other things, like me, I'm a seamstress and people would come to me to do sewing. After the shooting I would take out the machine, put it on the veranda, sit down there and start sewing. There was shooting every two or three days, whenever they liked, at any time they felt like shooting.

At that time there was incident with a tenant of my mother. The tenant's wife was abusing my mother because she had asked them to leave the premises. The man had two wives and we were all dwelling at my mother's house but they were not cleaning the compound and my mother couldn't clean it by herself. She said "You should clean your surroundings, so tell your wives to clean around this place. When they finish cooking in the kitchen let them clean it."

The man got offended and started abusing my mother and his wives also abused her. They all quarreled that day. Mama gave him notice to leave the house but he said he would not leave. The next day he said "Margaret is the one who is disturbing this place. She is the one who told her mother to drive us from the house. We are going to kill Margaret." I said "You don't have the power to kill me," not knowing that he meant it.

Two days later I was going to church and I saw the tenant and some soldiers coming toward me, one with a gun in his hand. I suspected something from the way he was looking at me and I went back to the house quickly and closed the door. They knocked loudly for me to go outside. The man had brought the soldiers who were his friends to kill me.

So they said "If she is not coming out, let us kill the mother." Another one said "No, the mother is old. We want to kill the daughter because she is the one who is spoon-feeding the mother everything." There was that tussle while I was indoors hearing their conversation.

They met my husband on the veranda and the tenant asked him to produce his wife or they would take him and kill him. Other soldiers came. I was hearing their voices. They grabbed my husband and somebody knocked and told me they were taking him away. I had to open the door. They were on the road holding my husband as if he were a thief. I said "Where are you taking my husband?" They said "Don't ask us, now you are here." Luckily for me the AFRC boss, Mr Jalloh, was in the office. They were taking my husband to Mr Jalloh to be put in the guard room and Mr Jalloh would pass the order to kill him. They never knew that I knew Mr Jalloh.

It pays to be good. It pays to be kind. I was kind and generous to Mr Jalloh. I used to cook for him. His place was just a stone's throw from my mother's. He was a soldier, a tall fellow. When I heard the Jalloh name I knew he was a relative of my mother. My mother's surname is Jalloh. She is a Fullah by tribe, and I was preparing food for them once in a while.

As soon as we entered his office Mr Jalloh stood up and said "Why? Why is this woman here? What has happened?" I explained to him in tears. I told him the man in the guardroom who they had just brought to kill was my husband so we went to the guardroom and he opened it. They released my husband and we went home. That was the way I saved his life on that day. If I had been a coward he would be no more.

Kamajors Drive Out the AFRC

Then, at a point in time, the Kamajors entered Bo and drove out the AFRC soldiers (during the Intervention in February 1998). The Kamajors were in control but they were fighting among themselves. Their fighting was just internal, over properties. They were quarreling over the items they stole from people's houses.

None of my relatives joined the Kamajors. They weren't willing to join. The Kamajors were forcing people to join them but the people in my house were not that type. The Kamajors were mostly villagers, speaking strong Mende. When they took control of Bo town they were moving from house to house causing problems. They said they had a list of people harboring AFRC soldiers. They just stood in front of your house and said "We are going to burn this house. Look at the name of the owner on the list." And indeed they burned down houses in Bo, and if they suspected that someone was a soldier they would take him and either kill him or beat him mercilessly.

One day they were passing on the street, and that day my husband was with us at my mother's house, sitting on the veranda. A group of them stood in front of him speaking in Mende, talking about him, saying "This man is a soldier, don't you see his looks? Let us take him along." I answered them in Mende that he was my husband and not a soldier. I told them he was a teacher and he wasn't going anywhere. They insisted and one of them grabbed him from the chair. I stood firmly by my husband and held him and said "If you are going to kill him you will have to kill two people." One of them said "Let us leave them. This is our Mende sister. For her sake let us leave this man whether he is a soldier or not." You see, that is what we were facing in the war.

The Kamajors didn't realize the AFRC and rebels were regrouping to attack them. The AFRC had a lot of war techniques, unlike the Kamajors. They had more weapons and more skills because they were trained, and that was the main reason they were able to return. One technique was to exchange footwear like their slippers, one would be given to another person so the two they were wearing were not the same, then if they came across anyone wearing two of the same shoes it meant you were an enemy. They were so sensible.

One day we were staying at my mother's house in the heart of the city. There was a heavy knock and men saying we should open the door or they would grenade the house. I was so afraid, but they persisted so I told my mother I was going to open the door. She held me so I couldn't go so I said "Mama, it's better for one soul to go than many. Let them not burn the house and the people here." There were so many people in our house who had come for safety. The severe knocking had opened the door slightly, so as soon as I touched it, it opened.

There were two of them—AFRC soldiers. They pointed their guns at me and one of them put his gun to my chest. He was so huge, so tough, and wore a white scarf tied on his head. They said "Where are the other people? Where are the other men? Call me the names of the men. Let them all come here or we will kill you." They started abusing me, using some abusive language.

I said "They have all gone." I stood there looking at them and they began threatening me. One said "Weh de money? Gi' me de money" and I said "I don't have money." Then they grabbed me and said they knew where women hide money. I wept, and the other one said "Oh, you de cry? We de come kill you. But gi' de money first."

They stripped me naked but couldn't see any money. In fact, on that day I was menstruating. Oh, my God. That was the way they disgraced me. Then they said "If you don't call the names of the men here we are going to count three, after which we will shoot you." The gun was still on my chest.

The first person I called was my husband and he came and stood by me. Then they said I should call another man so I called my son David who was seventeen years old at the time. They started addressing him, saying the youth were disturbing them, not joining hearts with them, so they were going to kill all the youth in Bo city. My husband was winking his eyes toward David as if to tell him to leave the place so they saw him and said "Oh, you de tell him le' him go? Well, na you we de come kill."

The other one looked at me in my eyes and said "You, I know you. Don't you know me?" I said "No, I don't know you." But of course I knew him, because at one time when I was going to church in the evening I had met him along the road where the AFRC soldiers assembled in the evening and he had proposed love to me.

But I said I didn't know him—maybe if I had said I knew him he would have really killed me so I could not prosecute him later. He said "OK, now you

The South: Self-Defense

Mahei Boima Road, Bo

are saying you don't know me, but I know you. The best thing is that we are not going to kill you people. We are leaving you, but other ones are coming behind us so pull out. Maybe when they come they will have no mercy on you. We will kill anyone who doesn't open the door in time."

Later we heard a gunshot and learned that one man was killed because he didn't open his door—one Mr Jalloh, my mother's cousin. So we got that message and started crying. Then another set of soldiers came and said "What are you crying for? You'd better leave this place" and we had to flee from our house. We jumped over the fence, along with my old mother. We were staying close to the Immaculate Heart Church St. Francis which shared a boundary with my mother's compound and we hid there for about two weeks while the fighting was going on.

We were very lucky because the ECOMOG soldiers arrived after that to save us, we the civilians. So they took over the city along with the Kamajors. It was nice that the war ended because it was no good. The children were not going to school. We were not working. Some of us who had old people to take care of, it was too much of a problem. Sometimes I had to carry my mother on my back. If the war hadn't ended I wonder what we would be doing by this time.

Volunteer

I was doing a voluntary job with KISS 104 FM in Bo when the fighting stopped in Bo and before the January 6th attack on Freetown. I used to go there every day, playing recordings of the voices of people who were stranded in Freetown, citizens of Bo who had gone there to buy goods or visit relatives. At that time, although Freetown and Bo were under ECOMOG it was still too dangerous to travel on the highways. The station manager went to Freetown and recorded the voices and we played them on the radio for tracing. A good number of people were traced through this program. There was no postal service at that time. People sent letters to relatives through the station manager who traveled to Freetown by helicopter.

To be very honest it is not easy to forgive those people, but if you are a Christian or a Muslim you are a child of God and we are all children of God, and for the sake of development in our country, and for the sake of de-traumatizing yourself, it is necessary. We who were workers of KISS 104 were moving around recording voices of people, counseling them, telling them to forgive and forget. They would say "OK, if you are telling me to forgive those people who did these things to me, I will accept it for your sake, but I will not forget."

I used to tell them "If you don't forget, every time you think about it you will make yourself stressful," so I was encouraging them to forget and forgive. To me it is important to forgive. I like the reconciliation because if it had not taken place there couldn't be peace. Some of us had training from NGOs like CCSL (Council of Churches in Sierra Leone) and I was one of those to disseminate the message that I learned in the training. After the war there were trainings going on like peace and reconciliation and trauma healing.

FREETOWN AND THE NORTH: CONFRONTATIONS

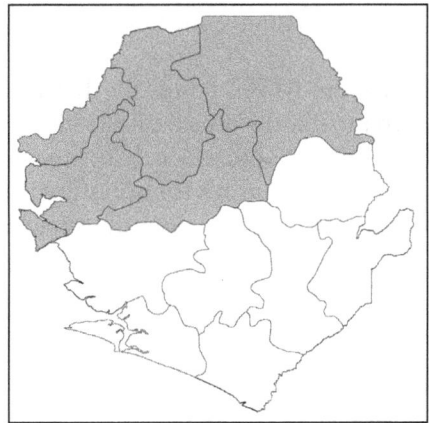

The rebels reached the north in 1994 and established a base in the Malal Hills in Tonkolili District, which they used to attack northern districts and the Western Area. They attacked Kabala in the far north the same year, moving on the town from Kono District.

After the AFRC coup in 1997 there were large-scale confrontations between the combined AFRC/RUF and the ECOMOG/Kamajor forces. In 1998 the AFRC/RUF were forced out of Freetown and they retreated to the north and east, committing serious atrocities against civilians with Operation Pay Yourself and Operation No Living Thing. They regrouped for their January 1999 attack on Freetown while fighting ECOMOG and Civil Defense Forces throughout the north and east.

The AFRC/RUF moved to attack Freetown in December 1998, taking control of Makeni, the largest city in the north, during their push to the capital. They attacked the capital on January 6, 1999 but were forced out after two weeks of fighting and they again retreated to the north and east. ECOMOG and the Kamajors followed them and retook some northern towns but weren't able to retake Makeni. The AFRC/RUF controlled around half the country and the government was forced to negotiate at Lomé.

In October 1999 the RUF expelled the AFRC from Makeni. In May 2000 they abducted peacekeepers in the north and again moved to attack Freetown,

Narratives

which led to a shootout at Foday Sankoh's lodge on Spur Road, Sankoh's arrest, and Britain's entry into the war.

In September 2000 the RUF began making attacks on Guinea from the north and east to support Charles Taylor in his war against LURD. In the north the RUF made incursions into Guinea from Kambia District which led to reprisals from the Guinean army and greater destruction in Kambia than in other northern districts. Fighting continued until the rebels were finally defeated in 2001.

The narrators describe the AFRC coup, the Intervention, preparations in the north for the Freetown attack, the attack on the city, the demonstrations and killings at Sankoh's lodge, and demobilization. Narrators include members of the AFRC and RUF who explain their reasons for opposing the Kabbah government, attacking Freetown, and carrying out atrocities in the north and Kono District.

1. Gibrilla
Trouble in Aberdeen
Civilian

Gibrilla is from Aberdeen, a town on Cape Sierra Leone near Lumley Beach that is connected to Freetown by a bridge. Three large hotels are located in Aberdeen and were used by various factions during the war. Gibrilla relates stories, rumors, and experiences from the period after the 1997 AFRC coup when ECOMOG shelled the city and clashed with the AFRC/RUF. After the Intervention in 1998 he was harassed like other young men who were suspected of being rebels. During the January 1999 invasion of Freetown the AFRC/RUF attackers didn't reach the western side of the city where he lived.

I was born in 1978. I live in Aberdeen in the Police Barracks. My father was a policeman. I didn't complete school because my father didn't have money to pay for it. I remember the NPRC time in 1992 when they took over. I was in class 3, but the real problems were when the APRC coup happened in 1997. I was around twenty years old then.

We saw RUF soldiers in town with AFRC soldiers leading their convoy to deploy them. In Aberdeen they stayed at the Bintumani Hotel. They had been called to back up the government and were deployed around town. Some were deployed at Johnny Paul's compound at Wilberforce. Kabbah ran away to Guinea in the morning the same day. Soldiers who didn't want to join the AFRC also left the country. They would have been killed if they hadn't joined. Some police also, and they teamed up with ECOMOG in Guinea to remove the AFRC.

The AFRC respected me a lot because at that time I had a gym—a weight-lifting room—and I was built. I was the coach in the gym. They even saluted me. I had no problems with the AFRC or RUF soldiers. Anywhere I went in town they thought I was a soldier, though I didn't join anything. At that time we called the RUF the People's Army. When they were called to Freetown by the AFRC they changed their name. If you called them RUF they would get annoyed. The AFRC were soldiers and the People's Army were rebels. There were a lot of women soldiers and some of them were more dangerous than men.

Most of the RUF had fought for five or more years. They were rough guys. They didn't respect any humanity. They just did what they wanted even though their boss (Mosquito) gave them an order that if they did anything to civilians he would punish them. If they killed anybody he would kill them. If they stole he would lock them in prison. That law was well known, but some of them weren't law abiding.

I saw RUF rebels threaten people several times at the hospital near the helipad in Aberdeen. There were trees where we used to sit and smoke and I saw a lot of confrontations there like woman business, and I saw them cock their guns to threaten people. They were all carrying guns and did everything with guns like in the bush.

There's one story at that time: there was one rebel who came from Kailahun and one day he told his companions he had a dream and that he should make some charity, some donations and prayers for the dream. His name was Soa. So they came and sat in a circle and poured some water on the ground. Then he took a gun and started shooting his companions right in the reception hall of the Bintumani Hotel. I was at the small beach across the street and we heard the shots. All of us, even the fish women, laid down flat thinking we were attacked.

Narratives

They took him to Cockerill Military Headquarters where they met Sam Bockarie (Mosquito) and he told them to go and kill him. They took him to the big roundabout in Aberdeen at Bintumani Junction. There was a kushu tree there and they laid him down near the tree. A lot of people came to look and they shot him and broke his head open, scattering his brain. I saw brain live on the ground. The dogs from the beach came and ate him. Most people regretted they went to see it, to see this kind of thing.

Aberdeen

ECOMOG Shells the City

After that ECOMOG came in a ship from Guinea to Government Wharf but at first the AFRC didn't allow them to come down. Finally they let them deploy after they told them they had come to reinforce their government. They deployed at the Mammy Yoko and Cape Sierra Hotels in Aberdeen, with the commander at the Cape Sierra Hotel. He was a Nigerian soldier, fair in complexion.

The next day, June 2nd, was the day ECOMOG and AFRC had trouble in Freetown. The AFRC knew ECOMOG had come to take them out. We heard shelling from the sea. A friend said "Gibbo, this isn't rain." We thought it was thunder. We heard shells traveling in the air and booms. In an hour we heard that a bomb landed at Whitepole at Wilkinson Road and killed some people. Even a devil was killed. Some guys had put on leaves (wore devil costumes) and were going to tell ECOMOG not to interfere.

ECOMOG couldn't overcome the AFRC. They tried in Aberdeen and at the military area but their manpower wasn't enough. The shelling killed people in other places. One old fisherman and his pregnant wife and grandson were killed at Aberdeen in their house. ECOMOG were crazy guys, just shelling anyplace.

From there the AFRC organized and decided to take care of ECOMOG. They attacked them at the Mammy Yoko Hotel. They came with a helicopter gunship and I saw them live coming from the sea, shooting shells at the Mammy Yoko Hotel. The third floor burned the whole day and night. After that the Nigerian soldiers surrendered, took off their uniforms, and they took them to Pademba Road Prison, some of them just wearing underwear.

They were also fighting in Lungi and Jui the same day. The AFRC and RUF attacked all of ECOMOG that day. Sam Bockarie sent RUF there to attack them but they couldn't take Lungi or Jui. A lot of RUF were killed there. They couldn't do anything. They just went there and died. A lot of my friends died there that day, friends who had gone to my house. They had brought looted things to our house to keep but my father told them not to keep looted things there because he was a policeman. My friend Abdul's room was full of looted things.

The RUF took five hundred ECOMOG to Pademba Road that they captured at Aberdeen and Jui. From there Johnny Paul allowed them to go back to Jui and they gave them their uniforms and rifles and they went back. Johnny Paul was a fool and a coward. A friend, one Fulani guy from Nigeria, told me they let him out and released him and they were the same ones who came back later for the Intervention. They never got the Nigerians dislodged from Jui. It was their base near town.

The shelling continued every day and ECOMOG ships were patrolling every day. This was the time of the embargo by land, air, and sea. They didn't allow anything to come into the country. ECOMOG was at Lungi Airport and patrolling the ocean. They would bomb any ship that came into Water Quay. I remember one time in the morning a Ukrainian ship came in. We called the ship A-Bomb. It was loaded with rice and weapons for the AFRC. The bombs landed in front or back but never hit the ship. They said it had a magnet in it to deflect the bombs.

ECOMOG and the ship caused a lot of problems at Kroo Bay (a small bay in central Freetown). ECOMOG tried to bomb and sink the ship but the magnets sent the bombs into the houses at Kroo Bay and a lot of people were killed. Every day ECOMOG jets bombed ships but it couldn't destroy A-Bomb. AFRC got the rice and the guns. One Lebanese guy was the winner that day. He paid for the rice and guns and brought them in. He was one of the main supporters helping the AFRC get food and weapons.

At that time we were eating rotten corn meal and corn flour with weevils in it. We cooked it like rice and ate it with fish. We used grenades and dynamite to kill fish and sell them and kept some to eat. Soldiers took apart unexploded bombs and sold the powder. We bought another fuse, lit it and threw it. A friend even converted a pineapple grenade into dynamite, but a grenade couldn't kill fish as well as dynamite. Life was simple for me under the AFRC because I had food and money.

Intervention

Later ECOMOG came with the Intervention. The whole night we saw planes come into Lungi full of Nigerian soldiers. We saw them fly over Aberdeen to Lungi the whole night. They came to take the AFRC/RUF out. ECOMOG had a radio station called Bush Radio 98.1 broadcasting from Lungi telling people the situation, that they were coming to take over, and they told people not to stand together in groups of more than three because ECOMOG would shoot them. They said not to be anywhere the AFRC had heavy weapons. If the AFRC heard anyone listening to that station they would beat them but everyone was listening to it. They even killed some people for listening to it.

In November and December cargo planes were coming in all night reinforcing ECOMOG. They took the troops to Jui by boat and submarine. It was a big operation. Abacha spent a lot of money here to bring Kabbah back, which is why they renamed a street after him downtown. A lot of Nigerian soldiers were killed here to reinstall Kabbah.

The ECOMOG soldiers fought from Jui into town, with Orogo Bridge as the boundary between ECOMOG and the AFRC. There was a lot of fighting in the east end. That was the toughest time. For ECOMOG to cross Upgun (a roundabout in eastern Freetown) took three days. All the people ran away and some were killed. They went upcountry or came to the west end. ECOMOG told people to stay where they were, not to cross the street though some were shot looking for food and water.

ECOMOG captured the State House so the AFRC were mostly staying around the beach because they knew the central part of town was rough. They were thinking of how to pull out of the city. I was there with them. They organized to pull out and left from the west of town where most of the barracks were, in Murray Town and Wilberforce and Juba where the AFRC were with their relatives. They didn't put up any resistance because the State House was taken, and they left down the Peninsula Road to Tombo at the bottom of the peninsula. They parked their vehicles there and took boats to the far coast. They left a lot of guns and bombs.

When they were leaving some of my rebel friends came to my house to ask me to go with them. My father talked to them while I stayed under the bed. These were guys from the country. They couldn't even speak Krio. They used to come to my gym and I said I would go to Kailahun and teach everyone to work out so they could have big muscles. Now they wanted me to go but I'm a city boy and I know my way around here.

Lumley Beach

ECOMOG in Charge

ECOMOG controlled the city and they called everybody to the Police Station in Aberdeen to address us. I saw Maxwell Khobe live. He looked like Foday Sankoh—fat and bald with a fair complexion. He told us to turn over any soldiers in our houses even if they were our brothers or sisters.

However there were more problems than before with ECOMOG controlling the city, especially for young men like me. We had to take off our clothes and they inspected us to look for boot marks or to see a mark on our shoulders from a rifle, or a mark on your finger from shooting a gun. Some guys were killed from these marks, wound marks or tattoos. Some guys took electric irons to cover their tattoos because they could be killed if ECOMOG saw them. For a year I just stayed at Aberdeen. My boss, Mr Macauley, told me to go for my salary but I didn't have an ID card and couldn't cross the bridge at Aberdeen or they would kill me. I looked like a soldier because I was doing physical training.

ECOMOG were catching boys they thought were collaborators and killing them. The ECOMOG commander called a meeting in Aberdeen and said that if he heard a gunshot in Aberdeen he would kill all the boys from the smallest to the biggest. They asked for ID cards and killed you if you didn't have one. A lot of people were killed at Aberdeen Bridge and Lumley Beach and at Lumley, Murray Town and Aberdeen Road. If you went down Lumley Beach Road you could see bodies all down the beach.

ECOMOG caught a lot of guys in Freetown and brought them to the beach to kill. They were tied with their hands behind their backs. The boys would shout "I'm not a rebel" but they would push them down on the ground and shoot them. A lot of people were killed because they resembled others or because others said something about them because of rivalry or jealousy. If someone told ECOMOG you were a soldier they would just catch you and take you to their camp. I saw a lot of dead bodies in the river that floated back to the beach. Nobody walked on the beach then or played football there. If you went to play football they would ask "How can you be glad when we're being killed?"

They knocked on doors and threatened to shoot the door if they didn't open. Inside they looked for young guys and told them to go out. When they took you out your parents would never see you again. They took a lot of young guys out in front of their parents. Once they took an old woman's only son and killed him. The woman went to ECOMOG and told them to kill her because they had killed her only son. She followed the ECOMOG soldiers anywhere and told them to kill her. At Aberdeen Bridge a man saw the boy's ghost at night.

We were all in trouble. We were all Sierra Leoneans and ECOMOG could see any of us as rebels. We could be punished and beaten. We even joked with each other when ECOMOG would beat guys in our area. I stayed on the street until one or two o'clock but they couldn't catch me because it was my area. The curfew was 3 PM to 6 AM but I couldn't follow it so they chased me.

One ECOMOG was named Evil Spirit. He was a twin. The AFRC had captured his twin and removed the skin from his palms and soles of his feet. They didn't kill him but he went back to Nigeria for treatment. After that time his brother was Evil Spirit. He killed hundreds of people and went out and hunted people to kill. No one in ECOMOG would stop him for fear. He had a group of

Aberdeen Bridge, connecting Freetown and Cape Sierra Leone

over ten security with him and no one could stop them. I always passed another way when he was around. He was a wicked guy. The worst in the western area.

January 6th Invasion

One month was fast month and my father forced all of us to fast. He woke us up to eat at four or five o'clock. My father told me to go and call a neighbor, a police officer, to eat with us. He was a man who always listened to the radio when he slept. I knocked: kong-kong-kong—"Mr Kanneh." He said "You came to wake me and you don't know what is happening?" I said "My father told me to call you."

We went and he asked my father "You don't know what is happening?" The AFRC had come back to town and already broken down Pademba Road. All the prisoners were freed. We ate fast and he went home. Nobody went to the mosque to pray. We all prayed at home that day. My father wouldn't let us go out.

A few days before I had a dream that I was going down the beach and some soldiers came behind me in three trucks. I called them "We are with you" but they said "You say you're with us but you go into the jungle and kill our brothers. We will come and treat the people in Freetown." I told my father about the dream but he didn't believe me, and that morning we heard they had come. My father said "My son told me this before." From then there was bombing, burning houses, and killing.

Narratives

When the AFRC left the first time (during the Intervention) people were pointing out AFRC collaborators. They were burning people, even big imams and alhajis, putting a tire around their necks and burning them. Even a big businessman they stripped naked and burned him for supporting the AFRC. So when the AFRC came back the second time (the attack on Freetown) they revenged on the people who killed their supporters and relatives.

They came early in the morning and started burning houses. They got information about those who killed their collaborators and retaliated against them. They opened the prison and gave guns to the prisoners. The whole east side was a problem, but ECMOG still controlled the west side from Congo Cross Bridge near the stadium up the hill to Wilberforce. But all of Kissy, King Tom, and the east was AFRC. ECOMOG finally drove them out of Freetown after a lot of fighting.

After that President Kabbah came back and the AFRC and RUF were in the provinces fighting each other. After that things were more normal in Freetown and we settled down. There was the problem with Foday Sankoh launching his political party, called RUFP. I was at their launching party at the Silver Wings on the beach. I saw Foday Sankoh live. After that people got fed up with Foday Sankoh and said "Enough is enough". All the time he was changing the things he said. They went to his house on Spur Road to demonstrate and forced themselves on him. Many were shot when they tried to capture him. His security shot many of them, but there were a lot of people there.

It's hard to forget about the war. It's still affecting people. So many breadwinners lost their lives and their families are suffering. A lot of women have children with no father to help them. For me, it only affected me because of my father. He didn't send me to school because he wanted to build a house in the village and have sheep, goats, and cows. He built the house instead of sending me to school, then the rebels came and burned the house and chopped (ate) all the sheep and goats. Now in the village we have nothing.

2. Heavy D
He was a Good Leader
RUF

Heavy D became a committed RUF fighter early in the war. He was present at, and gives his own interpretation of, major events including the RUF joining the AFRC in Freetown after the 1997 coup, the Intervention in 1998, and the attacks on Kono, Makeni, and Freetown. He was a bodyguard and driver for Foday Sankoh and was present at the taking of peacekeepers in Makeni and the demonstration at Sankoh's lodge in Freetown on May 8, 2000 which led to his arrest, along with Sankoh's. Heavy D refers to AFRC soldiers as juntas or SLA (Sierra Leone Army) juntas.

I was a Sierra Leone Army soldier and was captured by the rebels in the Kono axis. I was a young boy and it was during the first big attack on Kono. When we were captured the rebels had us carry loads and mine for them.

One day we were mining when General Mosquito called our group back to Kailahun, so we carried our loads and left the Kono axis back to Kailahun. From Kono to Sandaru, to Sengema, we crossed the Moa River to Giehun and we came right inside Kailahun. From there we were taken down to Buedu where Mosquito had his base.

We were introduced into the camp then taken to training. I was trained at Bunumbu Camp Lion, Foday Sankoh's base. This isn't Bunumbu where the college is, but up in Kailahun District near Dia Junction. The training instructor there was Mattia—I can still remember his name. He too was a captive when the RUF attacked Kono and was a government soldier. The rebels didn't kill him but used him to train other rebels because of his military background. Foday Sankoh said that when they captured government soldiers they should give them the RUF ideology and advanced guerrilla training so they would know much about the bush.

From 1993 to 1994 the Kamajors used to come to sabotage our missions. First they called themselves "Hindo-Hindo" (man-man) but when Kabbah took power they called themselves Kamajors. I saw the Tamaboros in 1993. They had magic but it couldn't withstand the sound of guns. After two hours of firing, birds will die if they are around because of the gas. If you have the sound of guns for three hours the honeybees will get tired and run away. (Tamaboros were known for their ability to change into birds and produce honeybees that attacked enemies.)

We used to go to Voinjama (in Liberia) to buy shirts and trousers and other things. The rebels used to wear jeans, combat shirts, and black boots. When we took long journeys we wore plastic sandals or slippers so we could move a long distance like seventy miles in a day. The whole place was bush and there was no place to sleep so we traveled day and night. There were Kamajors around and if you were alone you couldn't resist them.

We did advanced training until 1996 when Sankoh went for the first peace talks in Yamoussoukro. He was with Tom (Nyuma), Maada Bio, and high authorities from the country. He left the command to General Mosquito. Mosquito deputized Issa Sesay, Morris Kallon, Augustine Gbao, and Mike Lamin. These were the senior authorities in the RUF movement.

Narratives

In Freetown with the AFRC

I was fighting in small villages until 1997 when the AFRC took power and we came together with them. The AFRC junta called us from the bush. We were on the Kono Highway then with Col. Issac. It was by Masingbi, Matoi, Makalie, Owaka, Walehun, Koekoe, Fomaya. We were attacking these areas while we were based at Kangayehe back of Makong (in the Malal Hills) in Tonkolili District.

We were there when the AFRC junta called for peace (asked the RUF to join them) and we entered into Freetown. We were just soldiers and took orders from our bosses. We were with the head of state, Johnny Paul Koroma. We were called to join them and were part of the government working with Johnny Paul. We were Mosquito's men and at that time Mosquito and Johnny Paul shared power. Foday Sankoh was in detention in Nigeria.

In Freetown we fought the ECOMOG soldiers. We were sent to Hastings and fought there, we went and fought at Bintumani (the attack on the Mammy Yoko Hotel where foreigners were being evacuated). We arrested 315 Ogas and put them in Tata buses, the government buses, and took them to Cockerill (Army Headquarters) and then to Wilberforce to the main Head of State who was Johnny Paul. He addressed the ECOMOG soldiers and told us this was peace time. He said we would release them but under good terms.

We handed over the ECOMOG soldiers at Hastings where they had their base, though some of the RUF didn't agree to the peace terms and wanted to be able to pass freely through the Freetown-Waterloo axis. This was because each time we passed there, ECOMOG would tell us to disarm. Mosquito said if these were the terms it was not peace, so we started using the peninsula route to Freetown.

So we fought in Freetown because we didn't agree to ECOMOG's terms. Later the Intervention attacked us and drove us out of Freetown. We went through the peninsula to Tombo where the people didn't want to give us boats to cross while the Intervention was attacking us. The Intervention was so heavy—jets, air gunships, cannons, and heavy cannons from Lungi, Ferry Junction, and Cockerill shelling against us. They used jets on us, so we ran and left Freetown by the peninsula bypass and reached Tombo. When the people refused to give us boats we sacked the town to get engines to put on the boats to cross. We were mixed RUF and junta soldiers.

So we crossed in the boats and we all met at Masiaka and moved to Makeni where ECOMOG attacked us again and we withdrew. From there ECOMOG chased us to Kono where we wanted to destroy the bridge on the Sewa River at Sewafe. We had a machine which was damaging the road and we wanted to use it to scrap the bridge. But as time went on, our authorities said we shouldn't damage the bridge because this was our country.

Operation No Living Thing happened because there was no pay for the soldiers, there was no food for the soldiers, so Johnny Paul said we had to take up Operation No Living Thing because ECOMOG tried to push us and oppress us. There was nowhere for us to go. If we went anywhere we heard guns. If we went that way there was a gunship. That's why Mosquito said we were under pressure and we had to take up a jungle—Operation No Living Thing. But you can't do that. I'm a living thing and I can't kill any innocent person but only that I would find a way to make myself reliant. That's why we said this jungle was a self-reliant struggle.

At the Sewa River we didn't destroy the bridge and they crossed and attacked us in Kono. I was in Kono when they burned Koidu town. It was because of suppression by ECOMOG. When we were retreating we made a "maximum of designing" to show them that we were there, that we are the Sierra Leoneans and they are just ordinary Nigerians. We gave orders to our small little boys to set fire so ECOMOG wouldn't have any place. We did things to show signs and to tell ECOMOG we were serious. So that was the maximum of designing.

View from the Sewa River Bridge near Njaiama Sewafe in the dry season, Kono District

We went back into the bush and moved through Kono, over the Moa River, and into Kailahun. There we regrouped to take up a fresh jungle (begin new attacks) to come back to Kono, Makeni, and Freetown. The authorities were in Kailahun town and we acted as security for them to guard their positions.

So we returned to Kailahun and while we were having a meeting in Kailahun town we heard on our radio set that ECOMOG had sent a jet. They shelled us, destroying houses and using cluster bombs. There were a lot of casualties. Some people lost limbs. We still resisted and took the injured men to Buedu.

Attacking Kono, Makeni, and Freetown
Before we started attacking Kono, Mosquito went to Libya to get us heavy support because ECOMOG at that time had modern support weapons, so we weren't able to stand there like that. He got support so we could capture Kono. There were more ECOMOG in Kono than in any other place in the country.

At that time we had the south, east, and north jungles for the RUF and SLA junta soldiers. South was Kono, east was Kailahun, and north was Makeni and Kabala. The war didn't penetrate much into the south of the country. We were concentrated in the middle of the north on the highway and the highway to Freetown. (They didn't penetrate the Southern Province because the Kamajors controlled it.)

We regrouped in Kailahun and started moving back to Freetown. We started attacking Kono first. The commander of the mission was Col. Akim. In Kono we captured the ECOMOG base at Five-Five (a place in Koidu town) and captured arms. Before the attack we sent Morris Kallon to set up a long ambush in Ngo Town (on the highway in between Koidu and Makeni) so when we ambushed ECOMOG at Five-Five they would retreat towards Makeni and be ambushed there. He would allow the ECOMOG convoy to go right into the ambush. I was there. We ambushed them, killed some, captured some, some escaped, and we took most of their armaments. The ones we captured live we took to Kailahun, around sixteen of them.

I didn't use any magic except that I have wounds on my head and arms from gunshots. The first was when we captured Kono, a bullet hit me as we were advancing. One of my friends who had an RPG launcher was shot dead by a Nigerian Oga who saw him when we were trying to bypass them to attack their position. After he was shot, we opened fire. The ECOMOG was staying up on a hill and we were below in a swamp crawling on the ground. A lot of our men got killed. This mission was led by Akim. We called him "War Tank" because he was the only guy who could crawl towards a war tank. He could attack an armored car face to face and arrest the drivers.

We went to Makeni first before attacking Freetown. In Makeni we drove out ECOMOG and captured six armored cars. The commander of this mission was Col. Akim. With the arms from Kono and Makeni we had enough arms to attack Tongo, and after taking Tongo we were the operational group in the jungle. When we captured a place we called other RUF to go and stay there while we moved to other places.

We made a jungle from Kono to Makeni but in Makeni a conflict rose between Issa and Superman. From defense headquarters in Buedu Mosquito told Superman to tell SAJ Musa not to give any orders in the northern jungle (not to carry out his own attack on Freetown) but when Superman went to Makeni he joined SAJ Musa's group. Later Mosquito ordered Issa to arrest Superman and this was how the conflict started when they sent Issa to arrest Superman.

Mosquito gave half of the RUF to the Northern Junglers to go to Freetown, a full squad to join the juntas to attack Freetown. I was included. Mosquito said to take up our jungle at Masiaka (meet in Masiaka to make the attack). From there we moved to Songo where we fell into an ambush with jets and had a lot of casualties. We went ahead to attack Benguema. Our group was led by SAJ Musa. He led the operation and was killed there.

SAJ Musa was an ordinary man to the revolution. They called him from overseas to join the revolution. Johnny Paul and the juntas called him as an advisor, so he didn't have any position except that he had been an authority in the NPRC. As we started reaching Benguema they started saying they would capture Freetown. SAJ Musa was in a different faction and went ahead. Because he was ahead of them and wanted to take up the power, they killed him. He was trying to rush ahead. (Most people believe that SAJ Musa was killed in an accidental explosion.)

We entered Freetown and came around Pademba Road to open it. That was J-6. On J-5 we were still in the eastern part of Freetown, around Calaba Town. On J-6 early in the morning we met up at the prison area. We met there to wait until half past 4 to 5 to make an attack to open the prison.

We had one soldier we called Bulldoze. He could bulldoze any obstacle or ambush. Some people call me Heavy D because I carry support. I can carry heavy weapons, like HMG (heavy machine gun) and flame thrower 3 in 1.

We went to Pademba Road and there were some government soldiers who wanted to resist but we flushed them out. We launched an RPG bomb on the door and it opened. We went inside and shot padlocks on the doors and opened the whole of the prison and took the prisoners to the State House. We released them because most of them were members of the movement who were captured during the Intervention by ECOMOG. All the juntas and

Narratives

RUF got out and some criminals. We made everybody free because it was war. Some of the prisoners took another route to go back to the government while some stayed with us. We were all over the area of central Freetown, like P-Zed (downtown) up to the stadium.

From there we tried to take up another jungle to Wilberforce (Military Barracks). We reached Wilberforce. At that time ECOMOG was there. They had taken all our people from the barracks hostage (families of AFRC soldiers staying at the barracks) and told them if their husbands or brothers were fighting us they would kill them all. We got information about the barracks from men and women we captured. They told us that if we attacked the barracks they would kill all our families. So we decided to withdraw. When we advanced we had many authorities like Bomblast and Bazzy. So Bazzy told us to withdraw. We withdrew and set up our security at the State House. ECOMOG started fighting us to flush us out so we withdrew to the eastern area, Calaba Town and then back to Waterloo (followed by their retreat to the north, Kono, and Kailahun).

Sankoh in the Government, Peacekeepers, and Spur Road

Foday Sankoh was released from prison in Nigeria and was back in Freetown in detention. Mosquito said that before peace could come he had to have a meeting with Sankoh. At that time the government was calling for ceasefire and peace. It was in June and July before they went for the peace talks. They released Sankoh and he took two helicopters to Kailahun. Around 3,000 armed men received them at the field and they sent us some footballs. He addressed us and the authorities and told us peace would come. They asked him how peace would come and he said he was on it.

When Foday Sankoh joined the government he said he wanted to be based in Freetown as RUF leader and Mosquito said to give him security if he didn't want to stay in Makeni at the headquarters. Skinny (Mosquito) said he would give him 3,000 armed men to secure him in Freetown. Sankoh said no, because the international community wouldn't allow so many armed men to stay in the city. So I was among the group Mosquito appointed to go to Freetown with Sankoh.

The RUF had a conflict with the West Side Boys. This was between the South, East, and Northern Junglers. Before the attack on Freetown Issa and Mosquito told SAJ Musa to stop activities in the northern jungle. They could no longer take patrols in the northern jungle, but they were still doing it. Issa Sesay set an example and shot three men because of that, for violence against people. He said this war wasn't for violence but we were fighting it for a purpose. We weren't fighting the war for killing innocent people or using innocent people.

The West Side Boys formed a faction after we split in Makeni. (This refers to AFRC leaders splitting from the RUF and moving to West Side Base nearer Freetown, attempting to rejoin the government.) So that was how the West Side formed. The conflict was between us and the northern group. The northern group started moving toward Lunsar with Superman and SAJ Musa (during the Freetown attack). Issa said, all those who turned to the West Side, we will fight you. If this is the way you are behaving we will attack you. After that Superman avoided the West Side movement.

After this conflict the RUF and junta separated. The juntas stayed in the Okra Hills (West Side Base) and started attacking people and government buses on the Okra Hill Highway. They said this area is their own area and the government will take care of us, not the RUF (meaning they would return to the army and support the elected government). At that time the RUF was fighting to get peace while the West Side was making another faction to fight. The RUF said this was a time for peace and nobody should attack another and not attack innocent people. Foday Kallay and Ibrahim Bazzy, Santigie Borbor Kanu, Gullit, Bomblast were the leaders of the West Side Boys.

I was in Makeni with Akim when the RUF arrested the Jordanian and Kenyan UN peacekeepers. Sankoh was working with the government and said the ECOMOG shouldn't disarm the RUF. They didn't trust them to disarm us because they used to fight us. They needed a neutral body to make peace, not the ECOMOG soldiers. (The peacekeepers weren't ECOMOG troops. ECOMOG had already left the country and a new peacekeeping force was doing disarmament.)

What led to the arrest of the Kenyans and Jordanians: there was a lady who was Morris Kallon's who fell in love with a Kenyan authority. She was a Sierra Leonean. One day Morris Kallon went to the authorities and met the woman, his wife, there. He asked her "What are you doing here?" and she couldn't give a good answer. From then fighting started between the RUF and the Kenyans in Makeni and Magburaka. Morris Kallon ordered the Kenyans back to Freetown. They started arresting them and taking their armored cars. Women are a big problem in war. Women can make plenty of men die in war or become injured. (It's more likely that Sankoh ordered the seizure of the peacekeepers.)

I was a real fighter at that time. I was with Foday Sankoh at 56 Spur Road in Freetown. I was with him until May 8th (2000) when they attacked us. I was with Foday Sankoh, I drove for him. I'm a black guy, I'm a good security to a leader. Foday Sankoh was a nice man, a friendly man, a good man and a good leader. Only that some of his people and politicians wanted to punish him to die. But we didn't want that. Foday Sankoh was a good leader because he was the one fighting for certain causes in the country. The problems that Foday Sankoh was fighting were: we don't need corruption, we need freedom of speech and we need a good ruler.

On Saturday May 6th the government told the people that we (the RUF) don't want peace. The government used people like the Women's Wing. They went to our residence (the women's demonstration on May 6th) and we told them we don't want to fight again. We want peace in the country, and the government tried to incite you to do things which are not too good. If you want to demonstrate you should do it peacefully. When you demonstrate with arms it means you want to destroy life. That brought the shooting on May 8th. When we told them on May 6th not to come again and throw stones and bottles and using arms. We told them not to do that.

They waited until Monday and came back. A big crowd came. "We are going to kill Sankoh." They said Sankoh didn't want peace. Our leader said we wouldn't fight to get power. If we fought again America or England wouldn't support us and we wanted to have an election, and that's why we formed the RUFP so we could have a party.

While I was staying with Foday Sankoh at Spur Road he gave us instructions to do disarmament. I stayed with Foday Sankoh until he was arrested. We were the ones who were charged along with him and taken to prison. They gave our leader a ninety-three count charge and indicted him to Special Court.

I was with him in prison from 2000. When the government started arresting us all the people started talking about us—"You were the causes of these problems" and nobody would talk for you again. No one would be able to talk for you because you are RUF or junta and all these other things they used to term us.

When they arrested us, people were glad and jubilated. They said the RUF and juntas were in prison. We were more than four hundred. Most of our junior boys died because they couldn't resist the prison conditions. There were doctors but no medicine. If you went to the doctor to complain they would just give us one tablet and say "You are the RUF. You are a fighter. You are the ones who destroyed the country." This was the malice we had in prison. I'm telling you. We suffered much.

The international world pleaded for us because we had support, and if we left prison with guns we would know how to do it again. The thing would start again. So the international world used to go and interview us in prison. Like the Red Cross. I have a paper from the Red Cross. I took five years in prison after the arrest of Sankoh. A Danish woman came to get information from us about prison conditions and I was the one who gave it to her. Pademba Road isn't good for human beings. Being there, I used to do exercises, jogging, and hard work. We were just from the jungle. We used to walk sixty, seventy, eighty miles a day so being under arrest we didn't take it for anything. We just took it as arrest, just like taking a rest.

Everything is Cool
Everything is cool now. There is no problem. People know me as an old fighter, an old rebel. People know me. Rebels are men who have a cane. It's a code for "gun". When you ask any old fighter if they know Heavy D they will know him. He was Foday Sankoh's security.

I was trained as a steel bender. I did it under the DDR program. I handed over my AK in Freetown. I was disarmed before I went in prison. Before that time I had a gun and who could control me or put me into prison? I had a gun. They just waited for us, after we gave them our guns they put us in prison.

At this present time in Sierra Leone the government is encouraging us, but we aren't feeling good. After fighting a ten or eleven-year war we are not able to receive the resettlement they promised us. They said they would build houses for us. We have a paper.

Many of us are on the streets and that's why problems are caused in the city. What they should give us they took it and own it themselves. You will make that guy disgruntled. So that guy is able to do any kind of bad thing to get something. Like we now, because our men are with the president we can keep ourselves cool. (President Koroma has former fighters as bodyguards.) Ask any person in the movement and they will give you the same answer, the same information. The only person who can give this information is someone who was involved in the war.

Nobody could stop the war because no justice came. If justice came everything would be finished. Even we who were fighting, we couldn't see justice. That's why the fighting was prolonged. Like the time Sankoh was in prison attending court (Sankoh's treason trial in 1998) and we were in the jungle. We said "If they don't leave Sankoh alone we will attack the city and do merciless destruction." So people would fear.

People knew Mosquito. When he said he would do something he would do it. He was the leader, the one who gave the instructions. He was second in command after Foday Sankoh. Only an international country like America could stop the war, but if it was the Sierra Leone government, we would flush

Narratives

them out! We would flush out all the sixteen intervention countries because I didn't believe them. Only an international country like America said "Go and stop your men." Finally George Bush told our leader to stop fighting and that is why we stopped. (Possibly referring to George W. Bush's phone call to Charles Taylor to step down.)

At this present time with my life I achieved some training and am now working in construction. I think if I didn't learn this job I would find myself doing something else. If I don't have I don't have. I have a job to sustain myself. I have two children, one two years and the other one year six months. I got married after everything was finished. Now I have two kids and I don't want any problems in our country again. Now we look up to our leader. He works with our men so I feel fine. I never argue or debate with people about the RUF. I just concentrate on my job. I see my RUF boys and they call me "Heavy-Heavy".

3. Samuel
   Freetown Attack
   AFRC Child Soldier

Samuel is from Kambia District. He was fifteen years old when the AFRC recruited him for their attack on Freetown, and he was trained at Rosos, a training base set up in the north after the Intervention. He took part in the January 6th invasion of Freetown and describes the attack from his own perspective.

After the AFRC/RUF were defeated in Freetown, he stayed in the Okra Hill area (West Side Base) and took part in fighting ECOMOG in Port Loko District. Samuel was fortunate to disarm before the West Side Base was attacked by British forces. He calls that attack the "British intervention".

I was born in 1983 and I'm twenty-nine years old. I was born in Kambia District, Madina village. I'm a Limba by tribe. I say thanks to God presently because some of my colleagues who joined the fighters with me have died.

What made me join them: in 1998 the SLA (AFRC) junta and RUF rebels came to burn our houses and kill our parents. They came from Kono together (after the Intervention) but split into different factions because they quarreled over arms and ammunition. At that time I was around fifteen years old and lived in the village. We wanted to fight them but some of our own brothers were among them. If you don't want to kill your own brothers what can you do? They wanted to burn the town and kill everybody, but those who were our brothers didn't allow it. They argued with each other that in Kono they agreed to destroy the villages but now others didn't want to do it when they moved to their own end. They said "Don't try us or we'll burn the village."

So they decided they should have boys from the village join them so they wouldn't destroy the area. My uncle came and told me this and I told him to go and give his own son to join, but by that time the news circulated all around the village and they took eight of us plus cows and chickens. When we were leaving I told the rebels I had an aunt in a village. We had already moved two or three villages and they asked when we would stop and see the aunt, but I told them I was just following them and we should go.

So I joined in with them and they trained us in Rosos. I was there three weeks—"cock and fire". Three of my colleagues ran away and hid and returned to the village. At that time I wasn't on good terms with my uncle and couldn't return so I decided to hold a weapon and if I died, I died.

Troops came to Rosos bringing SAJ Musa. SAJ Musa said we should head for Freetown and "Nothing will stop us" but first we had to go back and attack Kambia because we didn't have enough arms and ammunition. When we attacked Kambia we shouted "Woooooo—Wooooooo!" with loud voices and the Kamajors and others all ran away.

When returning, our team went to Mange first but ECOMOG soldiers were there and they attacked us at the bridge. We fought them like dogs. We captured the bridge and that was the only way to exit the town. We succeeded because we killed the guy who was using the anti-aircraft gun, so we relaxed for awhile.

At that time we had no food so we diverted from the route to Port Loko and took a bypass toward Makeni and Lunsar. We didn't travel on the highway but used the cleared path under the power lines that bring power from Bumbuna Dam to Freetown. We went to torment the ECOMOG because they were at our backs and we needed to clear it before heading to Freetown.

Death of SAJ Musa
We rehogged in Lunsar. A convoy came from Kambia with SAJ Musa's group and we decided to head to Freetown. We advanced to Masiaka and captured it then moved to the checkpoint at Mile 38. From there we took a bypass to Songo and Benguema. SAJ Musa addressed us and said he was happy they had captured the barracks where he was trained (Benguema was an army training base). He said he was fighting for his people. He was dressed with a military helmet on his head. We took some arms and decided to burn down the iron door (armory) and it was during that process that SAJ Musa was killed in an explosion.

After the explosion they took SAJ Musa to a hospital near the barracks. We saw a nurse coming down and asked her how he was and she said he was dead. I felt bad when I heard that because he was our leader. So some guys wanted to shout and cry and said they would disarm because our leader was dead. The first guy who started crying was shot in the foot by a rebel commander named Fifty. He said "Don't cry here." They didn't need noise in the jungle. At that time there was no cooking and we couldn't break banga (palm kernels) to eat because of the noise, because the ECOMOG jets were in operation and they were hunting us.

We buried SAJ Musa and after that everybody was hungry so we all ate banga. Even the colonels and brigadiers were eating it because we didn't have any food. We were there three days and on the third day the Kamajors attacked us in the daytime. We fought them and ran after them, chasing them up to Hastings and Jui.

After that we came back to our base at Benguema because the wives and children were there. At night we went up to Hastings to spy and saw the ECOMOG helicopters bringing in troops from Freetown. In the evening at around 6 PM we attacked them. We captured the place and took the arms and food and moved on. I was happy because I hadn't had food for a long time.

This was in early in January, before January 6th. We attempted to capture Kossoh Town but some went another direction through Allen Town and there weren't enough of us to capture it. We were repelled at the bridge by ECOMOG. At that time the jets were bombing us. We called them "wo-wo boy" (ugly boy). We retreated and followed the other group through Allen Town. We were chased back to a small village though I don't know the name of it, and people were poisoning rice to give to us and some of our colleagues died from eating it. They would cook food, poison it, and run away so if you saw it and ate it you died.

When we captured Nigerians and killed them we took their combat (uniforms) and wore them so other ECOMOG thought we were the same. Even twelve year old boys were wearing the ECOMOG combat. We returned back toward the Freetown highway and when we reached Hastings a rekky plane (reconnaissance plane) saw us and alerted the Nigerians at Lungi and they bombarded our position. There were casualties from the jets but usually we managed to take cover when they came. We knew the jets would take an hour to survey the area and drop bombs if they saw targets. We were trained how to maneuver from jets. If we were in an open area we would stand straight and still like a stick, only that you had to cover the barrel of your gun or other metal objects with your hand or your uniform so the jet couldn't pick it out. We knew how to fight jets!

That night I was sleeping and they stole one of the magazines from my AK-58 which I called "run-belly" ("diarrhea" meaning it fired continuously). People would come and take everything when you were sleeping. Some even sold stolen arms to barter for goods. Later I was woken up by my boss and told we would advance to Freetown but I didn't see my magazine, so I went and stole one from someone else.

Advance into Freetown
We advanced to Freetown and captured Kola Tree, Wellington, and Calaba Town. This was on January 4th. We moved into town and captured the ECOMOG checkpoint at Ferry Junction. There was heavy fighting at that point because it was where the ferry brought ECOMOG soldiers from Lungi. After that we moved to Upgun Turntable and there was heavy fighting there again. We were in the advance team moving with our bosses, Akim and Lion, and they said we should conquer the area.

At Upgun the group separated into two, one taking Kissy Road and the other Fourah Bay Road. We did this so they couldn't defeat us. We who took Kissy Road went by Mountain Cut to Pademba Road to free our brothers who were captured and locked up during the first invasion of Freetown (the Intervention). There were so many of us and we were so mixed up junta and RUF that we were killing each other.

When we arrived at the gate of the prison we used an AA and machine guns against the door but it didn't open. Two of our guys, Tito and Col. Pikin said to use an RPG. We shouted and told our guys inside the prison to lie on the ground. They heard us and were all set. I was there facing the door. In the end we succeeded in destroying the door and we told all the prisoners to come out. There were over 2,000 prisoners, both men and women, and we freed everyone. Some didn't join us but we didn't kill them. The government planned to kill most of our commandos who were locked in the prison and so they were glad when we freed them.

At that time we controlled Kissy, the State House, and Pademba Road and the government controlled the stadium area. We advanced to capture the stadium. Maxwell Khobe, the Nigerian Commander, didn't have control over the city and we were abusing his mother like a dog. After that we used a lot of our ammunition and didn't have support coming. Mosquito refused to send support because he thought SAJ Musa was trying to get power and he didn't know he was dead.

My initial boss was named Mitto. He was killed at the State House. He didn't like women. If he saw a woman he would kill her. He used to shoot people indiscriminately. When he was killed I was disgruntled because I didn't have a boss. At that time everybody was bloody. I had an axe and if I told someone to put his hand down, if he refused I would cut off his nose. In fact I was so hungry I could eat anybody's nose. If we saw a dog we shot it and put it on a fire because we couldn't pick what to eat. Dog meat is good, and we called dogs "town commandos" because they could sustain us in town.

The ECOMOG soldiers found out we were using axes to butcher people and we didn't have ammunition. At that time the Guinean soldiers had moved behind us into Freetown with a 40 barrel gun which they used to bombard us from the rear, and we were locked into Freetown. We decided to attack the 7th Battalion at Wellington by the Star Brewery to get weapons and ammunition but we couldn't get there because of the Guinean soldiers, so we had to take bush paths.

We took a bypass to Kola Tree and decided to go back to Waterloo where our commanders were. By then the RUF had left Makeni (referring to the reinforcements sent by Mosquito) and entered Waterloo and they took all the things and money we looted in Freetown. Mosquito's boys took all the things from us junta boys. They said we hadn't done anything—just rushed into Freetown and we didn't stay there. They took everything from us. We called it "counter-loot". Myself, I came from Freetown with a motor car and different things. I didn't drive it myself but I commandeered a driver to bring me. I ordered him to go anywhere I wanted.

West Side Boy
From Waterloo we received an order to retreat to Makeni but I refused and stayed with the group from Freetown. The jets were seriously bombarding us. Once I saw a jet drop a bomb that tore a small baby into two and wounded the mother. She asked me to give her water but, at that time, if you gave water to someone who was wounded they could die immediately.

In the SLA (AFRC) and RUF there were positions. I was a sergeant. Even a small boy could be a sergeant in charge of a small boys unit. They appointed me to the position and I had to accept it. The loyal army troops planned to attack and kill us though we thought they were with us. One morning they started shooting us with cannons and we retreated to the Okra Hill area and rehogged by the Rokel River (where the West Side Base was established). I was in the jungle with no protection from guns on my body and no ammunition. I only thank God for protection. I only have a mark on my back from an RPG fragment.

We cut off the road at Makolo on the highway (near Songo) so no armored car or military vehicle could come from Freetown. We dug the road to cut it off. We were in Makolo when a message came that Col. Kallay (Foday Kallay, who became leader of the West Side Boys) should go to Gbere Junction to attack the Oga and Kamajors there.

Waterloo

We went at night and saw lamps the Oga put to make us think there were troops in many places. We succeeded in taking the junction then moved to Port Loko to fight with Malian soldiers who were part of ECOMOG. When we attacked Port Loko they were firing while we advanced on them. I really admired our Sierra Leonean armed boys because we could advance and fire at the same time. We captured one Malian and gave him a heavy chop with a cutlass and that made others start surrendering. We brought them to the West Side.

Later they told us they wanted to come and talk peace. Caritas told the West Side to disarm the small boys and they would take care of them but Kallay thought it was wrong and captured the British Soldiers when they came to negotiate. We gave them food that they had never eaten and which they didn't like. Every morning we gave them a heavy flogging—50 lashes. The government wasn't happy how we were treating them so a message came that there would be an attack to release them.

I left at that time, before the British intervention, and I went to Lungi to surrender. A lot of Kallay's men did that. I disarmed with a 10-battery gun—a gun that took ten cartridges. We called it an American Chakabula. I went alone to surrender. I was lucky to leave then. Many of our boys died in the British intervention.

Narratives

4. Alfred
Brima Lane
Civilian

Alfred was in eastern Freetown during the January 6, 1999 invasion of the city.

I'm presently twenty-six years old, born in 1985. I was in Freetown when it was attacked by the AFRC and rebels in 1999. I was thirteen or fourteen years old, living in eastern Freetown in an area called Brima Lane. We were there when we heard that the rebels were fighting to enter Freetown. In the morning we heard they were at Four Mile. The fighting continued and soon after that they reached Waterloo. Later, one night we were sleeping and we heard people shouting and crying as they were escaping into the city to get away from Waterloo and Calaba Town. They were carrying bundles and other things, trying to get inside the city. We didn't move out of our house, though, because it was nighttime and our father wouldn't allow us to leave. It wasn't until early morning that we went outside.

We saw that a lot of people were killed. We saw bodies in the streets and a lot of burned-out cars that people were driving into the city. Myself, I saw one ECOMOG soldier at Texaco Junction who was dead, lying in the middle of the street. Someone had taken his boots off his feet. I saw one family who had all been killed—the parents and children were all dead. Some people were killed inside their vehicles. The area was very long, from Porty Junction up to Shell you saw dead bodies on the road. It was very frightening.

The rebels entered Freetown by putting their guns and ammunition inside bundles they were carrying, then putting the bundles on their heads like they were their possessions. They would cry like they were civilians escaping the rebels, and some acted like ECOMOG soldiers calling people out of their houses to move into the city. In that way they mixed with the civilians and when they reached inside the city they would start shooting and killing people.

So, we were still at Brima Lane in the morning. The situation was too serious because the rebels were entering houses. One time a rebel entered our compound and threatened to burn our house. We were inside and he broke the glass windows and hit the door, which was made of steel so he couldn't break it down. There were many people in our house, both family and neighbors. At that point another soldier called him and said they had to move on. The rebels were looting everything from houses, taking vehicles and also young girls. Getting food was difficult.

We moved to Ferry Junction and stayed in one church, St Martin's at Blackhall Road. When we were running there I saw the body of a man in the street on a traffic island where there was a statue. He was kneeling back against the statue and his hands were tied behind his back and he was shot in the chest. His body was swollen because he had been shot for some time.

At night the fighting went on. There were ECOMOG forces around and the rebels would attack at night to fight them. We and many other people were hiding in the back of the church. They didn't enter the church compound because it fronted the street and ECOMOG was guarding the area, so the rebels couldn't succeed in getting near us. When ECOMOG came we went out to greet them and gave them water.

We stayed in the church for a long time but I can't remember how many days. The Catholic mission was giving us food like beans, bulgur, corn flour, and oil. ECOMOG soldiers were around and the rebels were attacking. One night I remember the rebels attacked the area but in the morning it was calm. After the rebels left Freetown we returned to our house on Brima Lane.

Diamonds and Corruption

One effect of the war for me was that it was a real experience because Sierra Leoneans had never faced war before. The country was moving smoothly and people were just enjoying their lives. It created something different in people's minds. During and after the war people went to different places and saw different things so when they came back they started implementing the same things here. It created some different things in people's minds.

Some went overseas in refugee programs so they had opportunities come their way. Countries donated money and a lot of NGOs came to help fix things that were spoiled and develop the country. People now think of more advanced ways to develop the country than before.

I know about blood diamonds—I watched the movie. A lot of people came into the war and into the diamond business and everything became corrupt. I

Narratives

have to reason that basically it was because of the diamond business. Kono was destroyed more than other places because it is a diamond area. For me it was because of the mineral riches in the country.

5. Isata
   Victim
   Civilian

Isata was a victim of the January 6, 1999 attack on Freetown.

My name is Isata. I was sixteen years of age in 1999 when the rebels entered the city of Freetown and captured me. I was staying at Jui, a small village east of the city. When the attacks started I moved and stayed in one of the government quarters in Cline Town. At that time I was seven months pregnant.

That day the rebels advanced deep into town with heavy gun fire and the quarters where my husband and I stayed was surrounded by gunmen. I was captured, my husband killed in front of my eyes and the quarters set on fire. As the fighting intensified ECOMOG fired on the rebels' position and I was taken away by a gunman. All the rebels were fighting to escape ECOMOG. We were carried away by force. If you mentioned God's name they would kill you or threaten to kill you.

We did not sleep in Freetown the day I was captured. On our way the rebels spoke different Sierra Leonean languages—Mende, Temne, Limba and Krio. I don't know the persons who captured me. There were plenty of them. Some disguised their faces with black and blue ink that made it hard to recognize them.

From Freetown we walked to a crossing point in the north on a bush path. My feet got swollen and my wrist and fingers also got swollen. The rebels took me to Gbalamuya, a village in the northern district of Kambia bordering Guinea close to Pamalap. At the crossing point to Gbalamuya village we used a canoe.

At Gbalamuya I was tied with a rope to a tree with my legs opened wide. There were many gunmen in the village and they were killing a lot of people. Some came around me and argued about the sex of baby I had in my uterus. One took a bayonet knife and tore my vagina and belly. I screamed. He removed the baby and went off. They abandoned me while I was crying and I fell unconscious.

Some who escaped reported it to the Guinean soldiers and they came and took me to Donka Hospital in Conakry and I was hospitalized and operated on. After the operation I couldn't walk for over one and a half years.

Women who were not pregnant were sexually abused. For those who refused, sticks were inserted into their vaginas and exited via their mouths. At the hospital in Guinea a rubber was inserted into my stomach. This made me feel severe abdominal pain. I have not menstruated since that trauma I underwent. The most unfortunate thing is I have no child. The pregnancy they destroyed was my first. Even now I stay alone.

6. Mahmood
A Devil Incarnate
Civilian

Mahmood is from Bombali District in the north. He experienced the January 6th Freetown attack when he moved to Freetown to escape attacks in his home district.

I was born in 1972. When the war started I was at Milton Margai College and the first experience we had about it was when one of my friends left for

Kailahun and was captured. He missed the exams but luckily after some time he resurfaced. He had gone on holidays and when the RUF made their first attack he was there. So we clustered around him. It was strange. He was telling us stories that we never believed.

Some of us actually thought the war was necessary though we never knew the impact we would see. Most people shared the view that it was about time for a change, you know, when there was this one-party system. Things were just very bad. But there were mixed feelings about the attack. Those who had the real picture were not happy, but others who had not had a taste of it would say "Ah, it's better the guys make some progress."

In 1994 I left college and was recruited as a teacher in Gbendembu in Bombali District, about twenty-two miles from Makeni. We were hearing awful stories about attacks in the east and south, then in 1996 we heard that the rebels were in Bombali District and were heading for Gbendembu. We ran to the bush and spent some days there, and indeed they came. They killed three people and advanced to some neighboring towns. They burned some houses but that was not very serious.

I remember one thing that happened during the Kabbah election in 1996. I was an election officer. In the place where I was in charge a small boy just ran up and said the rebels were coming. Any time I heard the slightest rumor that these guys were coming I would always run. I ran to the bush and I got myself messed up in the mud, only to realize it was not true. With my white election T-shirt—I was pretty ashamed that the election officer was covered with mud. A small girl had to find me another T-shirt and I had to go for a bath.

So sometimes, the slightest rumor—if it is a lie it's better I go to the bush and come back than to be caught and slaughtered or amputated. There was a woman called Adama Cut Hand, the commander, the lady in charge of the flank that amputated people. She was the one who cut off people's hands. When we learned that she was coming I sent my wife and family to Freetown and I went to Makeni. At that time both the government soldiers and Kamajors were defending us. The Kamajors were mostly in the east and south but sometimes when the rebels were concentrated in one place they would come to support.

Makeni and Freetown

In Makeni there were a lot of killings. Sometimes somebody could just say "This one is a rebel" and anyone could just execute the person without much investigation. It was very difficult to verify the authenticity of the accusation so there were just killings here and there. A summary execution was when you had a good number of suspected people and lined them up and killed

Downtown Makeni

them. Once I saw three people killed. Some people said they were rebels, that they saw them when they attacked their village. Actually these were difficult situations. Sometimes the rebels could come to Makeni township to spy, to find out the security situation, get food, then link back with the rebels at their bases. The only trouble was, sometimes innocent people could be accused and killed.

I saw that Makeni wasn't safe and I went to Freetown in 1998 and enrolled at Njala University (the university had moved to Freetown after the attack on its campus in the south in 1995). During our first term exams the biggest attack on Freetown took place. I was staying in Kissy and was alone in my room reading when we heard gunshots. We were worried but somebody said "Don't worry. It's the ECOMOG trying to assert their authority." But then we found ourselves surrounded by rebels.

I wanted to run, to go to my family, but a pastor advised me not to venture out and it was actually good that I listened to his advice. Three ladies who left, who I wanted to travel with, were killed. It took me some time to leave Kissy and go to my sister's house at Crook Street. There was a lot of risk running to the house but it was good that we were all there because the house was set on fire three times. If we had not been there it could have burned down. I was there with the children and my sister's children and other family members. My wife wasn't there. She had traveled to the village and was trapped. She couldn't travel back to Freetown.

We realized that the house was not safe because there were constant threats, and they were in particular looking out for young men to help in the war so some of us decided to go to a nearby mosque. The mosque was called Temne Mosque. We thought they would spare the mosque but we were not spared. The imam there was imprisoned once by the government as a rebel collaborator so sometimes he came around to tell the rebels not to hurt us. Sometimes they had sympathy for him but he had to be there constantly. If he wasn't there they could come and something terrible might happen.

They kept raiding constantly. The rebels warned us to be quiet because we were in their own area of operation as they were being pushed by ECOMOG, but in a place with hundreds of people you can't be certain of quietness so they killed three people to make sure we knew they meant quietness when they said quietness. So I was there with my children until finally ECOMOG flushed them out.

After the Kamajors and ECOMOG took over Freetown there were accusations and counter-accusations. I left my house once to see if something had happened to my brother, but on my way back some ECOMOG guys confronted me. I was lucky I had my university identity card, otherwise they were going to kill me. So from then on I decided to stay put because that was a warning these were dangerous times. When you went to Connaught Hospital you saw corpses left in the open being eaten by dogs, vultures, and rats. They had open trucks they used to gather corpses and deposit them by the hospital so when you got close to the place it smelled so much. I saw that thing myself. These were people suspected of being rebels, that kind of thing.

Living by Chance
The war went on and on. It was a question of you not knowing when to die. It was a question that life was, like, you are living by chance. You live today, nothing happens to you, you have to say thanks to God. You don't even know. It came to the point that some of us were not afraid of death again because death was in evidence everywhere you went.

During the war people sometimes took the risk to travel to do business. If you were lucky the road was clear and you could travel quickly. Life had to go on. People had to find a means to make money, and if you were willing to risk it to go to the villages and bring back food you could make more money. People took the risk and a lot of them got killed. There were rebels on the main highway between Freetown and Masiaka and a lot of other places. The attackers were moving all the time. Sometimes they would just come around a place without you knowing. You would be thinking this place was safe until one or two vehicles were ambushed and people killed.

When you turned on the radio you heard foreign countries condemning the war but we didn't see them taking sides or coming to help us. Particularly England, we had the hope that they would come to help us but it was only later when the rebels were flushed out of Freetown and the West Side Guys wanted to create another problem that we saw them in action. They finally came and they actually helped to put a total end to the war. But they came so late!

Foday Sankoh, to me, was a devil incarnate. The RUF started all the violence against civilians because they weren't able to take over power and the only way they could make people realize they were a force to reckon with was to attack innocent civilians because they were the people they could easily reach. You cannot leave Kailahun and come to Freetown so easily to attack the government. The only way they could send their message was to create mayhem as they did, on innocent people.

About child soldiers: to me, when you empower children to do anything they have nothing to be afraid of. The children were more terrible. You give them guns and they can do things an adult may be afraid to do. They don't have responsibilities. When I was in the bush if I saw a small boy with a gun I would make sure I distanced myself. Children are not afraid. They could do anything. They could penetrate any security.

It's possible that the idea to use child soldiers came from Liberia. There were interactions between Liberia and Sierra Leone. The war itself emanated from Liberia, so the techniques used in Sierra Leone may not have been different from those in Liberia. And using children makes an outcry. They always did things that people condemned so the international community would listen to them.

I remember Charles Taylor's first interview when the war was in Liberia and they asked him if he had the intention of coming to Sierra Leone. He said it was anybody's guess, and indeed we had war here. So to me it was like Charles Taylor wanted to create a system where Sierra Leone was going to be governed by rebels, Guinean rebels, Liberian rebels, everywhere within the West African sub-region. He wanted revolution in Africa, particularly West Africa, particularly those countries he could control.

I remember in our own situation here sometimes Charles Taylor gave them direct orders. He talked to Mosquito directly when certain things happened and they listened to him. So it was actually like he was in charge. I remember when I listened to the BBC we heard that Charles Taylor was going to tell these guys not to burn houses and that kind of thing when they attacked Freetown.

Where were the rebels getting their supplies? Some say government forces gave them supplies. And this diamond thing, we learned that diamonds were sent to Charles Taylor and he got weapons and sent them through Liberia to Sierra Leone.

The effects on society were many. Everything came to a standstill. A good number of children could no longer go to school. During the war parents wouldn't let their children go to school so education was at a standstill, particularly in the provinces. You couldn't let them walk to school. Anything could happen, so we had to make sure that if there was an attack you had your children around and you could find a safe place.

Society got to a place where the thing we call trust among ourselves was highly questionable. Sometimes we accused ladies of being rebel collaborators. They would go to the rebels to do business. There was trade going on and when you saw somebody moving—he goes to Bo and comes, he goes to Mile 91 and comes—you would be quick to say he was a collaborator. Maybe he had some link with the rebels. These are people who supply them with arms, these are the people who give them food, that kind of thing. Little to wonder then, that when the rebels were flushed out some people were accused as collaborators and killed.

Agriculture went down because sometimes when you farmed you didn't even harvest because the rebels would just come and take everything. People were dying in the bush of starvation. Imagine if you leave your house and go to the bush with all the wild animals and snakes and no good food. If you are sick you will not have medical facilities. If you got sick and were in the bush for two weeks, I mean, you died.

Reconciliation
Generally from the experiences people got from the war I have seen that absolutely no one wants to see this situation happen again. Therefore to me the concept of forgiving one another is being realized. The war gave everybody a bitter experience. War is not good. Those of us that went through it, anything that entertains war, I wonder if there is any Sierra Leonean who will entertain that again. You have some youths who will spark up political violence but it is very easy to quiet them down. You talk to them, and when talking to them you make reference to the war.

The reconciliation is working perfectly well. Yesterday I was told of one youth around us who was known to be a rebel commando but people don't even talk about that these days. Actually we are very forgiving and these people are reintegrated. I think we are working well with them. Sierra Leoneans are very peaceful, so to me it is that tendency of being peaceful that is the driving force behind forgiving one another.

This does not mean the perpetrators are not within our midst but normally we don't know them as perpetrators. We interact with them. People are trying to forget about the war unless you want assistance somewhere, for project funding, I mean "We've gone through this", that kind of thing so that you can get help. But generally people are putting the war behind them. When it comes to real, individual business we hardly talk about war. We now talk about development. Sierra Leoneans are involved in work, education, getting food and daily life. That is Sierra Leone.

7. Kaiku
They Were Against Us
AFRC Child Soldier

Kaiku is from Koinadugu District. His story takes place late in the war, from the Intervention through the attack on Freetown to disarmament. Kaiku joined his AFRC Limba brothers in the bush after the Intervention when ECOMOG was in control of the main northern towns. He explains the war from the AFRC point of view, including their reasons for continuing to fight ECOMOG after the Intervention and why they committed atrocities while moving to attack Freetown. Kaiku was in Makeni in October 1999 when the RUF forced the AFRC out of the town, and he demobilized after that incident. He refers to the AFRC as the "junta".

Presently I'm twenty-nine years old. I am a Limba by tribe. I was nine years old when the war started and was living in Mokanje (Moyamba District). One day I had trouble with my father so I left home and went to a village called Levuma and was there when the rebels attacked. Somebody saved me and brought me back to Mokanje. That caused my father to take us to our home in Fadugu in Koinadugu District and we were there for five years. In that area there are three major tribes: the Limba, the Mandingos and the Fullahs, but the Limbas are the majority. We were in Fadugu when the rebels captured it. There was nowhere to go so we just stayed there.

When the AFRC came to power in 1997 most of our Limba brothers were government soldiers and supported the junta. After being scattered by ECOMOG (in the Intervention) our brothers rehogged in the bush. Most of the Limba thugs came from our area because almost none of them went to school, so when ECOMOG came into the town most of our brothers didn't support them, but tribalism came in and people pointed out the houses to ECOMOG where there were Limba juntas staying.

ECOMOG would do away with anyone they saw in those houses whether it was a child or an old grandmother. We knew where our brothers were in the bush and we were in constant communication with them, and we decided to go to the bush and join them because of pressure from ECOMOG, though some people stayed in the town.

Living and Fighting
We had local people staying with us and we would send them to the bush to get bush yams and bananas. We also had local people make farms for us. All the towns under our command had to contribute to our food. We were the government of the area. If they didn't pay we would raid them and take away everything. When they paid we would give them a slip and any time a junta soldier came to the village they would show them the slip and the soldier would move on to another village.

We slept by guard duty. We would sleep for two hours then change guard. We had some laws, for example, if you fell asleep and they were able to take your gun from you they would kill you. It would cost you your life, so we always slept holding our guns. Colleagues would steal guns from each other if you were careless. If someone stole your bullets you would also have a problem. They would beat you for losing your rounds. While you were sleeping someone could even take the magazine out of your gun, steal the bullets, then put the magazine back.

They had weapons inspection during morning parade. If something was missing they would take action. In the parade anyone who committed a crime would be called out and given work to do. Every day they told us why we were fighting. They would also repeat and reaffirm the laws every day which is why they gave no one mercy. During the parade we prayed and they had both pastors and imams. We sang the Sierra Leone National Anthem because we were AFRC junta, not rebels. At six in the morning they raised the Sierra Leone flag and at six in the evening they lowered it. No one could move when they were lowering it. The flag was more honored at that time than it is now.

What brought the war? According to what they used to tell us, some said it was because of tribalism. Others said they wanted to change the nation, which is why the RUF was fighting. The AFRC junta went into the bush because they were disowned by the government. We were the government army, appointed since colonial days, so we felt they couldn't just disown us like that and we had to fight for our rights. The government was siding with the Kamajors against us. When we went to fight we were dying because of lack of support while the Kamajors were succeeding because they were supplied with arms. This gave us the cause to stay in the bush. The world didn't know our problems, that we were the Sierra Leonian soldiers who were condemned after Kabbah came back, so this led us to keep fighting as the junta. They sent a lot of Kamajor and ECOMOG soldiers against us.

We were torturing people because it was a method of making the government afraid of us. We thought the government would stop the war because we were torturing a lot of people. Especially when ECOMOG bombed our positions and killed a lot of our soldiers we would do a lot of torture so they would be afraid of us.

Raping took place in the bush but if it was reported to headquarters and they caught you they would kill you. They killed a lot of men in front of me. Other punishments were "fifty cuts", another they shot you on your hand and another they shot you on your foot. In another one they would beat you to death. I've seen all these punishments carried out in Kamabai. There was a guy known as Mustapha who stole chickens from a village that had already paid us and he was reported to headquarters. He killed one of his colleagues who reported him so he was beaten to death and it was done in front of me.

At times there would be a shortage of ammunition and we would raid the Guinea border posts, killing their soldiers and taking their ammunition and food. In this type of operation everyone had to be involved regardless of your rank.

The ECOMOG soldiers were chasing people in the bush and killing them so our brothers decided to retaliate because it was our land and we couldn't sit back and see that going on. This led the brothers to have the first attack on Kabala led by SAJ Musa, because that was where ECOMOG was based. This is what was called the First Portfolio of SAJ Musa to Kabala.

In Kabala some renegade soldiers (loyal to the government) had joined ECOMOG so it wasn't easy. We attacked but it was difficult because of the support they had from other Sierra Leonian soldiers and we couldn't take the town so we retreated back to our bases in the bush. We decided to go back to Fadugu and we attacked it and succeeded in taking it over from ECOMOG. When we were there ECOMOG sent jets to bomb our positions and the elders took a decision that whatever happened, it would bring us together and we would all fight against ECOMOG.

Attack on Freetown, Infighting, and Disarmament
We used our communications to call our soldiers back to Fadugu. The bosses there were Five-Five, Wudits, and SAJ Musa. We agreed that they shouldn't bring an army from another country to overtake us and that we should go to Freetown to fight against them if necessary. Whatever was going to happen,

Narratives

Shops in Kabala

let it happen, and this gave us a cause to take the city jungle (a reason to attack Freetown). Since the pressure from ECOMOG was coming from Freetown we decided to go there and overrun them to lessen the pressure. This was in late 1998.

As we moved to the city we collected other fighters, but things changed as we moved because people started amputating hands, especially on the Temne line to Freetown. During this jungle our way was blocked by ECOMOG and they killed a lot of our brothers which led to the amputations to send a message that we were coming. We decided to recruit anyone on the way to increase our numbers. If they refused we would do anything to them to send a message to Pa Kabbah. We also padlocked peoples' mouths, sealed their mouths, or cut their mouths off. This made ECOMOG fear us which caused them to retreat to the city.

When we reached Freetown we faced a big obstacle from ECOMOG which made us retreat. After that I was sent to the northern jungle again. I was with a commander called Mr Savage or Mr Die. Later I saw this man in prison when I worked as a prison officer and now he has been released. During the war he controlled the entire Koinadugu District. Five-Five, Jegeh, and Komba Gbondema were in charge of Bombali District. Peleto, who was a rebel, Superman, and some junta soldiers were in charge of Magburaka up to Lunsar.

The UN called representatives of all the rebels in the bush for a meeting in Makeni. I was there with an adjutant named Viper who is now dead. I was with him because I had completed Form 1 and could write. I was responsible for writing reports and filing them.

That day Foday Sankoh and big men from other countries were there for the negotiations. The UN told them they wanted the war to come to an end. They talked by turn, and some of them said they were tired of fighting and wanted to end the war. They asked the child soldiers which of us wanted to go to school and some of us raised our hands, but some of our senior colleagues said the UN just wanted to capture us and take us to prison in Freetown.

Johnny Paul agreed to end the war and this brought infighting between the junta soldiers and the rebels. What really brought the infighting was that, when the junta agreed to stop fighting, the RUF thought the UN would give the junta weapons to fight them. So Johnny Paul and his men agreed with the UN to leave the bush but Foday Sankoh didn't agree. Foday Sankoh formed his own group to hunt and kill the junta soldiers. I was with the junta and we fought the rebels for three days in Makeni. The rebels wanted to kill Johnny Paul and Koneh Mani, the advisor to Johnny Paul and the Chief of Staff.

The fighting stopped in Makeni and Johnny Paul and his men met with the UN in Kabala. I went with them and we took all our weapons in case they attacked us. In Kabala the UN told us that we were government soldiers so we didn't have to surrender and that they would help us by teaching us skills and sending the children to school. Some agreed to this and others didn't.

There were around two hundred in the first group who agreed and we were taken by helicopter to Lungi in three trips. From there we were taken to Lakka Beach in Freetown, though the place wasn't decent so we started making rudeness, so they split us up and our group of eighteen was taken to Lumley near the Police Station.

Caritas made a place for us to go to school. However, because my parents were living in Freetown they told me to stay with them. Caritas paid for us until I sat to the WASSCE (end of secondary school examination). After that they wouldn't give me any more support. To me it was because Johnny Paul ran away to Liberia so he wasn't there to support us with the UN.

I hadn't seen my father since I went with the junta. When the war ended everyone I knew was glad for me. In the war I learned a lot of things. I'm disciplined though this doesn't mean I'm not wild, but I can only be wild if I'm provoked.

Narratives

8. Edward
Trying to Seize Power
Civilian

Edward is from Kambia District. He describes the January 6th invasion of Freetown, attacks on Kambia District, and the demonstration at Foday Sankoh's lodge on Spur Road in Freetown.

I was born in 1966, October 14th, in Kambia District. I was in Rokupr in 1995 and I stayed there working as a teacher for more than two years and the area was quiet. However, the rebels attacked Rokupr town on the 20th of February, 1998 in the morning hours (as they moved into the north after the Intervention). After three days they came again. At that time I was at home with my father.

There was a group of rebels resting near my house, a group of five officers with some younger guys. There were thirty or more of them. The officers called me to go to them and asked me what I was doing there. I told them I didn't see any reason to run away. Their bodyguards came and surrounded them.

The five of them interrogated me. I sat down and told them I didn't see that they were doing anything wrong. I told them what they wanted to hear so they wouldn't do anything to me. I was the only person around. I told them "Gentlemen, I have seen you fighting a just cause." One of them asked me "What do you mean by a just cause?" I showed my rough palms because at that time I was just engaged in agricultural activities. That was the only way I was earning a living because teachers weren't being paid.

One asked me how I felt about their revolution. I told them I thought it was timely because I was someone who had completed education up to HTC level and I had taught for so many months and years and had not been paid. Look at my palms. So I don't think what you are doing is actually wrong. That was how they came to accept me to sit by their side.

After that I took permission from them to go home and get food for them. They asked me if they were selling palm wine around or something else to drink and I told them I would help them get these things. There were others nearby who feared joining them and there was a man who was tapping poyo, called Pa Alimamy, who was hiding somewhere and saw me discussing with the rebels. He didn't show himself until he saw how long I had spent with the rebels. After an hour or so he decided they weren't going to harm me. He showed himself and greeted us and I said "Thank God you're here. These guys are asking for palm wine." He brought it. It wasn't far from where they were seated and we all sat and drank some. We spent up to two hours resting. This was after they were through with their operations in downtown Rokupr, fighting and looting. Two people were killed in that attack.

So, we were seated there drinking the palm wine and they told me to go with them on a walk. They were asking me if I could join them. We talked for a long time about their operations and what they planned to do next. I told them I would join them when they visited me the next time. They told me not to be afraid and if there was anything I wanted they would help me get it. I accompanied them up to Mambolo Junction at a village called Royanka. They gave me their addresses and junta names which I don't remember now. I didn't ask them their tribes but they were mixed, one was a Mende but I didn't know the tribes of the four others.

At the end of 1998, in October, I applied for a course at Milton Margai College, so I was in Freetown when the January 6th invasion took place. I was staying at Circular Road. On the 5th the Ministry of Education asked us to go to Lungi to collect our last salary. Lungi was an important place then. All the highways from the provinces were blocked so it was the only accessible way to travel to Freetown. Even people from Makeni traveled through Port Loko to Lungi to cross over to Freetown.

I spent the whole day at Lungi and late in the evening I took the ferry to Freetown and was seated at Sunny Mark, a bar on Garrison Street. I was there drinking with some friends not knowing the rebels were around. I left at midnight and traveled back to Circular Road and just three hours later the rebels started entering the town. They spent the night moving from Waterloo and Hastings on foot. In the morning they asked everyone to welcome them and some of us were in the street watching them pass by. They were shouting "We have come and we want to liberate everybody." They were asking both women and men to take white pieces of cloth to wave as a sign of peace. They didn't harm anybody that day. They were just moving with vehicles and no one was harmed except those who were secretly harmed.

On the 7th they also didn't do much. That day I walked from Circular Road to Eastern Police to see the situation. They were passing everywhere with vehicles and RPGs and other weapons. It was on the 9th that they started harming people,

Ferry that crosses the harbor from Freetown to Lungi

because people had been reluctant to recognize them and welcome them. ECOMOG was in town and they knew they would try to repel them from the city. It was then they started burning houses and shooting people.

There were some of them who were taking refreshments at Firestone, behind Circular Road near the British Council. Some of us were spending our leisure time drinking with them there and they weren't too harmful until the 9th when ECOMOG started repelling them and they started looting. ECOMOG was firing on one side while they were firing on the other side. Most of them were at city center in Freetown. ECOMOG were at Wilberforce and the State House. They started fighting the rebels downtown and pushing them toward the eastern part of town and the rebels started burning and killing.

That night nobody slept in their houses because they were just burning houses. Freetown was almost on fire and nobody was at home. Some of us slept in the valley between the British Council and IPAM. Some were fortunate and had their belongings. Others left their houses when they were on fire. A lot of people were lying down in that valley while houses were burning and there was looting and shooting here and there all night. I spent the night in a broken toilet hearing what was happening.

The next morning I left Circular Road and went to stay with my cousin in Sorie Town. Nobody was able to move out of Freetown because the ways were blocked. I was trying to find my way to Rokupr because colleges were closed and there were no activities going on. Even the seas were closed. Nobody was allowed to move out of Freetown.

I traveled by sea back to Rokupr as soon as I could leave. I was in Rokupr in 1999 when the rebels attacked Pamalap (at the Guinean border). By that time Freetown was liberated by ECOMOG. The AFRC and RUF had left Freetown and some of them stayed in the north. They brought over fifty vehicles to Rokupr. They were Peugeot taxis which they looted from Pamalap where there are a lot of vehicles because it's a crossover point between the countries. The Guineans were launching artillery directly into Kambia District to fire on the rebels. It wasn't safe in Kambia.

Demonstration at Spur Road

The other experience I had was during the May 8, 2000 demonstration at Foday Sankoh's house. College had reopened and I was in Freetown. We were on campus that day when two buses arrived in the morning and alerted students to go to the demonstration. So some of us dressed and went to the place. Some of us were right at the front of the demonstration. There were so many vehicles that it was hard to get near Foday Sankoh's house. So many people wanted to see what was happening. We were there up to 10:30 or 11:00 AM.

People were trying to enter the gate and a good number had entered but Foday Sankoh had his own military guys there. When the crowd put pressure on Foday Sankoh's bodyguards the firing started. Actually he never meant to kill anyone that day. If it had been his objective they could have killed hundreds of people. There was one thing that brought the damage: it was one officer who shot an RPG. I think he just did it to get people to leave the compound but when it was fired it brought turmoil in the whole compound. People were just moving here and there. Everybody lost focus. I sustained a lot of injuries when a wall fell on me and I still have the scars.

Foday Sankoh was still trying to seize power. Before the demonstration he told people he was going to take power in three days. In fact that demonstration was a blessing to Sierra Leoneans. It caused a lot of causalities but it was a blessing. Foday Sankoh was bent on doing worse things. If he hadn't been captured he would have caused more trouble. He was an over-ambitious person. The government gave him prominent positions. He was working closely with Johnny Paul. They went together to Milton Margai with President Kabbah to address us, the students, to tell us they would put the country on the right track, though Kabbah never stood up during the entire meeting. He said it was possible that they could shoot him.

To be candid I was never attacked by a rebel that would lead me to vengeance. Nobody in my family was affected. The war was worse in the south and east than in the north. It was almost at the end when the war came to the north and there wasn't much destruction.

The violence of the war came from wickedness. They were wicked from drugs, from what they were eating, drinking, or smoking and taking into their systems. Sierra Leoneans can become wicked from drugs or drinking excessively. I think this is the reason things became so wicked. Drugs were in abundance during the war. Some of the youths had never taken these things—jamba, cocaine. It can make people do things. They were led into it, of course, and it was the only way the leaders could see of doing it, by getting their minds mixed up. If you drink to excess you will behave like a mad dog.

The problem with Foday Sankoh was, at the beginning he had all chances to win the revolution but he lost his focus. Sierra Leone was peaceful in the 1970s to the early 80s. Sierra Leoneans started facing trouble in the 80s when the OAU meeting was staged in Freetown. That was when Sierra Leone started facing financial problems. There was a one-party state, the judiciary was corrupt, education wasn't going on as was expected. Things started going the wrong way.

We were in a big mess before the war started, after Pa Siaka's regime. Momoh couldn't handle the country. He also contributed in bringing the war. If Momoh had noticed he could have minimized some of these irregularities but instead he fueled it and just became weak and gave room to all these things happening.

When Foday Sankoh came, I don't know if it was lack of knowledge or illiteracy, but he lost his focus completely. If Foday Sankoh and his men had thought of persuading Sierra Leoneans to see the reasons why he launched the revolution, possibly it would have succeeded, but he couldn't control his soldiers.

At this time the youths are still neglected. There is still something boiling with the youth which is the reason they have to preach peace for the elections. The government should really set its eye on youth. Education needs to be improved for them so they have worthwhile activities to do. They need vocational training and something meaningful. They need to be kept busy. If not, somebody can come from the blue, regroup them, and think of evil.

THE END OF THE WAR

After the abduction of peacekeepers and Foday Sankoh's arrest in May 2000, Freetown was generally peaceful and the focus of the war moved to the Guinean border where the RUF was fighting for Charles Taylor.

The RUF fought the Guinean army in the north in Kambia District, but the heaviest fighting took place in the east along the Guinean border in Kono and Kailahun Districts and in Lofa Country in Liberia. The war finally ended when the RUF was defeated by LURD, the Guinean army, and Sierra Leonean fighters in April 2001. RUF forces under Issa Sesay continued holding Kono District until peacekeepers arrived there in August 2001.

These narrators describe events in Kono and Kailahun Districts during the last years of the war including the fighting in Guinea, diamond mining by the RUF, and disarmament.

1. Mohamed
   These Were the Thugs I Saw
   Civilian

Mohamed is from Bumpeh, a diamond mining town a few miles west of Koidu. At the beginning of the war he was sent to his family village for safety. He returned to Kono in 2001 when the ceasefire was in effect, the RUF controlled the district, and the peacekeepers hadn't yet arrived. He witnessed diamond mining by the rebels, disarmament, and the Cutlass War.

Narratives

I was born in 1987 so I wasn't old enough during the first part of the war to remember anything. I lived in Bumpeh, Kono District with my uncle. When the rebels first attacked Kono in 1992 my uncle took me to stay with my grandmother and an uncle in our family village called Wasaiya in Bombali District.

Early in 2001 we went back to Bumpeh. There were still terrible things happening. It was the ceasefire and the rebels had their own government and did anything they wanted. There weren't many people because they thought it was still dangerous. People didn't start coming back to Kono until disarmament.

The rebels who stayed in Koidu town and the larger towns went to villages to get food and they also had supplies from their leaders in Liberia. They didn't tell us where they got ammunition but I know they got it through the Liberian border. We were seeing them with all kinds of ammunition and arms. They had vehicles. There was no fuel so they used palm kernel oil.

Issa Sesay was the rebel commander. They called him "Master". He was living in Koidu in an up-garret in a place called Small Lebanon. I never saw Charles Taylor with my eyes. I saw Komba Gbondema, I saw Superman, I saw Blackstone, I saw Saquee and Peleto, Colonel Tarrick, Tigerman, World Warrior. These were the thugs I saw.

My uncle was mining diamonds in a big field at Nyamadu Bridge near Bumpeh and Issa Sesay also had a mining operation there. One day I went to take food to my uncle and his workers, and Issa came. When Issa came to the diamond mines, if people were working they had to raise their shovels up and hold them up while he was talking. They said "The General is coming" and nobody could move. He had a black jeep that Tejan Kabbah gave him with open Landcruisers before and behind for his bodyguards. His bodyguards didn't have only two magazines, they had five or more. That was the requirement to be his bodyguard.

Diamond miner washing gravel

Issa commanded that all miners had to give half of their gravel to the rebels and they could keep the balance. It was called "two pile". They had to wash the rebels' pile of gravel in front of them to see if there were any diamonds and the rebels would point their guns at them while they were doing it. The rebel pile was called the "government pile". The jula (diamond businessmen) were paying money every month to Issa and my uncle was collecting that money in Bumpeh. He was chairman for the jula. This was before disarmament. I was just staying at home. There was no school.

The area commander for the rebels was Commander Bankuta, a Kono man. He had two wives, one Mandingo and one Fullah. Bankuta had a dancehall in Bumpeh and we used to go there to dance and watch films. Once in Bumpeh Issa flogged Colonel Bankuta twenty-four lashes in front of his wife because he set up a checkpoint late after he was ordered to do it.

There was a bad rebel named Peleto who beat up a Maraka man until he urinated, then another man pressed his arm against a stick until it broke. They would get important men together and make them stand where there were black ants, then play a tape and make them dance while the ants were biting them. One man lost his life when they did that. The commanders Bankuta, Pele 2, and C.O. Sam and a hundred fighters were there during that incident. Presently I don't know where any of them are. I haven't seen any of them since disarmament.

The rebels captured some boys and took them to Yengema Secondary School to train to fight at the border area. They would come into houses early in the morning and search for young boys of around fifteen to twenty years. They took two boys who were working for my uncle. This happened before the peacekeepers came later in 2001. Rebels were going to the Guinea border to fight and there was heavy fighting there. A lot of rebels were killed there like Komba Gbondema, the commander in the north, and Superman.

Sometimes when they came back they brought heads of enemies they killed and danced around with the heads on sticks to celebrate, just shouting and carrying the heads around in a vehicle. This stopped when the peacekeepers came (beginning in August 2001) and the training base at the school was closed. It became the headquarters for the Pakistani peacekeepers which they turned into a big camp for disarmament. The UNAMSIL peacekeepers were based in Yengema at the airfield and at Yengema Secondary School. The rebels were there but weren't causing any problems.

Disarmament and The Cutlass War

They had a big meeting in Koidu town (on September 4, 2001) before disarmament. President Kabbah, Nigerian President Obasanjo and another president who I can't remember attended and other African big men as representatives of other countries. I went to the meeting with my uncle.

Before entering the hall the fighters had to leave their guns at the gate. In the meeting Issa wanted to introduce himself as "General" but they told him "No, you are no longer a general." Issa had a gold chain with a 16-karat diamond on it. Obasanjo said "Look at the way you are dressing. Generals don't dress like that."

After that we started seeing a lot of UNAMSIL vehicles coming to manage disarmament. We the civilians were happy when we saw them and happier when we saw the rebels disarming. The disarmament took place at the Yengema Secondary School compound. I saw all of it. During disarmament some rebels had three or four guns each. When they disarmed they gave them a blanket, blended (corn-soy blend), a tarpaulin, money, oil, and other things and cooked food for them. They had ID cards to get food. There were women the Pakistanis paid to cook. When you came to disarm first they gave you food to eat. There was a queue, a long line. Some people brought bombs and grenades along with their guns.

UNAMSIL stayed a long time, at least a year. While they were here they did a lot of building and repairing. They built mosques and other buildings. They cooked food and passed it out in the towns. They did it every Friday. People brought their plates and they passed out the food. Another organization passed out sheep and goats.

After disarmament there was the Cutlass War in Koidu which was called *Kono-ma-kwe* or "Kono man's business". The Cutlass War came about when the Koidu people wanted the rebels to leave the town. The rebels were staying there after disarmament, digging diamonds. They didn't have any guns so the people wanted to drive them out. To find people who weren't Konos they would ask a password in the Kono language—*kolonto* (nine) and if you didn't respond *tahn* (ten) they would kill you because it meant you weren't a Kono and that you were a rebel. Or if they asked *nya-guma* (cat) you had to say *tua* (rat).

The fighting was serious and caused us to run to Masingbi. The Pakistani Peacekeepers were in Kono at that time and tried to put the situation under control, but it was difficult because everyone was using cutlasses and big sticks or pieces of iron to fight each other. No one had guns but they had all kinds of other weapons.

They killed one Koranko man who was a thug named Demba Marrah. This was a rebel who killed a whole village and didn't leave anyone. Demba Marrah was in Koidu and he was a strong fighter with some followers. People used to worship him like a god because he had a very strong charm and everyone was afraid of him because he had magic and could disappear or turn into any kind of person. When they went into his room he was trying to get his magic but he wasn't able to and they killed him. He was killed at the cotton tree in Koidu. They danced around town with his body and threw it in a well on Sahr Lebbie Street. The well is still there but it's only used now for garbage.

A Senseless War
What caused the war to happen? Foday Sankoh started the war. He was fighting for power. He wanted to become president. They were fighting a senseless war. They were fighting for no reason. Killing for no reason, looting property, raping, just feeling like they wanted to do it. They did it so Foday Sankoh could become president.

What happened here was one of the worst things that has happened in Africa. The young men who were fighting have really come to their senses and know that what they were doing was wrong and have resolved never to do it again. The kind of suffering we had, we pray will never happen again. Some people didn't experience it, but for we who went through hunger and hardship, walking long distances, we felt the pain. We did all kinds of things to survive. The war has made people realize things. Before the war people didn't realize things.

2. Fallah
I Never Want to See Such Things Again
RUF Child Soldier

Fallah was captured by the RUF late in the war when he was around eight years old, and sent to a rebel camp in Kono District near the Guinean border. He was involved

Narratives

in food-finding expeditions and the 2000-2001 fighting in Guinea, when the RUF attacked the LURD forces who were trying to overthrow Charles Taylor, though in his narrative he misunderstands the reason for the fighting.

Fallah left the rebels in Guinea but was caught by Kamajors, underwent Kamajor initiation at the very end of the war, and disarmed in Kono District. Fallah gives the most detailed description of RUF torture practices and indoctrination of child soldiers that we heard. He refers to torture as "punishment".

I'm a young man and I've decided to help myself at this time by working and studying. I was born in 1989 in a village near Gueckedou in Guinea. My parents are both Guineans but came to Sierra Leone to find money and we were staying in a small village in Kailahun District. I don't know anything about the beginning of the war. What I remember is that when I was seven or eight years old my father and I were captured by the rebels. Our house was attacked at night. My mother and sister ran one way and my father and I went another way. I was captured in Kailahun District and at the end of the war I explained this to IRC (International Rescue Committee) and they helped me find my mother.

It was afternoon when they captured us. We were walking along a bush path when we met them and they took us to a town. We were sitting outside and they thought my father and two young men would escape so they shot them. I was there. They called them and they stood up and were shot.

They called people to carry the bodies away. Nobody could help me because they were all thinking about their own lives. I decided to stay with them because there were a lot of other people who were caught together and because I didn't know where I was from or where I could go. So for these reasons I decided to stay.

I remember a lot of what happened to me during the war. After I was captured they took me to a camp. We walked with a big group of people and some escaped on the way. We walked for three days and two nights carrying loads. We only rested sometimes, lying down on our loads, but we walked day and night. They didn't provide any food. If we found food in some of the villages we ate it. We walked on a bush path, not the main road. I was too small to know where I was. We were taken to a camp near Daru where I met many other children, some who were older than me and some who were younger, and this gave me the courage to stay. That is where we were trained.

Those who were old enough were trained to fight. Those who were younger they only trained by telling them things, because if you're a young child you can't tell what is good or bad but whatever they tell you, you might see as the truth. They told us a lot, that they were fighting for rights, that the ones who were young now would be the future leaders and so we had to be serious. But

The End of The War

the war was going on and we were children and weren't able to fight though there was a group of little boys who wanted to go and fight right away.

I didn't receive training in 1997 when I was captured but at the end of 1998 I started training. First they trained us to run long distances, then to run with loads. They put sand in a bag and gave it to you to carry while you were running. Next they trained us to crawl on our elbows on the ground. There were many other things and at the end they gave you a gun and trained you to sight and shoot. They told us that we couldn't attain a position (rank) by age but by our performance.

Some of the training was dangerous but you didn't think about it because you wanted to gain a position. You think that what I'm doing might make me a very big man so I'll continue doing it. And there was no one there to tell you that what you were doing was bad. If you killed someone they would say "Good boy, good boy." If you hit an old man they would say "You're a very good boy." So people continued doing very bad things, you see.

The gun I had was an AK-47. I took all the wood off the handle and from under the barrel because it was too heavy and put cloth in place of the wood. I was only able to use one magazine when men could use two or three, and I also had to remove the bayonet but some men could use two bayonets. If you fire a gun a lot it will become hot, so you put it on the ground and urinate on it to cool it off.

After the training we were divided into twenty or more groups. My group was fortunate to be sent to the far east of the country to Kombayendeh in Kono District, right at the border with Guinea. Our boss at the time was Major Jusu. He was killed by the Kamajors later. I saw his body.

Fighting for Food

When we were at Kombayendeh the time came when we had no food and we had to start fighting. We didn't fight the war. We were fighting for food. They would tell us "You people, go to a certain place and bring this back." You don't just request food. It's not easy to get. When you go there you have to strike. There were people living around the border of Guinea. The villages were Kolobengu, Kokuma, and Gbongor. The last is in Sierra Leone but the first two are in Guinea, so we first attempted to strike Kolobengu and we went and succeeded. We attacked it to get food and also salt. Salt was a problem then.

It was a night battle. We left for the attack at four o'clock in the afternoon. First we stayed behind the river on the boundary between the two countries. They sent three of us to spy who could speak the Kissi language and who people in the town would think were only refugees, not rebels. The three of us crossed the river one after the other. I know how to swim. After crossing I met some boys by the river. It was near the end of the rainy season when rice farms were almost ready for harvest and the boys were scaring birds from the rice with slings. We walked around the place and observed everything then returned with the information.

You have to learn how to spy, to know how to identify who each person is. They give you money to buy things while you are surveying the area. I did it more than once. You observe the soldiers and what kind of weapons they have. When you come back you are compensated by the commanders, for example, they will give you a package of jamba.

Some people may suspect you are a rebel. One of my colleagues was suspected and killed, but they don't know everyone in the area and wouldn't automatically suspect you if you went to buy food, and also there are many people in the market so they can't easily identify you.

After you give the information to the commander they sit and plan how to attack the town. This was a general attack with the commanders present and it was agreed that if we are attacking for food we don't kill people. If you kill someone you will be punished. You have to know where to attack to give space to the civilians to escape.

We attacked at around 8 PM. The river was very high and we had ropes, knives, and matches. We used the matches to signal others when we were in trouble. If you are lost you light a fire, burning the bush. You move away from it and when your friends see it they will come to find you. Local people won't suspect that rebels are setting the fires.

One of the soldiers went first and he swam across with the rope and tied it on the other side. The others followed using the rope. When crossing the river you put your gun in the water to hide it. The water can't stop it from firing. There were seventy-five in our group and we crossed in three groups of twenty or more. Most of us were under eighteen years old. They assigned one man to start shooting.

The village had seven to fifteen Guinean soldiers guarding it. When we attacked we fired our guns in the air. Some people escaped but we also captured some. We looted the entire village and put everything in loads and told the civilians to carry them. They took them and when we came to cross the river some lost their lives because the water was fast and some of them were just young men who had never done it before. Even some of our colleagues lost their lives. It was very dangerous. If you lost hold of the rope the water would carry you away.

We killed three Guinean soldiers on that raid and one civilian was also killed. He ran out of his room naked when he heard the firing and someone shot him because it was night time and they thought he was a soldier. So we got back to the camp at Kombayendeh.

Another time I went as a rekky (spy) to Gbangandu for three days. I returned on the fourth day and on the seventh day we attacked the town. I pretended to be a refugee and met someone I knew and stayed with him and for three days observed the situation. When I was a rekky it wasn't possible to escape from the rebels because there were others behind me and because I didn't know where I was or where to go, and also because I might fall into the hands of other people like the government soldiers. Also, when they sent you to rek they wouldn't send you in the direction of your home. However, by that time, even if they let me go I wouldn't try to escape because I was used to the situation and civilians might identify me as a rebel and I would be killed.

That was where I was shot, when we went to attack Gbangandu. We fought for about fifteen minutes. I can't explain the whole story because I was shot in the first ten minutes and my friends carried me back to Kombayendeh where the doctors were.

Life in the Rebel Camp

The rebels were from many different tribes. Major Jusu, who I was telling you about, was a Mende and was the commander in charge of the camp. In the camp we had morning parades. We sang and did soldier parades. If you were late your punishment would be greeping or the butterfly. In greeping you have to crawl along the ground using your elbows. For the butterfly you hold your arms out straight for a long time, fifteen or twenty minutes. If you do that for fifteen minutes you will know how hard it is. You have to hold your arms out straight at your sides. You can't move them down or up. If you can't do it they may flog you. If you were guilty of offences, like if you were called by the commander but failed to go, if you tried to run away, or disobeyed the commander they would kill you. You will not exist. So it happened.

I had some special responsibilities in the camp. I was a training master, commander of all the colleagues my age. That is why I was given two names before the end of the war. At first I was called "Small". There were many boys named "Small" or "Small Boy". Anyone who was brave and who was small was called "Small". Next, when you had a position and a responsibility they called you "Wonder", like "wonderful", but they just said "Wonder".

In Kombayendeh I was in charge of the store. I was living with my commander's wife and men were cooking and doing everything. I had the task of giving them what to cook and telling them when to cook it and how to do it. My commander's wife loved me a lot. When my father was killed and I went to the first camp it was the same commander's wife who took care of me, so when Commander Jusu was transferred to Kono I went with him and his wife. Because I was staying with her I didn't have to fight when I was very young. I only fought when I wanted to. I decided to fight because I saw my friends going and bringing things so I also decided to go and not just stay in the camp.

Kombayendeh, in the far east of Kono District, near the Guinean border

Sometimes big commanders would visit us. I remember one man, I don't know if he was Superman or Butterfly, once came to the camp. In Kono we had Issa Sesay. I knew him well but he didn't know me. When they came we would gather and they would say that we were fighting to have our rights. Because there was a lot of violence in the country they said we had formed our own group and when the war was over we would be the ones to benefit. They said "All of you standing here will be the future soldiers and leaders of tomorrow" and everybody would clap because we didn't know what they were saying.

The commander didn't attend all the battles. They arranged groups to go out. Sometimes everybody had a gun but not always. In fact, in the end sometimes fifteen people would have only three guns—five people per gun. The others used knives and bayonets. There were so few guns at the end because of attacks from the soldiers and Kamajors. Whenever there was an attack some people would run away and leave their guns. Possibly if you ran away with the gun and there were no bullets in it civilians you meet may kill you.

They always had reasons to send out groups whether it was to search for food or ammunition or to capture territory. If they wanted to capture more villages they would send people to attack them and settle there. Sometimes they would go out to attack the Kamajors. We won most of our battles and when we won we had parties. When we came back after a victory we would arrange a party with smoking, drinking, enjoyment, even killing some people who were prisoners from the jo-jo or the cell.

If you wanted to have a wife you could. Some of them had two or three wives but you couldn't beat or flog them. They were only there to help you, so no man could be seen taking advantage of them. There were no other responsibilities for a man to his wife. The wives cooked and washed but we also had other cooks and workers as well. The wives were of any age but not above forty. Forty and above weren't really accepted unless they were very fit, but the old people usually lost their lives quickly. Even some twelve-year-old boys had wives and could be in control of two wives. The boy was not responsible for feeding them so he could leave for a week and go out on a mission and when he returned maybe they were in the hands of another person. The wives were just for play. You played with them for some time then gave them to another person.

I worked for my commander and slept at his place and knew many of his secrets like some of his worships and how he came into the society, because they came into a society to form the rebels, the RUF. Sometimes my commander sat with me and explained these things. They had different types of societies. One, if you are washed a bullet cannot enter you. In another, you will be given something to take with you wherever you go as your protector. It could be a handkerchief, a rope to tie on your waist or arm, or a piece of clothing or cap which you always wore. The witch doctors were in the camp with us. There were more than three in our camp. They did things for the commanders, not for the boys. We boys had to fight with our minds. Only the commanders were protected. Wherever a commander went the witch doctor went along to protect him.

Participation and Punishment
I want to explain how people were given leadership depending on their participation. If you are one of the fighters and want to have a post it is from things you do that it will be given to you. For instance, if somebody is captured as a suspect and if you are very wicked or very strict with the person, like you can't take any joke or you can't forgive anything, these are the people that are given posts. When people are captured some of them are old, some are children, some are breast-feeding mothers. If you have sympathy in you, you will let them go free. But some people are so strict they won't let anyone go and these are the people who will be given posts.

Narratives

If someone is captured as a suspect and that person is handed over to you the leaders will be sitting and watching what you do. If you kill the person directly, even though you were told to do it, that won't impress them. Only if you punish them, they will be very happy. Like putting them on the floor and putting a drum on top of them and putting a fire in the drum.

Another kind of punishment is flogging. People were flogged until they could no longer move. They would flog people until they died. If someone is lying on a table and I am flogging the person, another person will stand behind me and another person behind that person. If I am not flogging the person properly the way the commanders want, the person standing behind me will flog me to teach me how to flog someone. So you see, these people were mercilessly flogged.

If you are found guilty, if you are a suspect, or if you try to play tricks, if you are a government soldier or a CDF or whatever, you must be punished. If you are a young man who is so strong that you can escape in twenty-four hours they can kill you because they know if you escape you will reveal their secrets.

There were other types of punishment. There were many. For instance there was a very big piece of iron, bigger than a bench. If you did something that wasn't good you had to stand and hold up the piece of iron for a long time until you got weak and fell down, then you would be flogged. In fact, some people fell down and they pulled them up and made them hold it again, more than five times.

Some were beaten and stomped on with their boots. That happened at a farm in Kombayendeh where we met a man with his wife and children. The man was not strong enough to leave the area and go to Guinea so he decided to stay in the bush. There were people around who knew he was there. They went there and the man hid himself. When his wife and children were captured he showed himself so he was taken to the commander and beaten until he died. That was one of the incidents.

Babies were beaten in mortars by their mothers. They made them do it just to show how wicked they were. They did this because they didn't want to travel with a lactating mother and also so the woman could be taken as the wife by one of the men. Sometimes they would make a woman pound one or two bags of rice in one day which is almost impossible. The skin on her hands would be peeled off.

As for the old people, if you were asked to walk and were unable to walk you would be killed. They didn't have time to spare for old people. Most of them were killed. It was done by shooting or tying them to a tree until they died. Once we were going to fight the Kamajors and we met an old man who

The End of The War

was the father of a Kamajor. They tied him to a tree and told him that if they won the battle they would set him free and if they lost he would be killed. They lost the battle and killed him. It was during the dry season and his body was tied to that coconut tree for three months. His whole body was black. When the rains came the body fell down.

Drugs

They gave drugs to young children such as marijuana. It was given to young boys because they knew it would make them do whatever they said. Most of the leadership posts were given to boys of twenty and below because they could "act" more. As I said before, you would only be given a position depending on your participation—how you punished people, did acts, burned houses. And this was the cause of some of these things because if you are given a drug that is more than your head you will feel as if you are going mad.

You could smoke jamba or eat it. If they cooked jamba everyone would eat it. They cooked it with only salt and pepper and ate it with rice like potato leaf. After everyone ate it some would be unconscious and wouldn't know themselves for some time. Sometimes they forced people to smoke it as well.

There were many other drugs that were with these people, but I was so small I couldn't differentiate them. There was brown-brown and cocaine. Sometimes they made cuts in their bodies and put it in the cut. That was done by the commanders and some of the other boys. It was very dangerous. Where did the drugs come from? You know, these people were supported by somebody, so maybe that person got it. Sometimes money was left behind because if you took it you wouldn't have any way to use it but if you saw drugs you took them because you would be using them. As soon as you had a pack of jamba you had friends by you.

Giving children these drugs made them commit very offensive crimes. They would shoot whoever they wanted or do anything they felt like. They weren't afraid of talking to anyone. Like, for boys of sixteen, seventeen, and eighteen, if you were given a post they would say you were a commander and you would act more (do worse) than was expected, and that could be done only when they used their drugs.

For the young men, if you refused to join the rebels you would be punished, if you accepted you wouldn't be punished. You only had to go through the constraints such as sleepless nights and the trainings and thinking you could die. They could remove boys from their posts. If you were given a post today and went against the rules and regulations they would take your position away from you and beat you, or they would kill you because if they left you, you could go out and reveal their secrets. Sometimes they locked them in the jo-jo or they would drive you out of the camp but send people to kill you. This was done many times in Kombayendeh by Major Jusu.

I was a young boy. What was I thinking about? There was nothing to think about, only that I wouldn't see my mother again. I had lost my mother, I didn't know where she was, and my father was killed. So all that could satisfy me was what I was doing no matter how wrong it was. In fact my mother can never come here now to see me because she is an old woman staying in Guinea with my younger sister. If she came I would stop going to school because I wouldn't let her suffer. I would work for both myself and her. She isn't doing anything in Guinea. My younger sister is married so they are taking care of her.

The entire time I was a rebel I felt very uncomfortable, except for a few days you feel comfortable, because the absence of your mother and father makes it very difficult. This is a reason why the young boys weren't afraid of doing anything, because you think you will never see your parents again.

There were no comforts there. When you are captured by the rebels you always have in your mind that you will be killed one day unless you are given a gun. You remember people who were there before who were killed, so you really just think you are there for a specific time. The feeling of the whole thing is not too good, except for some times. This is the reason why most people took drugs. Thinking too much, sometimes if you took drugs it would go out of your mind. Maybe drugs will make you joyful, because sometimes if you are drugsick you will feel happy and forget about the issues ahead.

The only things they did for enjoyment was take drugs, play tapes, listen to the radio, like that, but sometimes we organized dances. We would call all our friends to come and enjoy with us for a night or a night and a day. Sometimes we would spend two or three days doing it. There was only that. Otherwise you just sat feeling uncomfortable.

Fighting In Guinea
In Kombayendeh we were attacked three times by the Kamajors around the time of the ceasefire. At first we and the Kamajors were staying near each other cordially. We were in Kombayendeh and they were in Saiama, the chiefdom headquarters. The government called for peace so we were all together. We listened to the radio about the ceasefire and followed instructions, however a quarrel came between us.

We had a big jamba farm and a lot of ammunition which they didn't have. One day they came and looted the entire farm of marijuana and carried it away, so our commander did not take this well and sent for their commander. When the commander came he was killed immediately, but the Kamajors were very smart. They didn't send their main commander. They just sent a boy, so he was killed.

The End of The War

Later they came back to attack us. They came along the main road from Saiama and attacked us when we were parading in the morning. We fought and defeated them. I saw that the situation was very serious so we went into the bush around the town. The Kamajors didn't stay. They just came and burned some of our houses and took some of our ammunition.

Because of this we contacted Kailahun where our main commanders were so we could surround the Kamajors in Guinea and attack them. We attacked Guinea because the Kamajors were there and they might come at any time to disturb our peace. However I was a small boy so I didn't really know why all this was happening. (They were actually attacking to help Charles Taylor fight against LURD.)

During the war if you wanted to send a message you had to send people. We had radios but you could only hear but couldn't speak into them. There is a road between Kono and Kailahun by way of Kamiandor and a man had to walk day and night for two or three days to take a message to Kailahun. You only stopped when you needed to smoke jamba and drink. The message told the rebels in Kailahun to meet us at the border.

A group from Kailahun entered Guinea through Liberia a few villages from Gueckedou. When we knew they had entered, we also went to Gueckedou by way of Kolobadu. When we got to Gueckedou our friends had already cleared it, so we went on to Kissidougou. On the way many of our men were killed by Guinean soldiers. They had dangerous weapons that I had never seen with my eyes. When you hear the voice of the weapon you will really know it is dangerous. Heh! But there it was so difficult to escape. Only a few people escaped. I was shot and injured near Gueckedou so I left the others and began to search for my mother.

I heard that my mother had died so I left the rebels and went there. I was able to go because I could speak the language and it was easy to get away from them because the place was so mixed up. You didn't know who was a rebel. Everyone was looking for a place to escape so nobody was watching each other. Maybe if they gathered and asked "Where is this man?" they would just think you had died or gone back. I decided to stay to look for my mother in Gueckedou. I left my gun in the street.

With the Kamajors

Unfortunately the Kamajors were in the town after they had chased out the rebels and I was captured as a suspect because some of them knew me from Kombayendeh. It was only because I could speak the Kissi language that I was freed. I told them I had been in Guinea for two years.

Narratives

Road to the Guinean border at Kombayendeh, Kono District

So I lied and was freed. The Kamajors saw that I knew everything about guns, so they gave me a gun and marked my arms and shoulders and many other places on my body for protection. They did this during the initiation which included being given a proper flogging that you will never forget in your life.

However, during the time I was a Kamajor I didn't fight because the war was almost finished. The rebels were driven out of Guinea. We, the Kamajors, came back and entered Kombayendeh and other towns on the road to Koidu but there were no rebels around. By the time we arrived in Koidu disarmament was going on. We saw a UNAMSIL helicopter dropping a lot of papers. The educated people read them and said they were papers of peace.

So we came to the center and were disarmed. I disarmed as a Kamajor and was taken to a camp, first to Yengema Camp and then to Funicor Camp in Kenema, then to Freetown. UNAMSIL took the child combatants to Freetown by helicopter. There were many big helicopters in the town at that time. They moved people away from their base of action so they couldn't return to fighting.

In Freetown they started giving the child combatants back to their parents but I couldn't find mine so I was helped by IRC. It was the NCDDR and IRC who helped me with my education in Koidu. At first they put me in class 2 but

The End of The War

I was too big and was very ashamed to sit in it, so the next year I went to class 4 and came second in the class. I never came third or fourth.

In Africa, people won't help other people's children. They only like to help their own biological children. We who suffered a lot should be helped. We who have no parents need to be helped by someone. That is why you see a lot of street children and criminals in our country.

What Brought The War

The commanders might have had a plan but they never revealed it to us. We were just fighting and being sent places so we had to protect ourselves. It was obvious they were taking over the country so Foday Sankoh would be president. It was explained every morning and every evening. When the commanders came together to drink, smoke, and laugh, because I was living with the commander, they would say when Foday Sankoh became president all of these child soldiers would be the soldiers of the country, and these commanders would be the members of parliament and whatever. They were hoping to be the rulers of the county. They were trying to make everyone afraid. That is why they cut off hands and killed people.

One of the older men was named Sam King. He had dreadlocks on his head. He refused all the positions and was only a killer. He didn't have any friends but just wanted to be alone and not have any problems. He was a Sierra Leonean, but was initiated into the society in Liberia when the war was there. You see, when the rebel war was going on in Liberia, Sierra Leoneans went there to join the society hoping the war would come to Sierra Leone. They knew, many people knew of everything.

What brought the war? For me it was because we, the Sierra Leoneans, are not fair. People will try to ruin you. We don't want to share with each other. There are rich black people who don't share their money with anyone while some poor people share with each other. I can even be laughing with you and at the same time killing you. This is one of the main things that brought the war.

When I see someone now who I was in the rebel camp with, we just greet each other and go about our business. If we have time to sit together we talk about the past. Some people want to explain their stories but not in front of just anybody, only with people who were there. I remember all my friends but don't meet them often. Most of them are miners now because they were not educated. Some of them are in the villages doing farm work. Some are still living in Kombayendeh. They were born there, they destroyed it, and now they are still there.

Sometimes people recognize me. In Kombayendeh I once set a man and his daughter free and I saw the daughter recently. She's a very big girl now. They were our prisoners and I was asked by my commander to go and hand them over to the killing commander for the morning ceremony killing. Early in the morning when everyone was still in bed, the first gunshot would be the killing of a prisoner. That happened at 5:30. Every morning they killed someone, except sometimes when there was no one to kill they just shot the guns five or more times. If there were people to kill they only shot two or three times to wake everyone up.

The commander told me to give them to the killer but when I took them there he was still in bed so I let them free and they went to Guinea. When I went back and the commander asked me if I handed them over I said "Yes, the man was inside and I left the people outside." My commander thought the killer was the one that let them free, not knowing it was me. He was punished, greeping with his elbows from his house to the commander's house, about a mile. They didn't suspect me because I left the people outside his door while he was inside and I had other work to do besides waiting for him. I only took them and said "I have come," so the man heard my voice.

His name was Killer. There is a place in Kombayendeh, if you go there you will see as many heads as you can count. People's heads. They would choose someone who was to be punished, or if you were suspected of wanting to escape, or if you were old. Since then I haven't seen Killer. For me I never want to see such things again in my life. If I have a friend who wants to get me to be a rebel I would run for I don't know how many miles.

Allan
Epilogue: Counseling and Reconciliation

Allan ends his narrative with a description of his work with an international NGO in Guinea and Kono District.

When I came back from Guinea and saw Koidu town I felt bad. We were just sleeping in burned houses and just bought tarpaulins to make roofs. I was fortunate that I came back with a small amount of money and I bought the place where I'm living now.

Before the war people valued culture so much but since the war they have been leaving their traditional culture. Now some boys refuse to be initiated into the Poro society and they are bringing other religious influences so things have changed drastically. Some aspects of this are good. People have gone to other areas and learned from other people and are trying to modify things. The belief in witchcraft isn't as strong as before though some people still have that belief. The war has opened people's eyes but it is a gradual process.

I started working for Center for Victims of Torture as a psycho-social counselor while in Guinea, going through trainings by technicians from America and Europe. We were doing counseling with refugees—group, family, and individual counseling, depending on the problems the clients had. We screened them and if there were, say, ten people with similar problems we would put them in a group and do group counseling.

People living in a destroyed house, Koidu

Some had behavioral problems, for example, those whose family members were killed by soldiers with knives. If they saw a knife they would think it was something bad. With such people we were doing cognitive behavioral counseling, that is, trying to change their cognition that a knife isn't something bad but that it was the circumstances they had faced. For example, you can use a knife to chop your food or for other things. Some people when you work with them a long time will be able to change their thinking.

Narratives

We were also doing family counseling. People who were separated from their families would be put into groups and we would have them discuss their problems together so they would know they weren't the only ones with the experience so it should not make them stop functioning. We would do that for around ten weeks and I think we were successful because many people were able to process their problems and become functional. Prior to that, they weren't able to do anything, isolating themselves from others and not doing any work. Some were just sitting and thinking. After working with them they were able to do things for themselves and even join in social activities.

When we came back to Kono I continued doing this work. We had some ex-combatants and did group counseling with them. All those who said they were forced conscripts were put into one group. Some had certain symptoms. They were hyperactive, stubborn, or restless because they couldn't forget what they had done in the jungle. We tried to work with them and learn how they were feeling with other people now, how they had felt with the rebels, how life had changed, and what their problems were now. We put them in groups and worked on the problems they posed. We didn't make decisions for them but tried to suggest how to find ways to overcome those things.

For example, someone would say "I saw so many killings, they were killing people in my presence, and because of this I'm not feeling fine." We gave them some exercises to do to get this stress out of their minds. There's one exercise we do in counseling: they sit on a chair and talk to the chair about everything that is at hand and how they want the problem to be solved. So we would do that with the guy for some time because it helped some people to voice out what was disturbing them. Maybe if you did that with them several times the degree to which it was disturbing them would decrease.

Women mostly had problems from sexual abuse. Some of them had problems with STIs so we did referrals to the government hospital, and IRC opened the Rainbow Center for counseling and helping women. There was group counseling for rape victims but women were in charge of that because some of the women were not open to men.

For children, most had problems with separation from their relatives and we were helping them to be reunited with their families. I believe that counseling also had a good effect with them. There were so many street children. The ones who were ex-combatants we identified by doing door-to-door sensitizations. We had pictures of problems affecting children and people would say if there were such children in the community—children with no parents, just walking about and sleeping in the market area—and we would go in search of them.

The End of The War

There was a woman who had an organization dealing with children called Brave Heart who referred children to us for counseling. We did individual counseling with those who had individual problems and group counseling with others. We succeeded because most of them were able to go back to their people and were accepted and started going to school. Those who opted for skills training were sent for that. We weren't doing family reunification, but it was done by IOM (International Organization for Migration).

When we went into communities one of the people's concerns was that their relatives had been killed, like at Maima where a lot of people were put in a house and burned. When the people returned they didn't have the means to do ceremonies and some of them thought that was the cause of their suffering. They said their crops weren't giving good yields, there was sickness among them, and so many other bad things which they thought were a result of that. So our organization gave them funds to do family cleansing, a Kono tradition.

They killed a goat and shared it, one part for the men and one part for the women. The men and women each cooked their own part. They brought it together, carried it to a sacred place, and offered it to their ancestors. They asked for good health, good yields, and for the cleansing of their land of the blood that was spilled. Others did personal ceremonies for their loved ones.

Our organization didn't do work on reconciliation between communities and fighters who had killed people in the communities. The only thing we did was, when the TRC (Truth and Reconciliation Commission) came to communities they had us show videos and talk to the community members to prepare their minds, because these were sorrowful videos which showed former fighters coming out and saying what they had done was not their wish, that they were under the influence of drugs, or that they had been forced to do it, and they were now coming to apologize and ask their communities to forgive them.

They would play these for people to realize that if there were ex-combatants in the community they shouldn't do retributive justice and accept the fact that some of them did not do it willingly, like the little boys, they were just held by some big men and conscripted into their fighting forces. That's what the TRC was trying to do.

The stories we listened to, things that happened here were terrible. It seems that now most people have coped and overcome most of their stress. You see everyone working hard for themselves. Formerly we all used to live in family houses but now everybody is trying to put up his or her own structure to live an independent life. That's a very big change that I admire. Everybody wants to be on his own.

Some rebels still think what they did was right. Most people don't accept that but there's one fact that remains: these guys were brainwashed. The rebel authorities told them they were fighting a just cause so some of them still have that opinion. You meet educated people who think the Rebel War was just.

The reconciliation came at a time when people wanted it. People were tired of running here and there. People wanted to be at home so they had to accept those who had done wrong to live in the same community. That's why you still see some violence going on, like here in Kono where there are so many ex-fighters. People are living with them as a price of peace. They don't want to go into any other war again.

War Memorial, Kabala

APPENDIX 1:
Groups and Organizations Involved in the War

AFRC: Armed Forces Revolutionary Council: The military government formed after the second coup of the war in 1997. They ruled until 1998 when they were forced out of Freetown by ECOMOG in the operation known as the Intervention, then led the attack on Freetown in 1999 and continued to agitate for reinstatement into the army.

APC: All People's Congress: One of the two main political parties in Sierra Leone with its stronghold among the Temnes and Limbas in the north. The party was founded by Siaka Stevens.

CDF: Civil Defense Forces: Civilian militias who fought the RUF and AFRC. CDF groups included the Kamajors, Tamaboros, Gbintis, Kapras, and Donsos.

ECOMOG: Economic Community of West African States Monitoring Group: An armed force organized by ECOWAS, mainly from the three member states of Nigeria, Guinea, and Ghana, who were present in Sierra Leone for almost the entire war. Nigeria had the greatest number of troops in ECOMOG. ECOMOG was also active in the war in Liberia.

ECOWAS: Economic Community of West African States: A regional group of fifteen West African countries created in 1975.

Executive Outcomes: A South African private military (mercenary) company hired by the NPRC to fight the RUF.

Kamajors: (pron. KAH-mah-joh) The largest CDF whose members were mainly from the Mende ethnic group.

LURD: Liberians United for Reconciliation and Democracy: A group supported by Guinea and enemies of Charles Taylor that fought Taylor in the Second Liberian Civil War. The RUF fought LURD in 2000 and 2001.

NPFL: National Patriotic Front of Liberia: The Liberian rebel group led by Charles Taylor that fought against the government of Samuel Doe and took part in the war in Sierra Leone.

NPRC: National Provisional Ruling Council: The military government formed after the first coup of the war in 1992. They held power until elections were held in 1996.

RUF: Revolutionary United Front: The Sierra Leonean rebel group organized by Foday Sankoh that attacked Sierra Leone in March 1991.

RUFP: Revolutionary United Front Party: The political party formed by the RUF before the 2002 elections.

Appendix 1

SLA: Sierra Leone Army: The army undertook two coups during the war, the NPRC coup in 1992 and the AFRC coup in 1997. The NPRC regime held power until the 1996 elections. The AFRC regime, however, was opposed by the International community which supported the return of the democratically elected Kabbah government. The AFRC joined with the RUF which resulted in fighting against ECOMOG and the Kamajors. Some Sierra Leone Army soldiers remained loyal to the Kabbah government during the AFRC coup.

SLPP: Sierra Leone People's Party: The rival political party of the APC, primarily the party of the Mende ethnic group and its allies in the south and east.

The People's Army: The RUF changed their name to The People's Army when they joined the AFRC junta after the 1997 coup.

ULIMO: United Liberation Movement of Liberia: Liberian fighters opposed to the NPFL and Charles Taylor. They were organized by the Sierra Leone Army in refugee camps in Sierra Leone and fought against the RUF/NPFL early in the war, then went to Liberia to continue fighting against Taylor.

UNAMSIL: United Nations Mission in Sierra Leone: The UN peacekeeping force that entered the country in December 1999, replacing a monitoring group with the similar acronym of UNOMSIL.

vigilantes: Civilian defense volunteers who fought alongside the Sierra Leone Army.

West Side Boys: AFRC/RUF soldiers who settled in the area between Okra Hill and Masiaka in Port Loko District after the Intervention in 1998. AFRC commanders moved the area in 1999 and established West Side Base. In 2000 the group abducted British soldiers which led to their downfall.

APPENDIX 2:
Leaders and Commanders

Abacha, Sani (General): Leader of Nigeria from 1993 to 1998. Abacha supported Nigerian military involvement in Sierra Leone. He was controversial because he was a dictator who violated human rights in his own country while he supported a return to democracy in Sierra Leone. He died in 1998.

Bangura, Hassan Papa (a.k.a. Bomblast): AFRC commander who was leader of the West Side Base with Ibrahim Bazzy Kamara. In 1999 he became a bodyguard of Johnny Paul Koroma. Bangura was convicted in September 2012 for attempting to bribe a Special Court witness and attempting to induce a witness to recant testimony during Charles Taylor's trial and served 12 months in prison.

Bio, Julius Maada (Brigadier): Sierra Leone Army soldier who took part in the NPRC coup. He took over the NPRC chairmanship from Valentine Strasser in a "palace coup" that led to the elections in 1996. Maada Bio ran for President in 2012 for the SLPP party but lost to incumbent Ernest Bai Koroma.

Bockarie, Sam (a.k.a. Mosquito, or Maskita in Krio): Battlefield commander and second in command of the RUF. Mosquito became leader of the RUF when Foday Sankoh was arrested in Nigeria in 1997. He left the RUF and went to Liberia in 1999 and was killed there in 2003, allegedly on the orders of Charles Taylor.

Brima, Alex Tamba (a.k.a. Gullit): An AFRC commander, he was part of the group that staged the AFRC coup and a member of the AFRC Supreme Council. After the Intervention Gullit formed an attack force in the north, then took over command of the forces that invaded Freetown in January 1999 when SAJ Musa died. Gullit was convicted of war crimes and crimes against humanity by the Special Court. A football player, he took his nickname from Dutch footballer Ruud Gullit. He died in June 2016 while in prison in Rwanda, of complications from a foot infection.

Campaoré, Blaise: President of Burkina Faso from 1987 to 2014. He supported Sankoh and Taylor in their wars by providing troops and allowing transshipment of arms through his country. Like Sankoh and Taylor he was an associate of Muammar Qaddafi.

Conté, Lansana: President of Guinea from 1984 to 2008, when he died. He supported the Sierra Leone Army, ECOMOG, and anti-Taylor groups based in his country to fight the RUF and Charles Taylor.

Appendix 2

Flomo, Boston (a.k.a. Rambo or RUF Rambo): A Liberian RUF fighter, he was killed by Dennis Mingo (Superman) in Makeni in 1999 during RUF infighting between Superman and Issa Sesay.

Fofana, Moinina: A Kamajor leader, he was convicted of war crimes and crimes against humanity by the Special Court. His position in the CDF was "Director of War".

Gbao, Augustine: RUF commander and Chief of Security who, in 2000 with Morris Kallon, led the attack on the DDR center in Makeni and the abduction of UNAMSIL peacekeepers. He was convicted of war crimes and crimes against humanity by the Special Court. Prior to the war he was a police officer.

Kabbah, Ahmad Tejan: President of Sierra Leone from 1996 to 2007, his term interrupted by the AFRC regime. Prior to the war he worked for the United Nations Development Program. He died in 2014.

Kallay, Foday: AFRC fighter who took over command of the West Side Boys in 1999 after Bazzy and Gullit went to Freetown to be bodyguards for Johnny Paul Koroma. He was a sergeant in the Sierra Leone Army but with the AFRC had the rank of corporal, then colonel. Kallay led the abduction of British troops and one Sierra Leonean soldier at West Side Base in 2000. He was arrested and imprisoned, and released in 2009.

Kallon, Morris: RUF commander who, with Augustine Gbao, led the attack on the disarmament center in Makeni and abduction of peacekeepers in 2000. He was convicted of war crimes and crimes against humanity by the Special Court.

Kamara, Ibrahim Bazzy (known as "Bazzy"): AFRC commander and member of the AFRC Supreme Council. He was involved in attacks in the north and east after the Intervention and on Freetown in 1999. He led the West Side Boys with Hassan Papa Bangura, then went to Freetown to be bodyguard of Johnny Paul Koroma. He was convicted of war crimes and crimes against humanity by the Special Court

Kamara, Idrissa (a.k.a. Leatherboot): A Sierra Leone Army soldier who joined the NPRC and AFRC junta regimes. Kamara was the AFRC representative to the Lomé Peace Talks. After the war he became a bodyguard to President Ernest Bai Koroma and was accused of involvement in an attack on the SLPP party office in Freetown in 2009.

Kanu, Santigie Borbor (a.k.a. Five-Five): AFRC commander and part of the group that staged the AFRC coup. He was a member of the AFRC Supreme Council, and was convicted of war crimes and crimes against humanity by the Special Court. Kanu was implicated in the 2003 coup attempt with Johnny Paul Koroma.

Khobe, Maxwell (General): A Nigerian army officer who was a commander with ECOMOG, first in Liberia in 1992. From 1997 to 1999 he was head of ECOMOG troops in Sierra Leone. Khobe organized the Intervention and the response to the 1999 attack on Freetown. He died in 2000 from shrapnel wounds sustained in Freetown.

Kondowai, Allieu: (spelled "Kondewa" by the Special Court) High Priest and the original initiator of the Kamajors. He was convicted of war crimes and crimes against humanity by the Special Court.

Koroma, Johnny Paul (Major): Head of the AFRC, he fled to Liberia in 2003 after being implicated in a coup attempt and is presumed dead.

Mansaray, Rashid and Abu Kanu: Two of the original RUF fighters who trained in Libya. They were committed revolutionaries but both were killed during Sankoh's purge of RUF fighters in 1993.

Massaquoi, Gibril: One of the original RUF commanders trained in Liberia. In 1997 he became spokesman for the RUF. Massaquoi was an insider witness at the Special Court.

Mingo, Dennis (a.k.a. Superman): A Liberian-Sierra Leonean RUF commando who was known for his fighting skills. He was killed in the fighting against LURD in 2001.

Momoh, Joseph Saidu: President of Sierra Leone from 1985 to 1992 when he was overthrown by the army, which formed the NPRC regime. Momoh had been head of the Sierra Leone Army but resigned his commission as Major-General to become president. He later joined the AFRC junta and was arrested for treason. He died in 2003.

Musa, Solomon Anthony Joseph (Lieutenant) (known as "SAJ Musa"): A government soldier and vice-chairman of the NPRC, Musa was sent to Britain following criticism of a summary execution of coup plotters that he oversaw. He returned after the AFRC coup and joined the AFRC Supreme Council. After the Intervention Musa organized a force in the north to attack Freetown but died at Benguema, near Waterloo, in December 1998 prior to the invasion of the city.

Norman, Samuel Hinga: A former government soldier and Regent Chief of Jaiama-Bongor chiefdom in Bo District, Norman was an early supporter of civil militias and became leader of the Kamajors, then Deputy Minister of Defense and National Coordinator of Civil Defense Forces under President Kabbah. He was indicted by the Special Court for war crimes but died in 2009 before a judgment was handed down.

Nyuma, Tom (Lieutenant Colonel): A government soldier who took part in the NPRC coup. Nyuma became commander of the eastern region and was famous for fighting the RUF. In 2008 he was elected Chairman of Kailahun District Council. He died in 2014.

Appendix 2

Obasanjo, Olusegun: President of Nigeria from 1999 to 2007. He withdrew Nigerian ECOMOG troops from Sierra Leone on becoming president but continued to take part in negotiations up to the end of the war.

Qaddafi, Muammar: Leader of Libya from 1969 to 2011 when he was killed in an Arab Spring revolt. He supported the wars in Liberia and Sierra Leone by training fighters and providing funds.

Sankoh, Foday Saybana (called "Papay"): An army corporal and later a studio photographer, Sankoh was the leader of the RUF. He died in 2003.

Sesay, Issa Hassan: Third in command of the RUF, he became interim leader in 2000 after Mosquito went to Liberia and Foday Sankoh was arrested for treason. Sesay led the RUF when the group fought for Charles Taylor against LURD and during disarmament. He was convicted of war crimes and crimes against humanity by the Special Court.

Stevens, Siaka: Autocratic leader of Sierra Leone from 1971 to 1985, first as Prime Minister then as President. He died in 1988.

Strasser, Valentine Esegragbo Melvine (Captain): A government soldier who became head of the NPRC government at age 25, the youngest head of state in the world. He was deposed in a "palace coup" by Julius Maada Bio and went to Britain to study at a university. He faced criticism from Sierra Leoneans in Britain and returned to live in Sierra Leone after the war.

Taylor, Charles McArthur Ghankay: Head of the NPFL and supporter of Foday Sankoh and the RUF. An associate of Muammar Qaddafi, his troops invaded Liberia in 1989. Taylor was president of Liberia from 1997 to 2003. He was convicted of war crimes and crimes against humanity by the Special Court in 2012.

Timber, Charles (a.k.a. Rambo): The first Rambo of the war, Charles Timber was a well-known Liberian commando who was killed in an attack on Moa Barracks in Kailahun District during the first year of the war. His loss was a setback for the RUF who had planned to move directly to Freetown on entering the country.

Turay, Akim: First a government soldier, then a Kamajor, then RUF. He was well known for his fighting skills and knowledge of all three factions. In 2014 Akim was serving as a bodyguard to President Ernest Bai Koroma.

GLOSSARY

AA: anti-aircraft
alpha man: Muslim magic man (Krio)
armored car: may be used to refer to a tank
banga: palm kernel, the inner kernel of the palm nut (Krio)
barrie: an open pavilion used for meetings and court proceedings
bauxite: aluminum ore
BECE: Basic Education Certificate Examination, a standardized examination taken at the end of Junior Secondary School (9th grade) for promotion to Senior Secondary School
blended: blend of corn and soy meal
bo: "boy", a word used informally to address any person
Boxing Day: December 26th, the day after Christmas (British holiday)
boy: used to refer to a boy or man up to around 25 years of age
brown-brown: brown heroin
brush: to cut down grass and bush
bulgur: cereal food made of wheat, distributed in relief programs by the World Food Program and UNHCR
Burkinabé: national of Burkina Faso or the adjective form of Burkina Faso
bus park: an area in a town where public transport vehicles park
bush: area of forest, brush, or uncultivated land
bush road: footpath through the bush
bypass: bush path, back road, back way
chakabula: single-shot rifle used for hunting
chief: traditional leader of a town, section, or chiefdom
chiefdom: political unit headed by a paramount chief. Each district is divided into a number of chiefdoms.
CO: Commanding Officer
combat: may refer to a combat uniform
compound: family house and outbuildings
condiments: items used in stew such as pepper, onions, and Maggi cubes

Glossary

controller: a magical object used by the Kamajors to deflect bullets and shells and to warn of attacks

cowrie shell (or "cowry"): shell of a sea snail found in the Indian Ocean, formerly used as currency in Africa and other parts of the world

CPP: Committee for the Consolidation of Peace: the agency set up after the Lomé Accord to oversee disarmament and other points in the accord.

crepes: crepe-sole shoes

CRS: Catholic Relief Service

DDR: Disarmament, Demobilization and Reintegration

devil: traditional dancer with his/her identity hidden by a mask who appears during ceremonies and holidays

dew: may refer to fog

facilities: in Sierra Leone this word can refer to any kind of benefits that people have, not only buildings

FGC: Female Genital Cutting, also called FGM, Female Genital Mutilation

Form (1, 2, etc): secondary school class levels under the British system

fufu: starchy paste made of cassava or yams

ganja: cannabis, marijuana, jamba

gara: cloth that is tie-dyed or wax print dyed

gari: grated and dried cassava

GMG: general machine gun

ghetto: a place in a town where jamba and drinks are sold

go-slow: a workers' strike

green-green: green camouflage combat uniform

groundnuts: peanuts

hammock: in the African bush a hammock may be used to carry people when traveling

Honorable: member of Parliament

HMG: heavy machine gun

HTC: Higher Teachers Certificate

IDP: internally displaced person, internal refugee within a country

IOM: International Organization for Migration, an international intergovernmental organization

Glossary

IPAM: Institute of Public Administration and Management, an institute in Freetown that is part of the University of Sierra Leone

IRC: International Rescue Committee, a non-governmental organization

ja-ja: food-finding mission

jamba: cannabis, marijuana, ganja

jege: a charm that includes cowrie shells, attached to the body for protection

jeke: gambling game played with spinning tops (Krio)

jet: may be used to refer to both fighter jets and helicopters

jo-jo: pit used to detain and torture prisoners (from "dungeon")

jula man: diamond businessman

jungle: used by the RUF to refer to areas of operation

junglers: used by the RUF to refer to their fighters

kamor: Muslim magic man (Mende)

karamoko: Kamajor initiator (Mende)

kimberlite: diamond ore

kola nut: bitter nut that is chewed, contains caffeine

lappa: cloth worn by women around the waist

LMG: light machine gun

Maggi: seasoning cube

mahei: chief (Mende)

Maraka: ethnic group from the Gambia who engage in diamond trading in Sierra Leone

mori man: Muslim magic man (Krio)

NaCSA: National Commission for Social Action, a commission formed after the war to effect rapid redevelopment

NCDDR: National Commission for Disarmament, Demobilization and Resettlement

NDMC: National Diamond Mining Corporation, phased out in the 1990s

nessi: magic oil used for protection (Mende)

NGO: non-governmental organization, any non-profit, voluntary citizens' group which is organized on a local, national, or international level.

NP: National Petroleum

O Levels: standardized examination taken at the end of secondary school in the British system, replaced by the WASSCE in West African countries

Glossary

OAU: Organization of African Unity, continent-wide body of African states, replaced in 2002 by the African Union

Oga: local name for Nigerian ECOMOG soldiers, slang for "boss" in Nigeria

oil palm: *Elaeis guineensis*, the palm tree from which palm oil, palm kernel oil, and palm wine are harvested

okada: motorcycle taxi

omole: local gin (Mende)

OPS: operation station, deployment area

Pa: used to refer to a middle-aged or respected man

palaver: a discussion or quarrel, to discuss or quarrel

palm kernel oil: clear oil made by pressing the inner kernel of the oil palm nut (palm fruit)

palm oil: orange-red oil pressed from the mesocarp of the palm nut (palm fruit), eaten with rice and used in plasas (stew)

palm wine: alcoholic drink tapped fresh from the oil palm tree

pan body house: house made of corrugated metal sheeting

PANAFU: Pan African Union, a student group formed at Fourah Bay College before the war

Paramount Chief: the traditional leader of a chiefdom, elected for life from one of the ruling houses designated for each chiefdom

paw-paw: papaya

pikin: child, children (Krio)

plasas: stew eaten on rice made of ingredients including oil, onions, peppers, seasoning, meat and fish, greens, peanut butter, beans, etc. (Krio)

poda-poda: passenger van

Poro Society: men's secret society

potato leaf: leaf from a local potato vine used in stew

poyo: palm wine (Krio)

properties: may be used to refer to personal belongings

RC: Roman Catholic

RDF: Rapid Deployment Force

rehog: to regroup

rek: to spy, to do reconnaissance

Glossary

rekky: a spy

ronko: woven shirt for men

RPG: rocket-propelled grenade

rum: can refer to any kind of liquor

rutile: titanium dioxide

Salone: this shortened form of Sierra Leone was originally used for the Freetown colony but now refers to the entire country

sebe: charm with Arabic writing decorated with threads, attached to clothes or near doors for protection (Krio)

shistosomiasis: also called bilharzia, a debilitating disease caused by a parasitic worm, contracted in streams and rivers

SLBS: Sierra Leone Broadcasting System, the government-run radio network (now SLBC)

SLMB: Sierra Leone Muslim Brotherhood

SMG: support machine gun

sobel: soldier/rebel, a word coined to describe soldiers who looted and committed violence against civilians like the rebels

soquihun: bush camp (Mende)

Sowei: chief initiator of the local woman's Bundu or Sande society who appears as a masked figure on ceremonial occasions

STI: Sexually Transmitted Infection

Special Forces: Forces trained outside the country at the start of the war

stumping: taking out tree stumps when preparing forested land for farming

town speaker: spokesperson for a town, the position directly under the town chief

TRC: Truth and Reconciliation Commission

turntable: roundabout (traffic)

UNHCR: United Nations High Commissioner for Refugees

UNICEF: United Nations Children's Fund

UNITA: Uniao Nacional para a Independencia Total de Angola, an Angolan rebel group

up-garret: two-storey building

vangahun: term the rebels used for foreign fighters

vigilante: voluntary support soldier

Glossary

VSO: Voluntary Service Overseas, a British volunteer development organization

ward counselor: representative of a ward (political division of a district)

wash, wash the body: to pour magic water on the body for protection

WASSCE: West Africa Senior School Certificate Examination, a standardized examination taken at the end of Senior Secondary School, used in West African Anglophone countries

WFP: World Food Program

worship: may be used as a noun to refer to a magical object kept for protection

zinc: corrugated metal sheeting, commonly used for roofing

FOOTNOTES

PREFACE

1. *Witness to Truth: Report of the Sierra Leone Truth and Reconciliation Commission,* Vol. 3A, Ch 4, Par. 24, p. 471

COUNTRY AND PEOPLE

1. United Nations Development Program, 2015 Human Development Report http://hdr.undp.org/en/composite/HDI
2. United Nations Development Program, 2015 Human Development Report http://hdr.undp.org/en/countries/profiles/SLE
3. Transparency International, Corruption Perceptions Index 2015 (https://www.transparency.org/cpi2015/)
4. United Nations Development Program, 2015 Human Development Report http://hdr.undp.org/en/countries/profiles/SLE
5. United Nations Development Program, 2015 Human Development Report http://hdr.undp.org/sites/default/files/hdr_2015_statistical_annex.pdf
6. Ibid.
7. *Human Leopards, An Account of the Trials of Human Leopards before the Special Commission Court with a note on Sierra Leone Past and Present,* London, Hugh Rees, Ltd,., 1915 (available online)
8. *Witness to Truth: Report of the Sierra Leone Truth and Reconciliation Commission,* Vol. 3A, Ch. 4, Par. 126, p. 497
9. World Bank Data (http://data.worldbank.org/indicator/SE.ADT.LITR.ZS)
10. *Female Genital Mutilation/Cutting: A statistical overview and exploration of the dynamics of change,* United Nations Children's Fund (UNICEF), July 2013

BEFORE THE WAR

1. *Witness to Truth: Report of the Sierra Leone Truth and Reconciliation Commission,* Vol. 1, Introduction, Par. 11, p. 10
2. Ibid. Vol. 3, Ch. 3, Par. 126, p. 120
3. Judgment, Special Court for Sierra Leone, Trial Chamber II, Case No. SCSL-03-1-T, Prosecutor v. Charles Gbankay Taylor, May 18, 2012, Par. 6767-6787, pp. 2395-2405

THE REBEL WAR: 1991-2002

1. *Witness to Truth: Report of the Sierra Leone Truth and Reconciliation Commission*, Vol. 3a, Ch. 3, Par. 541-545, pp. 207-208
2. *Sierra Leone: The Extrajudicial Execution of Suspected Rebels and Collaborators*, Amnesty International, 1992
3. Judgment Summary, Special Court for Sierra Leone, Trial Chamber II Case No.SCSL-03-1-T, Prosecutor v. Charles Gbankay Taylor, April 26, 2011, Par. 65, pp. 13-14
4. Jackson, Michael D, *In Sierra Leone*, Duke University Press, 2004, p. 143
5. *Witness to Truth: Report of the Sierra Leone Truth and Reconciliation Commission*, Vol. 3A, Ch. 3, Par. 423-424, pp. 184-185
6. *A Revolutionary United Front (RUF) camp near or in Zimmi; a fight with government soldiers in 1994 (1991-1995)* Immigration and Refugee Board of Canada: [SLE41276.E], 26 February 2003 (available at ecoi.net: European Country of Origin Information Network), quoted from *Sierra Leone: Fighting Intensifies in Africa Research Bulletin: Political, Social and Cultural Series* (ARB), Oxford, 24 April 1994. Vol. 31, No. 3, p. 11375
7. *Witness to Truth: Report of the Sierra Leone Truth and Reconciliation Commission*, Vol. 3A, Ch. 4, Par. 118-124, pp. 496-497
8. Judgment Summary, Special Court for Sierra Leone, Trial Chamber II Case No.SCSL-03-1-T, Prosecutor v. Charles Gbankay Taylor, April 26, 2011, Par. 65, pp. 13-14
9. *War for Diamonds: Executive Outcomes in Sierra Leone;* Soldiers of Misfortune (website) http://www.soldiers-of-misfortune.com/history/eo-sierra-leone.htm
10. *World News Briefs: Sierra Leone Civil War Is Causing Starvation*, New York Times, August 31, 1995
11. Sierra Leone Web, News Archives, March 9, 1996
12. *Witness to Truth: Report of the Sierra Leone Truth and Reconciliation Commission*, Vol. 3A, Ch. 3, Par. 662, p. 237
13. French, Howard W, *African Rebel With Room Service*, New York Times, June 23, 1996
14. Special Court for Sierra Leone, Case SCSL-03-1-T, Judgment Summary, April 26, 2011, Par. 86, p. 20
15. Special Court for Sierra Leone, Case SCSL-03-1-T, Judgment Summary, 26 April 2011, Par 113, p. 27
16. *Witness to Truth: Report of the Sierra Leone Truth and Reconciliation Commission*, Vol 3A, Ch 3, Par 651-652, p. 235

17. Judgment Summary, Special Court for Sierra Leone, Trial Chamber II Case No.SCSL-03-1-T, Prosecutor v. Charles Gbankay Taylor, April 26, 2011, Par 121, p. 29
18. Sierra Leone Web, News Archives, May 7, 1997
19. Witness to Truth: Report of the Sierra Leone Truth and Reconciliation Commission, Vol. 3a, Ch. 3, Par. 693, p. 247
20. Sierra Leone Web, News Archives, June 6, 1997
21. Judgment, Special Court for Sierra Leone, Trial Chamber II, Case No. SCSL-03-1-T, Prosecutor v. Charles Gbankay Taylor, May 18, 2012, Par. 5874, p. 2060
22. *Sierra Leone 1998—A year of atrocities against civilians*, Amnesty International, Report AFR, 51/22/98 London, November 1998, p. 14
23. Judgment, Special Court for Sierra Leone, Trial Chamber II, Case No. SCSL-03-1-T, Prosecutor v. Charles Gbankay Taylor, May 18, 2012, Par. 5840, p. 2044
24. Judgment, Special Court for Sierra Leone, Trial Chamber I, Case No. SCSL-04-14-T, Prosecutor Against Moinina Fofana, Allieu Kondewa (Kamajor Judgment), April 2, 2007, Par. 383-386, pp. 122-123
25. *Witness to Truth: Report of the Sierra Leone Truth and Reconciliation Commission*, Vol. 3A, Ch. 4, Par. 151-153, 303, pp. 505, 546-547
26. *Security Council Meets in Open Session to Consider Situation in Sierra Leone*, Africa Focus 12/18/1998 Press Release SC/6613
27. *Witness to Truth: Report of the Sierra Leone Truth and Reconciliation Commission*, Vol. 3A, Ch. 3, Par. 932, p. 306
28. Judgment Summary, Special Court for Sierra Leone, Trial Chamber II Case No.SCSL-03-1-T, Prosecutor v. Charles Gbankay Taylor, April 26, 2011, Par. 73, p. 16
29. *Sierra Leone: Human Rights Developments*, Human Rights Watch, Archives, www.hrw.org/legacy/wr2k/Africa-09.htm
30. Onishi, Norimitsu, *Pacts Reached on Congo and Sierra Leone*, New York Times, July 8, 1999
31. *Human Development Report 1999*, United Nations Development Program, p.128
32. Mathers, Colin D et al: *Healthy Life Expectancy in 191 Countries*, World Health Report 2000, The Lancet, Vol. 357, May 26, 2001
33. Judgment Summary, Special Court for Sierra Leone, Trial Chamber II Case No.SCSL-03-1-T, Prosecutor v. Charles Gbankay Taylor, April 26, 2011, Par.114, p. 27

Footnotes

34. Witte, Eric, *Summary from Charles Taylor at the Special Court, 12:00 Witness describes attacks around West Side Base*, Testimony of witness Alimamy Bobson Sesay, April 24, 20308, http://www.ijmonitor.org/2008/04/1200-witness-describes-attacks-around-west-side-base/
35. *Witness to Truth: Report of the Sierra Leone Truth and Reconciliation Commission*, Vol. 2, Ch. 2, Par. 398, p. 88
36. *Humanitarian Intervention: Britain in Sierra Leone*, BBC News Report (video), www.youtube.com/watch?v=Dp7Q018O6s4
37. Judgment Summary, Special Court for Sierra Leone, Trial Chamber II Case No.SCSL-03-1-T, Prosecutor v. Charles Gbankay Taylor, April 26, 2011, Par. 118, pp. 28-29
38. Harden, Blaine, *2 African Nations Said to Break U.N. Diamond Embargo*, New York Times, August 1, 2000
39. Sierra Leone Web News Archives, Sept 11, 2001
40. Thokozani, Thusi and Sarah Meek, *Monograph 80: Sierra Leone, Building the Road to Recovery, Institute for Security Studies* (ISS), March 1, 2003, Ch. 1, pp. 33, 35
41. *Witness to Truth: Report of the Sierra Leone Truth and Reconciliation Commission*, Vol. 2, Ch. 2, Par. 536, p. 105

SOURCES

BOOKS

Abraham, Arthur, *Mende Government and Politics under Colonial Rule*, Sierra Leone University Press, 1978

Coulter, Chris, *Bush Wives and Girl Soldiers: Women's Lives through War and Peace in Sierra Leone*, Cornell University Press, 2009

Gberie, Lansana, *A Dirty War in West Africa: The RUF and the Destruction of Sierra Leone*, Indiana University Press, 2005

Jackson, Michael D, *In Sierra Leone*, Duke University Press, 2004

Kabbah, Tejan Ahmad, *Coming Back from the Brink in Sierra Leone: A Memoir*, Excellent Publishing and Printing, Accra, 2010

Keen, David, *Conflict and Collusion in Sierra Leone*, Palgrave Macmillan, 2005

Peters, Krijn, *War and the Crisis of Youth in Sierra Leone*, Cambridge University Press, 2011

Waugh, Colin M, *Charles Taylor and Liberia: Ambition and Atrocity in Africa's Lone Star State*, Zed Books, 2011

Woods, Larry J. and Timothy R. Reese, *Military Interventions in Sierra Leone: Lessons from a Failed State*, Combat Studies Institute Press, Fort Leavenworth, Kansas, 2011

ARTICLES AND PAPERS

Arkley, Alfred, *Slavery in Sierra Leone*, M.A. Thesis, Columbia University, 1965

Farah, Douglas, *Harvard for Tyrants*, Foreign Policy, March 4, 2011

Igwe, Leo, "Witch-Gun" and Superstition in Guinea and Sierra Leone, Sierra Express Media, September 8, 2013

Kamara, Tom, *Liberia – Meaningless UN Sanctions*, The Perspective/Africa News, July 7, 2000

Leboeuf, Aline, *Sierra Leone: List of extremely violent events perpetrated during the War, 1991-2002*, published March 5, 2008, Online Encyclopedia of Mass Violence, http://www.massviolence.org/Sierra-Leone-List-of-extremely-violent-events-perpetrated

Malan, Mark, Phenyao Rakate, and Angela McIntyre, *Peacekeeping in Sierra Leone: UNAMSIL Hits the Home Straight*, Institute for Security Studies Monograph 68, January 1, 2002

Marcus, Jonathan, *Analysis: "Mission creep" in Sierra Leone?*, BBC, Friday, 19 May, 2000

Mufson, Steven, *U.S. Backs Amnesty in Sierra Leone*, Washington Post, October 18, 1999

Sources

Perbi, Dr.Akosua, *Slavery and the Slave Trade in Pre-Colonial Africa*, Paper delivered April 5, 2001 at the Univ. of Illinois (www.latinamericanstudies.org/slavery/perbi.pdf)
Polgreen, Lydia, *A Master Plan Drawn in Blood*, New York Times, April 2, 2006
Thusi, Thokozani and Sarah Meek, *Monograph 80: Sierra Leone, Building the Road to Recovery*, Institute for Security Studies (ISS), March 1, 2003
Timmerman, Kenneth R., *Jesse, Liberia and Blood Diamonds*, Insight Magazine, July 25, 2003
Utas, Mats and Magnus Jorgel, *The West Side Boys: Military Navigation in the Sierra Leone Civil War*, The Journal of Modern African Studies, Volume 46, Issue 03, September 2008, pp 487-511
Waterfield, Bruno, *Charles Taylor: how Naomi Campbell 'blood diamond' evidence was critical*, The Telegraph, April 26, 2012

REPORTS

IMF Approves Third Annual ESAF Loan for Sierra Leone, Press Release Number 97/23, International Monetary Fund, 700 19th Street, NW, Washington, DC, 20431, May 5, 1997
Liberia: The key to Ending Regional Instability, International Crisis Group, Africa Report No. 43, Freetown/Brussels, April 24, 2002
Nigerian Intervention in Sierra Leone, Conciliation Resources, 1997 (http://www.c-r.org/sites/c-r.org/files/NigerianIntervention_199710_ENG.pdf)
No Peace Without Justice, Conflict Mapping in Sierra Leone: Violations of International Humanitarian Law 1991 to 2002, International Criminal Justice Program, March 2004 (www.npwj.org/ICC/Conflict-Mapping-Sierra-Leone-Violations-International-Humanitarian-Law-1991-2002.html)
Sierra Leone 1998 – A year of atrocities against civilians, Amnesty International, Report AFR 51/22/98, London, November 1998
Sierra Leone: A disastrous set-back for human rights, Amnesty International, Report AFR 51/05/97, October 20, 1997
Sierra Leone: Human rights abuses in a war against civilians, Amnesty International, Report AFR5/05/95, London, September 1995
Sierra Leone: The Extrajudicial Execution of Suspected Rebels and Collaborators, Amnesty International, 1992 (www.amnesty.org/en/library/info/AFR51/002/1992/en)
Surviving the First Day: State of World's Mothers 2013, Save the Children, May 2013
Witness to Truth: Report of the Sierra Leone Truth and Reconciliation Commission, Vol. 1-5, 2004 (www.sierraleonetrc.org)

Sources

Youth, Poverty and Blood: The Lethal Legacy of West Africa's Regional Warriors, Human Rights Watch, Vol. 17, No. 5 (A), March 2005

TRIAL JUDGMENTS (VERDICTS)
Judgment, Special Court for Sierra Leone, Trial Chamber I, Case No. SCSL-04-14-T, Prosecutor Against Moinina Fofana, Allieu Kondewa (Kamajor Judgment), April 2, 2007
Judgment, Special Court for Sierra Leone, Trial Chamber 1, Case No. SCSL-04-15-T, Prosecutor Against Issa Hassan Sesay, Morris Kallon, Augustine Gbao (RUF Judgment), March 2, 2009
Judgment, Special Court for Sierra Leone, Trial Chamber 1, Case No. SCSL-04-16-T, Prosecutor Against Alex Tamba Brima, Brima Bazzy Kamara, Santigie Borbor Kanu (AFRC Judgment), June 20, 2007
Judgment, Special Court for Sierra Leone, Trial Chamber II, Case No. SCSL-03-1-T, Prosecutor v. Charles Gbankay Taylor, May 18, 2012
Judgment Summary, Special Court for Sierra Leone, Trial Chamber II Case No.SCSL-03-1-T, Prosecutor v. Charles Ghankay Taylor, April 26, 2011
United States Court of Appeals for the Eleventh Circuit, No. 09-10461, United States of America vs. Roy M. Belfast Jr., Appeal from the United States District Court for the Southern District of Florida, July 15, 2010

WEBSITES
Global Security.org (articles on Sierra Leone, Liberia and Guinea)
International Justice Monitor (testimony and commentary on the Special Court trial of Charles Taylor) http://www.ijmonitor.org/charles-taylor-background/
Sierra Leone Web, News Archives, http://www.sierra-leone.org/archives.html
Special Court For Sierra Leone, http://www.rscsl.org/

NARRATORS: Year and original language of interview
2010: Bobby (Mende), Jeneba (Mende)
2011: Alfred (Krio), Ansumana (Mende), Baby Seiya (Mende), Bolo (Krio), Fallah (English), Foday (Krio), Gibrilla (English), Jasper (Krio), Jusu (Krio), Kaiku (Krio), Lucia (Mende), Makambo (Krio), Mohamed (English), Mr Tucker (Krio), Sheku (Mende)
2012: Abdul (Mende), Allan (English), Borbor (Mende), Edward (English), Finda (Krio), Heavy D (Krio), Jammie (Krio), Kumba (Krio), Mahmood (English), Margaret (English), Massah (Krio), Michael (English), Momodu (Krio), Samuel (Krio), Tamba (English)
2013: Fatmata (Krio), Isata (Krio)

INDEX

Abacha, Sani, 55, 68, 222, 285
Abidjan Peace Accord, 52-54, 58, 91
Abuja (Nigeria), 54
Abuja Ceasefire Agreement, 87
Adama Cut Hand, 67, 131, 134, 246
AFRC (Armed Forces Revolutionary Council): coup, 54-55; junta, 55-61, 137-139, 149, 202-205, 218-222, 228; conflicts with RUF, 56-58, 65-67, 70-71, 77-78, 79, 82-83; Intervention (AFRC junta forced out of power), 61-64, 139, 149, 189, 205-210, 222-223, 228-229; AFRC/RUF renegade after return of government, 65-75, 77-78, 79-80, 82-83, 86-87, 140-141, 149-150, 160-172, 228-232, 251-255; convictions, 92-94. *See also* army (Sierra Leone Army), and Freetown, attack on city
amnesty, 67-69, 76
Amnesty International, 36, 58-59
amphetamines, 43
amputations, 28, 50-51, 65, 67, 74, 104, 131, 134, 144, 154-155, 158, 167, 176, 180, 246, 254
Annan, Kofi, 76
APC (political party), 21-23, 36, 50, 55, 102, 105, 113, 115, 118, 176
arms, weapons, 35, 89, 119-120, 128, 133, 138, 200-201, 262
arms shipments, 26, 27, 39, 53, 59-60, 69, 76-77, 83, 85, 107, 133
army (Sierra Leone Army), 22; early fighting and NPRC coup, 31-41, 135-137; guerrilla warfare period, 41-51; soldiers committing crimes ("sobels"), 44-45; SLPP in power after elections, 51-54; conflicts with Kamajors, 48, 51-52, 53-54, 137, 188-189; army troops loyal to government (following AFRC coup), 54-55, 57, 61,

66, 67-68, 74, 83-84, 87, 89. *See also* NPRC, and AFRC for the two junta periods of the war
atrocities, 28-29, 32-33, 37, 41-43, 50-51, 61, 64, 65-66, 67, 70, 73-75, 92-93, 104, 108-109, 131, 143-144, 161-163, 164-171, 181-182, 244-245, 253-254, 271-274
Bangura, Hassan Papa ("Bomblast"), 77-78, 232, 233, 285
Bangura, John, 21-22
Base Zero, 45, 59, 61, 63, 187, 189
Bazzy (aka of Ibrahim Bazzy Kamara), 56, 65, 77-78, 80, 92-94, 232-233, 285
Benguema (army training base), 71, 136, 191, 231, 237-238
Bio, Julius Maada, 37, 50, 227, 285
black magic: *see* witchcraft
Blair, Tony, 84
Blama (town), 51, 153
blockade, of Freetown harbor, 58, 221-222
Bo (town), 24, 41, 44, 58, 59, 61-64, 81, 93, 180-182, 183-184, 189, 194-216
Bo District, 33, 44, 51, 60, 89, 173-174
Bockarie, Samuel: *see* Mosquito
Bomaru (town), 31, 100-104, 127
Bombali District, 67, 75, 89, 130, 168-169, 245-247
Bonthe District, 33, 44, 45, 47, 50, 59, 89, 173-174, 187-188
Branch Energy, 48, 60, 148-149
Brima, Alex Tamba: *see* Gullit
Britain, 3, 8, 12, 18-20, 39-40, 44, 57, 58, 60, 64, 75, 81, 83-88, 95, 234, 249
British troops, abduction of, 86-87, 241
brown-brown, 43, 134, 273
Buedu (RUF Headquarters), 41, 65-67, 69, 71, 121, 130, 133, 136, 139, 227, 230, 231
Bundu society, 14-15

Index

Bunumbu (town, college), 36, 100, 108, 122, 126, 139-140, 145, 153
Bunumbu Camp Lion (RUF training base), 227
Burkina Faso, 25-26, 86, 106, 119, 121, 122, 134, 175
bush wife, 41, 43, 102-103, 130, 133, 162, 185-186, 271-272
Bush, George W, 94, 235
Calaba Town, 73, 231-232, 239, 242
Camp Naama (training base in Liberia), 27, 29, 174-175
Campaoré, Blaise, 25-27, 86, 285
Campbell, Naomi, 59-60
cannibalism, 12, 37, 143-144, 152
Caritas, 80, 241, 255
ceasefire, 40, 52, 76, 87, 130-131, 134, 262, 274
Center for Victims of Torture, 153, 279
chief, paramount chief, 7, 20, 36, 45, 58, 101, 102, 105, 108, 115-116, 122, 167, 182-183, 184, 187, 197, 202, 204
child soldiers, 43, 78, 80, 89, 93, 249, 281; AFRC, 236-241, 251-255; Kamajors, 51; RUF, 104-114, 164-172, 265-278. *See also* Small Boys Unit
Christian, 5, 11, 19, 177, 193, 216
Civil Defense Forces, development and role, 39, 44-45, 51-52, 53-54; fighting, 48-49, 59, 61, 63-64, 66-67, 74, 83, 87-88; disarmament, 80, 89
Cline Town, 18, 74, 244
Clinton, Bill, 68, 76
cocaine, 43, 128, 134, 166, 175, 260, 273
Cockerill Military Headquarters, 56, 57, 220, 228
colony, colonial government, 3, 12, 18-20, 24, 25, 32, 55, 160
Committee for the Consolidation of Peace, 79, 82
Commonwealth, 58
Conakry (Guinea), 87, 150, 245
Conakry Peace Plan, 60
Congo Cross Bridge (Freetown), 74, 226

Conté, Lansana, 27, 78, 286
Cook, Robin, 81
corruption, 7-9, 12-13, 20, 22-23, 28, 35, 108, 243-244, 260
coup d'état, 21, 23, 25-26, 37, 50, 52, 54-55, 57-58, 68
coup plot, 22, 39-40, 54, 83, 91
Cry Freetown (documentary), 81
Cutlass War, 89, 264
Daru (town, Moa Barracks), 32, 43, 51, 70, 101, 106-107, 113, 120-121, 127, 136, 140-141, 193, 266
DDR (Disarmament, Demobilization, and Reintegration), 76, 79, 80-82, 85-90, 112-113, 124, 130, 132, 134-135, 158, 171, 199, 234-235, 241, 255, 262-264, 276
demonstrations, 23, 55, 58, 78, 82-83, 139, 233-234, 259
diamonds, diamond mining, 2, 4, 8, 20, 22; during war, 28, 33, 43, 47, 48, 67, 75, 89, 137, 145-146, 147-150, 166-167, 174, 243-244, 262-263, 264
diamonds for arms, 39, 58, 59-60, 69-70, 76-77, 81, 82, 83, 85-86, 88, 123, 250
disarmament: *see* DDR
Doe, Samuel, 25, 27, 175
Donso (Civil Defense Force), 39, 45, 150
drugs, 43, 134, 163, 260, 273-274
ECOMOG: formation, base in Liberia, 27, 59-60; fighting RUF, 40, 44, 47, 147; AFRC coup, Intervention and after, 54-55, 57-68, 138-141, 147, 149-150, 156-157, 168, 209-210, 220-225, 228-233; leaving Sierra Leone, 80, 81-82, 92. *See also* Freetown, attack on city
ECOWAS, 27, 47, 52, 58, 84, 85, 87, 94
education, 10, 12-16, 22-23, 26, 171, 250, 256, 260, 277
effects of war, 104, 124-125, 144, 155, 178-179, 265, 278-282
elections, 21-22, 49-52, 75, 125, 148-149, 154-155, 186, 234, 246

303

Index

England: *see* Britain
ethnic groups: *see* tribes
Executive Outcomes, 48-49, 52-54, 60, 147-149
FGC/FGM, 15
Fofana, Moinina, 51, 92-93, 188, 286
Fogbo (town), 48, 63
food finding, 41, 129-130, 140, 165-166, 168, 252, 267-269
Fourah Bay College, 12, 19, 23, 74
Freetown Peninsula, 1, 17-19, 61-63, 74, 139, 223, 228
Freetown: early history, 1-2, 12, 18-20, 22-23; beginning of war, 32-33, 36; NPRC in power, 37, 39, 44, 47-49, 51; AFRC in power, 54-64; 218-223; return of government, attack on city, 64-75, 223-226, 230-232, 236-240, 242-244, 244-245, 247-248, 253-254, 257-259; to end of war, 79, 81, 82-84, 87, 91, 93, 226, 232-236, 259-260
Fullah (ethnic group), 3, 120, 141, 153, 160, 163-164, 178, 213, 251, 263
Gandorhun (town), 33, 39, 65, 67, 122-123, 145, 146-148, 157, 159
Gbao, Augustine, 82, 92-93, 227, 286
Gbarnga (Taylor Headquarters in Liberia), 27, 99, 115, 174-175
Gberibana (town), 77-78, 86-87
Gbinti (Civil Defense Force), 45, 198
Gbondema, Komba, 75, 88, 254-255, 262, 263
gender issues: *see* women and girls
Ghana, 25, 27, 47, 55, 82, 123, 193, 283
Gio (ethnic group in Liberia), 25, 27, 101, 108, 144
girls: *see* women and girls
God, 5, 10-11, 118, 142, 160, 164, 171-172, 177-178, 194, 200, 216, 236, 241, 248
Green Book, 23-24, 195
Gueckedou (town in Guinea), 87-88, 150, 155, 164, 266, 275
Guinea, 1, 5, 18-19, 22, 32, 37, 47, 50, 55, 60, 66, 75, 120; Guinean army, 27, 32, 47, 55, 140; fighting on border, 70, 75, 76, 78-79, 85, 87-88, 253, 259, 261, 267-268, 274-276
Gullit (aka of Alex Tamba Brima), 56, 65, 67, 70-71, 71-73, 80, 92-93, 233, 285
Hastings Airfield, 55, 61, 71, 73, 228, 238, 257
hostages, 47, 58, 78, 82, 86-87, 120, 232
Human Rights Watch, 75
IDP camps (Internally Displaced Person camps), 40, 44, 47, 51, 153
IMF (International Monetary Fund), 23, 53
independence, 3, 8, 12, 20-21, 160
International Rescue Committee, 266, 276, 280
Ivory Coast, 25, 26, 52-53, 94, 174-175
Jackson, Jesse, 68, 76
jamba (marijuana), 43, 127, 175, 190, 198, 208, 260, 268, 273-275
Johnson, Ellen Sirleaf, 95
Joru (town), 33, 175, 177
Jui (town), 55, 58, 61, 63, 73, 139, 221, 222, 238, 244
Kabala (town), 43, 47, 66, 67, 80, 130, 134, 147, 217, 230, 253, 255, 282
Kabbah, Ahmad Tejan: election, 50, 148, 154; in power, 51-54, 148; government-in-exile, 55, 57-64; return to power (Intervention), 64, 67-69, 70, 75-76, 78, 79, 82, 83, 84, 89-90, 91-92, 134, 222, 253-254, 259
Kailahun (town), 32, 33, 41, 67, 84, 100, 105-107, 108, 111, 112-113, 115, 116, 117-118, 121, 130, 136, 230
Kailahun District (RUF headquarters), 99-100; early fighting, 29, 31-39, 40-44, 52, 100-124, 136-137, 227; AFRC/RUF combined, 65-67, 69-71, 140-141, 156-157, 230; after Freetown attack, fighting in Guinea, 75, 77-78, 78-80, 82, 84, 87-89, 275-276

Kallay, Foday, 80, 86-87, 233, 241, 286
Kallon, Morris, 57, 65, 82, 92-93, 113, 140, 227, 230, 233, 286
Kamajor (Civil Defense Force): formation, initiation and beliefs, 44-45, 157-158, 186-188; early fighting, conflicts with army, build-up, 44-45, 48-49, 51-52, 53-54, 137, 183-184, 188-189, 199-202; fighting AFRC/RUF, 55, 58-67, 71, 74, 156-157, 167-168, 178, 184, 189-190, 202-210, 213-214; late fighting, disarmament, convictions, 80, 83, 87-89, 92-93
Kamara, Ibrahim Bazzy: *see* Bazzy
Kamara, Idrissa (aka Leatherboot), 76, 286
Kambia (town), 66
Kambia District, 47, 70, 75, 79, 87-88, 89, 218, 236-237, 244-245, 256-257, 259, 261
Kanu, Santigie Borbor, 56, 65, 92-94, 233, 287
Kapra (Civil Defense Force), 45
Karina (town), 67
Kenema (town), 33, 43-44, 51, 54, 58, 59, 61, 63-64, 70-71, 81, 134-135, 141
Kenema District, 2, 32-33, 41, 61, 89, 99-100, 111-112, 137, 153
Khobe, Maxwell, 55, 64, 139, 223, 239, 287
Kimberley Process, 81
Kissidougou (town in Guinea), 87, 275
Koakoyima (town), 66, 149, 163, 168
Koidu (town): early fighting, 33, 39, 43, 48, 122-123, 145-149, 151-153; AFRC coup, Intervention and after, 64-67, 70-71, 75, 149-150, 164-168, 229-230; end of war, 89, 155, 171, 261-265, 276-277, 278
Koinadugu District, 39, 43, 65, 67, 89, 251-254
Koindu (town): early fighting, 32, 104-106, 119-120, 136; after Intervention, 67

Kombayendeh (town), 267-278
Kondowai, Allieu, 45, 59, 92, 93, 178, 188-189, 287
Kono (ethnic group), 3, 39, 45, 145, 150
Kono District, 2, 20, 145-146; early fighting, 33-35, 37-40, 43, 48, 58, 122-123, 146-149, 151-153, 154-155, 159-160; AFRC coup, Intervention and after, 64-67, 69-70, 75, 77, 139, 140-141, 149-150, 153, 156-157, 160-164, 164-171, 228-232; fighting for Taylor, end of war, 79, 81-82, 87-89, 171-172, 261-282
Koribundu (town, barracks), 60, 64, 189
Koroma, Johnny Paul: AFRC coup and junta, 37, 54-60, 137-139, 202; Intervention, 61-67, 77-78, 139, 153, 221, 228-229; head of CCP, disappearance, 79-80, 82-83, 91-93, 255
Krahn (ethnic group in Liberia), 25, 27
Krio (ethnic group), 3, 5, 19-21
Krio (language), 3, 19, 124, 152, 153, 210, 223, 244
Lamin, Mike, 33, 79, 140, 227
Lebanese, 4, 166, 196, 222
Liberia, Liberians, 1, 2, 12, 18; early fighting in Liberia, 24-29, 249-250; early fighting in Sierra Leone, 31-33, 36, 37-39, 40-41, 47, 52, 100-101, 103-104, 106-109, 113, 114-116, 119-125, 127-128, 133-134, 136, 142-144, 174-178, 195; Intervention and after, 59-60, 63-64, 67, 69, 71, 76-77, 150; RUF fighting for Taylor, end of war, 78-79, 81, 84, 85-88, 90-95, 142, 249-250, 262, 275-277
Libya, 23-24, 26, 53, 77, 122, 175, 195, 230
Limba (ethnic group), 3, 21, 45, 48, 61, 236, 244, 251-252
Lofa County (Liberia), 32, 79, 84, 87, 94
Lomé Peace Accord, 68, 76-77, 79, 84, 92, 112, 113, 286

Index

looting: as tactic, 28, 36, 41-43, 63, 78, 108-109, 111, 113, 121, 123, 147, 161, 167, 176, 198; by "sobels", 44, 202; incidents, 31-33, 55, 56, 58, 63-64, 65, 70-71, 83, 180, 184, 189, 195-196, 205, 209, 221, 240, 257, 258, 259, 268
Lumley Beach, 1, 49, 84, 224
Lungi Airport, 27, 55, 58, 60, 61, 83-84, 88, 90, 221-222, 228, 238-239, 241, 255, 257
Lunsar (town), 43, 47, 66, 75, 82-84, 140, 142, 232, 237, 255
LURD, 78-79, 81, 85, 87-88, 94, 142, 145, 218, 261, 275
Magbeni (town), 77, 86
Magburaka (town), 40, 60, 71, 81, 82, 233, 255
magic: *see* witchcraft
Makeni (town), 20; early fighting, 40, 146-147, 151-152; AFRC junta, Intervention, Freetown attack, 58, 65-66, 71, 75, 130, 139, 140, 142, 228, 230-231, 246-247, 257; Lomé Accord, Peacekeepers, 77, 79, 81, 82, 87, 232-233, 255
Malal Hills, 43, 228
Mandela, Nelson, 59, 68
Mandingo (ethnic group), 3, 27, 50, 163, 251, 263
Mano (ethnic group in Liberia), 25, 27, 101
Mano Dasse (town), 184, 195, 197
Mano River, 33, 60
Manowa (town, ferry), 33, 108, 122, 139, 140
Mansaray, Rashid, 26, 33, 40, 109, 110, 287
Margai, Albert, 21
Margai, Milton, 21
marijuana: *see* jamba
Maroons, 18-19
Masiaka (junction), 63, 66, 75, 78, 83, 86, 198, 228, 231, 237, 248

Masingbi (town), 40, 43, 51, 151, 169-170, 228, 264
Massaquoi, Gibril, 41, 105, 129, 287
Matotoka (town), 43, 54, 151
Mattru Jong (town), 47, 187, 195
Mende (ethnic group, language), 3, 20, 80, 105, 113, 114, 144, 152, 244, 257, 269; in tribal politics, 21, 28, 48, 51-52, 173; Kamajors, 45, 48, 153, 201, 213
mercenaries, 26, 48-49, 53, 54, 69, 109, 123, 147-149, 180, 283
Mile 91 (junction), 43, 64, 75, 137, 198, 250
Mingo, Dennis: *see* Superman
Moa Barracks, 31, 32-33, 70, 81, 84, 99-100, 106, 107, 120, 127
Moa River, 32, 33, 41, 99, 120, 122, 145, 227, 230
Momoh, Joseph: president, 23, 26, 36-37, 103, 125, 171, 260; NPRC coup and after, 37, 49, 50, 64, 68
Monrovia (Liberia), 24-25, 27, 94; in Sierra Leone war, 66, 69-70, 78, 81, 85-86, 142, 174-175, 178
Mosquito (aka of Samuel Bockarie): early fighting, 40, 54, 109, 111-112, 129, 133-134, 137, 177, 227; AFRC period, attack on Freetown, 56-58, 60, 65-75, 140, 171, 192, 219-220, 228-231, 239-240, 249; Lomé Accord, death, 77, 79, 80-81, 85, 92-93, 232, 235
Mosquito Spray Squad, 79
Moyamba District, 43, 47, 89, 137, 138, 179-184, 195, 251
Murray Town Barracks, 74, 139, 223, 224
Musa, SAJ, 37, 39-40, 57, 65-67, 70, 161, 231, 232, 237, 253, 287; death, 71, 231, 237-238, 239
music, 4, 123, 127, 201
Muslim, 4, 5, 15-16, 19, 104, 128, 177, 178, 193, 216

negotiations: Abidjan Peace Accord, 49, 50, 52-53; Conakry Peace Plan, 60; Lomé Peace Accord, 75-77; UNAMSIL hostages, 84; British hostages, 86; Taylor indictment, 92, 94-95

Newton (town), 48, 63

Nigeria, 19, 54, 55; Nigerians in ECOMOG, 27, 49, 55, 81-82, 94, 141-142, 147, 210, 221, 229; Nigerian civilians, 73; Nigerian government, 44, 47, 68, 75, 81, 95, 222, 263-264

Njaiama Sewafe (town), 65, 170, 228-229

Njala University, 47, 182, 184, 197, 247

Norman, Samuel Hinga, 44; build up of Kamajors, 51-52, 54, 57, 137-138; Intervention, 59-60, 64, 189; conviction, 92-93,

NPFL (National Patriotic Front of Liberia): formation, fighting in Liberia, 25-27, 29, 31, 36; fighting in Sierra Leone, 27, 31-33, 37, 39, 71, 78; expulsion from Sierra Leone, 37-39, 108-109, 118-123, 143-144

NPRC (National Provisional Ruling Council): coup, 37; junta, 39-40, 41, 44, 47-49, 110, 136, 147-148; palace coup, 55

Nyuma, Tom, 111, 136, 177, 227, 288

OAU (Organization of African Unity), 22, 24, 52, 58, 260

Obasanjo, Olusegun, 81, 89, 263-264, 288

Okelo, Francis G, 76

Okra Hill, 63, 78, 198, 233, 241

Operation Barras, 86-87

Operation Khukri, 84

Operation No Living Thing, 65, 160-164, 164-168, 217, 229

Operation Palliser, 83

Operation Pay Yourself, 63, 129-130, 139

Operation Stop the Election, 50

Pademba Road Prison, 54, 64, 68-69, 73, 81, 101, 117, 138, 178, 221, 225, 231, 234, 239

palm nuts, palm oil, 6, 20, 102, 141, 158, 237, 262

palm wine, 6, 163, 209, 257

Pamalap (town in Guinea), 87, 245, 259

PANAFU (Pan African Union), 23-24, 26

Panguma (town), 61

party politics: *see* tribal politics

peacekeepers: *see* UNAMSIL peacekeepers

People's Army, 56, 219

Peyama Camp, 43, 99, 111, 126, 137

political parties: *see* APC, SLPP, RUFP

Poro society, 14-15

Port Loko (town), 66

Port Loko District, 47, 71, 89, 237, 241, 257

Portuguese, 17, 19

protectorate, 8, 19, 20

Pujehun (town), 33

Pujehun District, 29, 31-33, 89, 174-177

Qaddafi, Muammar, 23-26, 53, 76-77

radio, 4, 56, 70, 73, 83, 112, 138, 139, 199, 216, 230, 249, 274; BBC, 63, 65, 68, 71, 73, 150, 249; radio stations, 35, 58, 64, 68, 222

railway, 20, 22, 185, 197, 200-201

Rambo, 33, 77, 106, 120-121, 286, 288

rape, 15; as tactic, 28, 37, 43, 65, 74-75, 103, 108, 117, 133, 143, 158, 180, 185; incidents, 36, 83, 117-118, 141, 162, 182, 209, 244-245; punishment, 131, 176, 253; Kamajor laws, 158; convictions, 93

rebels: *see* RUF

reconciliation, 124, 216, 250-251, 278-282

refugee, refugee camps, 19, 27, 33, 40, 47, 51, 67, 88, 94, 101, 178, 243, 269, 279; in Guinea, 66, 87-88, 109, 120, 124, 150, 155, 160, 163-164

Index

reggae, 4, 123, 192
regional politics: *see* tribal politics
reintegration: *see* DDR
religion, 5, 10, 11, 68, 279
rice, 5-6, 18; during war, 58, 115-116, 127, 130, 151, 160, 164, 180, 201, 206, 221-222, 238, 268, 273
rice ration (army), 36, 53
Richards, David, 83-84
Rogbere Junction, 75, 241
Rokel Creek, 77, 86, 241
Rosos (training camp), 67, 70, 237
RUF (Revolutionary United Front): formation and early fighting, 27-41, 100-106, 119-122, 175-177; guerrilla warfare, 24, 41-44, 48-49, 52, 54, 111-112, 128-129, 179-183; life with RUF, 106-107, 127-128, 177, 269-274; RUF joined with AFRC, 55-77; conflicts with AFRC, 56, 58, 65, 77-78, 79-80, 82-83; in government, fighting for Taylor, ceasefire, 78-90, 232-236, 261-278. *See also* army, AFRC/RUF renegade after return of government; and Freetown, attack on city
RUF anthem, 112-113
RUFP (political party), 53, 76, 91, 226, 234, 283
rutile: *see* Sierra Rutile
sanctions, on Liberia, 86, 88
Sandline, 60
Sankara, Thomas, 25
Sankoh, Foday: pre-war, formation of RUF, 22-24, 26-29, 174-177, 210; first attacks, 31-41, 102, 106-111, 115, 121-122, 133-134; guerrilla warfare, 41-49, 111-112; elections, Abidjan Accord, 49-53, 148-149; arrest in Nigeria, AFRC period, 54-57, 139; treason trial, attack on Freetown, 68, 70, 73; Lomé Accord, in government, 76-77, 79-83, 226, 233-234, 255, 259-260; arrest, trial and death, 84-85, 90, 91-93, 260, 265, 277

secret societies, 14-15, 271, 278-279
Segbwema (town), 24, fighting, 33, 43, 70, 107, 126-127, 140; disarmament, 80, 113, 130, 142
Sesay, Issa, 56-58, 65-67, 69-71, 77, 79, 109, 140, 163, 227, 231-232; leader of RUF, 85, 87, 89, 261-264; conviction, 92-93,
Sewa River, 65, 228-229
SIEROMCO (mining company), 47-48, 180
Sierra Leone Army: *see* army
Sierra Rutile (mining company), 2, 47-48, 137-138, 180, 191
skills training, 89, 124, 134-135, 260
slave trade, slavery, 3, 7, 17-19
SLPP (political party), 21-22, 35, 50-51, 58-59, 105, 138, 148, 173, 176
Small Boys Unit, 43, 108, 110, 133, 241
sobels, 44-45, 176
Songo (town), 63, 231, 237, 241
sorcery: *see* witchcraft
South Africa, 48, 59, 82, 147-149, 180
Special Court, 28, 53, 59-60, 61, 83, 84, 89, 91, 93-95, 234
Spencer, Julius, 70
Spur Road (Sankoh's Lodge), 79-80, 83, 218, 226, 233-234, 259
stadium (Freetown), 73, 83, 139, 226, 232, 239
State House, 54, 61, 73, 138, 222-223, 231-232, 239, 258
Stevens, Siaka, 21-23, 50, 173
Strasser, Valentine, 37, 40, 50, 178, 288
Superman (aka of Dennis Mingo), 48, 65, 67, 77, 88, 129, 138, 231-233, 255, 262-263, 287
supernatural powers: *see* witchcraft
tactics, strategies, 12, 28-29, 35-36, 41-44, 48-49, 57, 70, 108, 128-129, 177, 253, 267-269
Talia (town), 59, 187
Tamaboro (Civil Defense Force), 39, 45, 147, 227

Taylor, Charles, 12, 23; pre-Sierra Leone war, 25-29; involvement in Sierra Leone, 31, 32, 33, 39, 47, 52-53, 54, 58-60, 66-71, 76-78, 174-177, 249-250; RUF fighting in Liberia, conviction, 78-79, 81, 83, 84-88, 90, 91-95,142

Temne (ethnic group), 3, 18, 20, 45, 61, 168, 244, 254; in tribal politics (with other northern ethnic groups), 21, 22, 48, 55, 59, 61

Tihun (town), 45, 50, 59, 183

Tombo (town), 63, 139, 223, 228

Tombodu (town), 65, 147, 152, 160-162

Tongo Field (town and mining area), 43, 54, 58, 60-61, 69, 75, 82, 99, 111, 117, 125-126, 137, 177, 231

Tonkolili District, 43, 89, 228

torture, 27, 31, 36, 37, 39-40, 43, 58-59, 61, 64, 65, 67, 69, 94, 155, 253, 266

treason trials, 67-69

tribal politics (party, regional politics), 7-8, 21-22, 48, 51-52, 55, 58- 59, 61, 89, 173, 251-252; in Liberian war, 25, 27

tribes (ethnic groups), 3, 7-8, 14, 19, 20, 21, 45, 101, 251, 269

Truth and Reconciliation Commission, 12, 23, 27, 36, 41, 52, 53, 64, 69, 76, 81, 89, 92, 281

Turay, Akim, 70, 113, 137-138, 157, 230-231, 233, 239, 288

Ukraine, 86, 123, 221

ULIMO, 33, 40, 176, 177, 180, 195

UNAMSIL peacekeepers, 80, 81, 82-84, 87, 88, 89, 171, 233, 261, 263-264, 276

UNHCR, 88, 150

United Nations Security Council, 58, 60, 66, 68, 80, 85-86

United Nations, 8, 50, 51, 52, 76, 86, 88, 91, 113, 155, 178, 180, 255

United States, 18, 24-25, 27, 68, 75, 81, 86, 94, 235, 279

UNOMSIL, 68, 78, 80

Vaahun (town in Liberia), 31, 103

war crimes, 28, 76, 84, 89, 91, 93, 95

Water Quay (Freetown), 74, 178, 221

Waterloo (town), 48, 55, 63, 70-71, 74, 136, 139, 228, 232, 240, 242, 257

West Side Base, West Side Boys, 63, 77-78, 80, 82, 83, 86-87, 232-233, 241, 249

Western Area, 2, 21, 43, 47, 48, 74, 136

Wilberforce Barracks, 54, 58, 74, 223, 226, 228, 232, 258

witchcraft, sorcery, magic, 10-12, 279; in war, 11, 12, 39, 45, 104, 128, 141, 153, 157-158, 178, 186-188, 264-264

women and girls: issues, 9, 10, 14-16, 89, 280; RUF female fighters, 27, 43, 131, 132-135; violence against, 43, 103-104, 141, 160-164, 170, 185-186, 205-206, 244-245

World Bank, 13, 23

World Revolutionary Headquarters, 24, 26

Yamoussoukro (Ivory Coast), 52, 148, 227

Yengema (town), 75, 263-264, 276

youth, young people: incidents, 22, 23, 37, 64-65, 120, 122, 149, 195, 201; issues, 14, 108, 122, 172, 250, 260

Zimmi (town), 33, 60, 175, 178, 191

Zogoda Camp, 41, 52, 99, 111, 173

ABOUT THE AUTHORS

James Higbie was born in Michigan and educated at Denison University in Granville, Ohio, and at the University of Hawaii. He worked in Sierra Leone for ten years, first in the Peace Corps in the early 1970s and again after the war in education programs in Kono District. He has also worked in Hawaii, Thailand, Laos, and South Sudan, and has published books on the Thai and Lao languages.

Bernard S. Moigula is from Moyamba District in Sierra Leone. He holds a Higher Diploma in Community Health and Clinical Sciences and a BSc (Hons) in Public Health, both from Njala University. He has worked in Kailahun, Bo, and Moyamba Districts in clinical and community medicine.

www.ingramcontent.com/pod-product-compliance
Lightning Source LLC
Chambersburg PA
CBHW080636170426
43200CB00015B/2859